Understanding the Bengal Muslims

Understanding the Bengal Muslims

Interpretative Essays

Edited by

Rafiuddin Ahmed

OXFORD
UNIVERSITY PRESS

OXFORD
UNIVERSITY PRESS

YMCA Library Building, Jai Singh Road, New Delhi 110 001

Oxford University Press is a department of the University of Oxford. It furthers the
University's objective of excellence in research, scholarship, and education
by publishing worldwide in

Oxford   New York

Athens   Auckland   Bangkok   Bogota   Buenos Aires   Cape Town
Chennai   Dar es Salaam   Delhi   Florence   Hong Kong   Istanbul   Karachi
Kolkata   Kuala Lumpur   Madrid   Melbourne   Mexico City   Mumbai
Nairobi   Paris   São Paolo   Shanghai   Singapore   Taipei   Tokyo   Toronto   Warsaw

with associated companies in   Berlin   Ibadan

Oxford is a registered trade mark of Oxford University Press
in the UK and in certain other countries

Published in India
By Oxford University Press, New Delhi

ISBN   019 565520 6

Typeset in Times New Roman
By Urvashi Press, 75, Gandhi Nagar, Meerut-250 001
Printed in India at Roopak Printer, Noida
Published by Manzar Khan, Oxford University Press
YMCA Library Building, Jai Singh Road, New Delhi 110 001

My friends and colleagues
whose help made this volume possible
and to
Dean Bryan D. Reddick
of Elmira College for his
continued support to my
scholarly projects

Preface

The purpose of this volume is to present to the reader a broadly inter-disciplinary and scholarly work on the Bengal Muslims. Although the essays in this collection do not revolve around a central question, or a chosen problem, the themes they address are not mutually exclusive and should help to provide an understanding of the dynamic of Bengal Muslim society in an appropriate historical context. The underlying question that pervades the essays, notwithstanding the diversity that charac-terizes the volume, is simple: How do we assess the muslim community of Bengal, its changing perceptions, ideas, and ideologies? More specifically, we seek to explore the origins of the Bengal Muslims as a community and examine the patterns of historical developments in their religious belief, social circumstances, cultural orientations, and political growth. We feel that a work such as this will be of particular value at this juncture in their history, especially of Bangladesh, which is charac-terized by a great deal of discussion and debate on identity, nationalism, communalism, authoritaranism, and religious fundamentalism.

Although several of our contributors have addressed questions that specifically relate to the Muslims of Bangladesh, our concern was to produce a volume that would take a broader historical view of the com-munity in its all-Bengal context. This was also why we did not get in-volved in debates specific to the emergence of Bangladesh as a sovereign nation, such as the Language movement (1952), the Bangladesh Liberation War (1971), and the Genocide of Bengalis by the Pakistan army in 1971. We do recognize the limitations imposed on us by the paucity of contributions on West Bengal. Similarly, the absence of in-depth discussions on economic issues, urban–rural dichotomy, Hindu–Muslim communalism, and the educational problems of the Bengal Muslims, make this venture somewhat partial and incomplete. A second volume is therefore planned to fill that lacuna.

The use of the terms 'Bengal' and 'Bengali' in this volume requires an explanation. The 'Bengal' in the title reflects the need to recognize existing divisions between the Bengali-speaking Muslims of Bengal as an ethno–linguistic category, and those who, though living in Bengal, have consistently refused to be identified as such. In the editor's

opinion, 'Bengal' used as an adjective, denotes a neutral space and ob-
viates the confusion between a 'Bengali' and a 'Bangladeshi' so typical
in present-day Bangladesh, and is thus a logical choice for the title.
However, no effort was made to impose consistency in usage on the
authors, though there does exist a marked degree of consistency within
their respective articles in favour of one or the other term.

What gives us particular joy at this moment is to acknowledge the
extent of cooperation received from the contributors. Without
remuneration, or any tangible benefit, they laboured hard to produce
their essays within a limited time frame and thus made it possible for
me to produce this volume. As its editor, I owe a deep sense of gratitude
to all of them for their efforts. Richard Eaton, Peter Bertocci, Shelly
Feldman, Clint Seely, and Joseph O'Connell have been particularly
helpful in numerous other ways for which I am grateful. Ralph W.
Nicholas has done us a great favour by permitting us to reproduce his
valuable essay, 'Islam and Vaishnavism in the Environment of Rural
Bengal', published earlier in *Bengal, Regional Identity*, ed. David Kopf
(East Lansing: Michigan State University, Asian Studies Center, 1969),
entitled 'Vaisnavism and Islam in Rural Bengal'. I am also indebted to
President Tom Meier of Elmira College for agreeing with Dean Bryan
D. Reddick and Associate Dean Steve Coleman to release me on sab-
batical leave for the academic year 1999–2000 to take up a fellowship
at the National Humanities Center in North Carolina. Karen Carroll of
the Center has been very helpful with editorial advice whenever I
needed it. Finally, Oxford University Press deserves our special thanks
for undertaking the publication of this work.

National Humanities Center   RAFIUDDIN AHMED
Research Triangle Park,
North Carolina
7 February 2000

Contents

Notes on Contributors

RAFIUDDIN AHMED is Professor of Asian Studies at Elmira College, New York, and adjunct Professor of History, Cornell Unversity. The author of *The Bengal Muslims 1871–1906: A Quest for Identity* (1981 and 1988) and editor of several volumes of essays on the Bengal Muslims, he is currently a Fellow at the National Humanities Center in North Carolina writing a book on 'Religious Symbols and Political Mobilization: The Bengal Muslims, 1905–1947'.

SONIA NISHAT AMIN is Professor of History at Dhaka University, Bangladesh. Her publications include *The World of Muslim Women in Colonial Bengal, 1876–1939* (1996) and several other articles on Bengali Muslim women. Currently a Commonwealth Fellow at the School of Oriental and African Studies, University of London, she was also involved with a documentary on the life of Begum Rokeya Sakhawat Hossein, which received the Bangladesh President's award of excellence.

PETER J. BERTOCCI is Professor of Anthropology at Oakland University, Michigan. His interests are in the comparative political economy of peasant societies, with special reference to Bangladesh where he has conducted fieldwork and on which he has published extensively. His doctoral dissertation titled 'Elusive Villages: Social Structure and Community Organization in Rural East Pakistan' (Michigan State, 1970), though never published, has been widely read and is still regarded as a classic in the anthropology of Bangladesh. His publications include *The Politics of Community and Culture in Bangladesh* (1996).

RICHARD M. EATON, Professor of History at the University of Arizona in Tucson, is a leading North American scholar of precolonial South Asian Islamic history and culture. His many publications include *The Sufis of Bijapur, 1300–1700: Social Roles of Sufis in Medieval India* (1978 and 1996), *The Rise of Islam and the Bengal Frontier, 1204–1760* (1993 and 1997), and *Essays on Islam and Indian History* (2000). He is currently editing a collection of essays for Oxford University Press, entitled *Indian Islamic Traditions, 711–1800*.

SHELLEY FELDMAN is Associate Professor of Development Sociology and former Director of the South Asia Program at Cornell University. She is co-editor of *Unequal Burden: Economic Crises Persistent Poverty, and Women's Work* (1992), *Informal Work and Social Change* (1998), and numerous articles on purdah, non-governmental organizations, rural cooperatives, and gender inequality in Bangladesh. Her current research is on the institutional history of the post-1947 period and the unfolding of Partition (1947) in what was then East Pakistan.

SHAHADAT H. KHAN taught history at the University of Chittagong, Bangladesh, from 1975 to 1987. His Ph.D. dissertation on 'The Freedom of Intellect Movement (*Buddhir Mukti Andolon*) in Bengali Muslim Thought, 1926–1938' (Toronto 1997) was a significant breakthrough in exploring the roots of rationalism in Bengali Muslim political thought in the early twentieth century

RALPH W. NICHOLAS is William Rainey Harper Professor of Anthropology and of the Social Sciences at the University of Chicago. One of the pioneers in Bengal studies in North America, he has done extensive field work in India and Bangladesh. At the University of Chicago, he has played a major role in undergraduate education: as chairman and staff member of a core social sciences course, as a teacher in the Indian civilization programme, and as Dean of the College. He also served as Deputy Provost of the University. He is now the President of the International House of the University. He has written extensively on Bengal and is the co-author of *Kinship in Bengali Culture* (1977).

JOSEPH T. O'CONNELL is Professor Emeritus in the study of Religion at St Michael's College, University of Toronto, Canada. He has published extensively on religion and society in India and Bangladesh. He has edited and co-edited a number of volumes, including *Bengal Vaisnavism, Orientalism, Society and the Arts* (1985), *Sikh History and Religion in the Twentieth Century* (1988), and *Organizational and Institutional Aspects of Indian Religious Movements* (1999). He is currently working on a historical anthology on the relation of Bengali language and culture to Muslim religious and communal values.

ENAYETUR RAHIM teaches South Asian history at Georgetown University, Washington, DC. The author of *Provincial Autonomy in Bengal, 1937–43* (1981), and several other publications on South Asia, he is also co-editor of *Bengal Politics: Documents of the Raj, 1937–47*

(1999). He is currently working on a project on the Bangladesh Liberation War, 1971.

CLINTON B. SEELY is Associate Professor of Bengali Language and Literature at the University of Chicago. An expert in nineteenth-century Bengali literature, his Ph.D. dissertation on poet Jibanananda Das (Chicago, 1976) is a classic in the field and reflects his mastery of the language and its literary heritage. His subsequent translation of Jibanananda's poems, undertaken with advice from the famed Bengali novelist, Buddhadeva Bose, entitled *A Poet Apart: A Literary Biography of the Bengali Poet Jibanananda Das, 1899–1954* (ca 1990) remains an authoritative work on the poet. His current interest is in the nineteenth century Bengali poet, Michael Madhusudhan Dutt.

MOHAMMAD SHAH is Professor of History and Chairman of the Department at the University of Chittagong, Bangladesh. Formerly a Commonwealth Fellow at the School of Oriental and African Studies, University of London, he is the author of *In Search of Identity: Bengali Muslims, 1880–1940* (1996) and co-author of the *History of Bangladesh, 1704–1971* (1992), and *Dinajpur: History and Traditions* (1996). He is currently working on a project on 'Pan-Islamic Cross-Currents in Colonial Bengal'.

Introduction

The Emergence of the Bengal Muslims

RAFIUDDIN AHMED

The essays in this volume deal with a number of interrelated issues on the Bengal Muslims, ranging from their social origins to recent social, religious, and political developments. Specifically, they relate to such issues as conversion and Islamization, religious ideas and practices, structure of social and political authority, patterns of orthodoxy, revivalism and pan-Islamism, radical-humanist religious and political thought, secularism and fundamentalism, language and literature, and, finally, the changing role of women. This wide variety of subject matter is matched by a diversity of disciplinary approaches. Our contributors thus include anthropologists, historians, linguists, political scientists, sociologists, as well as generalists. Beneath this variety, however, all of them share a common concern: to understand and describe the dynamics of Bengal Muslim society, from its beginnings in the medieval period to our own time. In other words, the principal focus of this volume is to explore what being a 'Muslim' means in the context of Bengal. Although none of our contributors specifically addresses the topic of how the Bengal Muslims emerged as a distinctive 'community', this could be a critical question, especially for the reader who would want to relate the different essays to their historical context and to gain an insight into the processes that led to the 'formation' of such a community. I will raise a few questions in this introduction—and I can do no more than attempt to formulate these questions, far less their resolution—focusing on how a self-conscious Muslim community developed.

The existence of a clearly defined community, based either on religion or ethnicity, is not a predetermined social fact. Although loyalty to a particular version of the sacred may provide a useful basis for the growth of a religious identity, it is often through a slow process of change and transformation, as well as the systematization and articulation of particular religious and cultural symbols, that the boundaries of a community actually take shape. The community, like the nation, is often an 'imagined' entity (to borrow the phraseology of Benedict Anderson),[1] perhaps with the exception of smaller village-centric groups, communities, castes, or the brotherhood of specific religious cults, sufi *silsila*s, and the like. However, the cultural boundaries of a community, whether religious or ethnic, cannot be appropriately articulated without reference to a socio-territorial identity, i.e. a linguistic and cultural heritage shared by its members who have collectively inhabited a common territory.[2] This parallels in some respects the concept of a nation, but is not coterminous with it. Indeed, a self-conscious religious or ethnic community is a much more compact, and well-defined, entity than the nation: the latter could, and often does, incorporate diverse religious, linguistic, and cultural groups and communities, as in India.

A religious community, without a socio–territorial base, is not real. Although 'united' by a few common rituals, it can at best be described as a brotherhood of believers, like the modern-day *tabligh* or *daw'a* movement in Islam, whose members share a common religious ideal but scarcely a common identity. Although they have an overriding concern to revitalize and reactualize Islam by encouraging stronger commitment to the Islamic *shari'a*, and occasionally come together to propagate their message to others, they do not form a community by themselves; they come from diverse social, cultural, and ethnic backgrounds, and essentially remain members of such 'communities' though they may share a common objective: that of 'purifying' the Faith.

For similar reasons, the notion of an Islamic *umma*, which categorizes Muslims all over the world as members of 'a community of believers' and rejects socio–territorial identity, is scarcely a meaningful 'community'. Contrary to Benedict Anderson's argument on the role of the sacred language in creating such communities in the medieval period,[3] and perhaps even later, the reality has always been different; notions of such communities may have existed in the imagination of believers, but could never be meaningfully articulated. Arabic as the sacred language of Islam may have served a limited purpose, especially of uniting the Arab Muslims against their enemies during the formative phase of Islam, and, later, in creating a sense of *communitas* at the level of Arabic learning and Arabic speaking Muslims from different parts of the world. It could however never contribute towards the creation of a world Muslim 'community' at any time, although such a perception may have existed. While the status of Arabic as the sacred language of Islam has never been in dispute, only a handful of Muslims, especially in the non-Arab world, could ever read and actually understand Arabic. Anderson himself acknowledges the limitations of his argument when he writes that 'even though the sacred languages made such communities as Christendom imaginable, the actual scope and plausibility of these communities cannot be explained by sacred script alone: their teachers were, after all, tiny literate reefs on top of vast illiterate oceans'.[4] Ironically, Arabic as the sacred language could not even ease rivalries between Muslims of different races and cultures, far less create a community of believers; the historic conflict between the Arabs and the Persians exemplifies this.

There can be little doubt that significant elements of Islamic religious culture—especially the sacred text and a set of sacred symbols, including the Five Pillars of Islam, namely, the profession of faith (*kalima*), ritual prayers (*salat*), fasting during the month of Ramadan, the giving of alms (*zakat*), and pilgrimage to Mecca (*haj*)—profoundly affect the lives of Muslims from all over the world, but these cannot separate them from their real life in different geographical and cultural settings. In other words, notions of a sacred language, a sacred text, or a particular set of religious symbols, divorced from the realities of life, could never be the basis of a 'community'. Even in the Indian subcontinent, ruled by Muslims for nearly six hundred years (ca thirteenth through the mid-eighteenth century CE), this did not happen. Argues Paul Brass, 'Muslim political élites in India in the nineteenth and twentieth centuries attempted to argue that the Muslims of the subcontinent formed a distinct nation . . . . It proved to be ephemeral because beyond the core of Islamic symbols, all other symbols proved to be divisive and could not be made congruent with the religious ones'.[5] Mohammad Shah's essay on pan-Islamism (chapter 4) demonstrates the superficiality of such a supranational identity. Pan-Islamic feeling, which had become quite powerful among sections of Bengal Muslims in the later nineteenth and early twentieth century, was symbolic of the emotional attachment that Muslims felt for each other, but it did not have the power to 'unite' them as members of a distinctive 'community'.

The experiences of the Muslims of Bangladesh suggest that socio–territorial identity plays a critical role in defining and redefining the parameters of a community. They equally point to the uselessness of trying to identify a fixed criterion for a definition of the cultural boundaries of such a community: a Bengali Muslim may have seen himself primarily as a 'Muslim' the other day, as a 'Bengali' yesterday, and a 'Bengali Muslim' today, depending on objective conditions, but on none of these occasions did his thoughts and his idea of destiny become separated from his territorial identity. Whether he likes it or not, his entire personality bears marks of this socio–territorial imprint. The songs he sings, the music he plays, the poems he composes, the literature he produces, his daily life, marriage rituals, dietary habits are all clearly linked to the territory of his birth. Attempts to forge closer links to an Arab or a Persian dream could scarcely distance him from his roots. He emphasized his differences with 'others' at different times in different ways, which dictated his choices of symbols. In 1947, he tended to distinguish himself more from his Bengali Hindu neighbour than any other and emphasized the Islamic content of his identity. This definition was somewhat modified in 1969–71 when language became a powerful political symbol, primarily in response to domination by the Urdu-speaking Pakistani élite, especially for those in eastern Bengal who lived under Pakistani colonial rule. It would however be too much to suggest that on any of these occasions he had either ceased to be a Bengali or had rejected his identification with Islam. Developments in Bangladesh, especially since 1975, indicate that the Islamic content of his personality continues to have great relevance to his role in society. Similarly, throughout this period of political turmoil, and even in pre-modern times, the socio–territorial pull continued to exert a powerful impact on him. This dual pull is often reflected in his continued hesitation to define the cultural boundaries of his identity in specific terms: 'Am I a Muslim first or a Bengali?' he keeps asking himself.

The language question did not become a critical factor in remoulding the identity of those who lived in West Bengal after the Partition of 1947. They have remained part of the larger Indian entity as Muslims and as Bengalis; if politics and government policies have affected them, the impact was different from what happened in Bangladesh and did not require an abrupt change in their choices of symbols which the Bengali Muslims of Bangladesh were required to make. In other words, the political divide of 1947, which separated Bengali Muslims of Bangladesh from their coreligionists in West Bengal, had a differing impact on their respective experiences, attitudes, and world-views. Consequently, the notion of a single Bengal Muslim community, that may have evolved over time, increasingly became pointless after 1947.

Despite the cultural ambivalence that has characterized Bengal

Muslim history since the medieval period,[6] a self-conscious community defining itself primarily as Muslim did emerge over time by the early twentienth century. This was the result of a *very slow* process of change and transformation since the dichotomy between a Bengali and a Muslim identity continued to persist. The masses of Muslims living in the countryside were so fragmented from within by caste-like features, and, more importantly, so widely separated from their upper class co-religionists (the so-called *ashraf* and the orthodox *ulema*, who did not even recognize the former as 'Muslims') that the notion of a 'community' could hardly exist. A veneer of culture unity emerged, in part, from adherence to a common faith—despite differing perceptions, rituals, and practices—and partly from common experiences of living in a territory marked by certain common geographical phenomena such as the subtropical forests, mighty rivers, frequent floods, flat alluvial land, and wet-rice cultivation. Nonetheless, a feeling of *communitas* cutting across various lines of distinction did not develop until late in the nineteenth century. Till then, there was little organized effort, if any, to articulate a sense of community identity among these disparate groups; nor were any institutional links forged. True, the clergy, such as the *mullah*, the *maulvi,* and the *pir,* propagated the ideals of an Islamic society, and perhaps succeeded in establishing some kind of institutional, as well as emotional contact with the Islamic world beyond the borders of Bengal, which became particularly evident during the so-called Wahabi trials in 1869–71.[7] It, however, touched only the relatively articulate segments of the population, especially, the *madrassa*-educated literati, the affluent farmers in the countryside who had links to the urban society, and members of the non-Bengali urban Muslim population, including the hide merchants. The larger community of peasants, artisans, and functional groups remained isolated from these trends.

Historically, at least, three dominant patterns of tension can be identified in Bengal Muslim society since the medieval period: (i) the social and cultural barriers that existed between a predominantly urban immigrant (the so-called *ashraf*) culture, oriented more towards northern India and beyond, represented mostly by the clergy and those who traced their descent from early immigrants, and the rural (the so-called *atrap*) culture of the Muslim peasants, artisans, and functional groups with their roots in the Bengal countryside; (ii) the tension between the religious values and ideals of those who professed to represent Islamic 'orthodoxy' in Bengal, such as the *mullah*, the *maulvi,* and segments of immigrant Muslims, and the 'syncretic–pantheistic' beliefs and practices of the majority of rural Muslims as well as the 'heterodox' Sufi sects; and (iii) the confusion and uncertainty characterized by the attitude of the dominant social classes towards Bengali cultural symbols, especially the language, which they categorized as a non-Islamic inheritance. This negative attitude towards Bengali language and culture affected the psyche of even the non-literate rural Muslims, and eventually came to be linked to the question of their social origins. We will return to this later in this Introduction.

These categories into which the Bengal Muslims have been broadly divided above were neither fixed nor homogeneous entities: lineage, sectarian division, education and existing social and economic condition all had a bearing on their social status and identity. They did not necessarily live as isolated groups, especially in urban areas, and may even have had some form of contact and interaction with one another, the *mullah* acting as a go-between, as is evidenced in medieval Bengali literature.[8] However, the notion of a 'community', encompassing the different social classes and functional groups, did not seem to have developed. In the late nineteenth century improved means of communication, modern education, the printing press, a powerful programme of Islamization launched by the Islamic revivalists, colonial reforms, and increased political tension between Hindus and Muslims gradually broke the isolation of the villages and brought about a certain degree of rapport between the 'high born' and the 'low born', and induced the mullah to aggressively articulate a sense of common identity. Yet, even then, educated and upper-class Muslims were still reluctant to accept the Muslim functional groups as 'true Muslims'.[9]

The poet Mukundaram's description of a sixteenth-century Muslim settlement in Bengal is indicative of the broad social and cultural affiliations of those who formed the core of the early Muslim presence in Bengal; this would also suggest that even in urban areas, where they mostly concentrated at this stage, the notion of a 'community' did not exist. The poet writes:

There came the Sayyids, Mughals, Kazis mounted on horses; the Bir [the Hindu hero of the story] gave them rent free land for their houses . . . . They rise early in the morning, and spreading a red *pati* [prayer mat] they offer their *namajes* [ritual prayers] five times a day . . . . They are very wise, they care for none, they never give up *roza* [fasting during the month of Ramadan] as long as they have life in them . . . . They wear on their head a *topi* [cap] which has ten sides, and what they call an *ijar* [paijama] tied tight round the waist.[10]

Evidently, those whom Mukundaram mentions were immigrants

from outside Bengal and were Shi'i Muslims, 'for they contribute[d] to decorate the house of [Imam] Hossain, and had their green flags and beat their drums',[11] and they had a lifestyle typically different from the locally converted Muslims who were theoretically Sunnis. The immigrants to this colony seem to have been familiar with the scriptural traditions of their religion, and followed those with some measure of scrupulousness. That, however, is not what we notice at the lower level of the society:

There are some people called *gola* [*goala*/milkman?]. They do not perform *roza* [fasting] and *namaz*. Those who accept the occupation of weaving are called *jolha* [weavers]. Those who drive bullocks are called *mukeri*. Some sell cakes and are called *pithari*. Those who sell fish are called *kabari*; they do not grow beards and always resort to lies.[12]

The list goes on and indicates the existence of various functional groups at the lower level of Muslim society, based primarily on occupational identity, somewhat analogous to the Hindu *jatis*. Such groups continued to exist even in the late nineteenth century.[13]

These two categories of Muslims, described by Mukundaram, broadly reflect early differences in lifestyle and identity between the immigrant Muslims and the local functional groups, and, equally, between those who followed the standard forms of Islamic rituals and others who did not. However, even at the level of immigrants, although Mukundaram refers to 'a' Muslim settlement, it would be incorrect to assume that the different racial groups who came from outside Bengal immediately merged into a brotherhood of believers. The mullah, as the priest and as the teacher of the *maktab* (elementary school with a heavy bias on religious education), may have contributed towards articulating a sense of Islamic identity, as suggested above. Equally, the experiences of living in a predominantly Hindu territory and adherence to a particular faith may have eventually helped coalesce those 'foreigners in town' into 'a community of believers', but none of these could have created the necessary conditions for integrating the lower functional groups within its fold. In reality, up until the late nineteenth century, a significant proportion of Bengal Muslims, especially the geat majority living in the countryside, were, in a certain sense, more a part of the larger Bengali community comprising Hindus, Muslims, Buddhists, and animists than any specific Islamic community. Ralph Nicholas's research demonstrates that their eclectic religious culture did not change fimdamentally in many areas of Bengal even in our time (chapter 2). Obviously, the mullah and the *maulvi*, among others, rejected non-

Islamic rituals and symbols and favoured closer ties to north Indian and Middle-Eastern Islam. However, excepting isolated instances where we may witness some limited participation by members of lower functional groups in these extraterritorial gestures promoted by the mullah, such as the *jihad* in the Nort-West Frontier Province in the nineteenth century,[14]—none of these had much real impact in creating a community consciousness at that level of the society until much later.

The question is: Why are we emphasizing the differences rather than the similarities, if there were any, at the beginning of this Introduction? Why are the dissimilarities, and, equally, the diversities, critical to our understanding of the processes through which a Muslim community may have eventually emerged in Bengal? Formulated differently, what defined the social and cultural boundaries of Bengali Islam? How were the cultural symbols and idioms chosen and the notion of a 'community of believers' articulated? Perhaps one useful way of approaching the problem is to revisit a familiar question (as Richard Eaton does in chapter 1) and ask: Who are the Bengal Muslims? Closely related to this question is the amazing fact that Bengal today, comprising Bangladesh and the Indian state of West Bengal, is home to 'the second largest Muslim ethnic population in the world, after the Arabs'.[15] A recent estimate put the number at 93 million, of which 81 million lived in Bangladesh and the remaining 12 million in the state of West Bengal. An unusually large concentration of them in the lower districts of Bengal, the so-called 'rice swamps', far removed from the centres of Muslim political power in medieval India, makes the question of their social origin particularly provocative. To the educated and middle-class Bengali Muslims, this has always been a particularly sensitive issue. Eager to project their image as the bearers of an 'authentic' tradition, they often react sharply to any suggestion or theory that challenges their claims to an 'Islamic', meaning Arab, Persian, or Central Asian, origin. One may read their autobiographical works, published especially in the first half of the twentieth century, and notice the remarkable consistency in claims to an 'Islamic', i.e. a non-Bengali, and often non-Indian, origin. Even when there were no tangible means of concocting a foreign genealogy, this did not deter many from making such claims. One such claimant thus felt no shame in making a 'conjecture' 'that the remote ancestor from whom my family sprang up might have been among the retinue of Murad Khan [a Mughal general]'.[16] One of the rare exceptions to this general tendency among the middle-class Bengali Muslims is Abul Mansur Ahmad's autobiography; he openly acknowledges his plebeian identity and explains that he had no pretensions to *sharafat* (Muslim aristocracy essentially based on claims to foreign ancestry).[17] Such modesty was however unusual at that time and does not reflect the dominant mood of the society even today. A modern Bengali Muslim historian of medieval Bengal was so upset with repeated references in colonial census reports to the 'low-caste' origin of the majority of Bengal Muslims that he thought it necessary to digress from the principal theme of his book and devote a considerable amount of time and space 'exploding' 'the theory'of low-caste origin.[18]

Why this sensitivity? One of the questions considered critical to defining a 'true' Muslim is to determine the 'appropriateness' of his lifestyle, language, and culture. Muslim scholars and theologians have tended to draw a sharp distinction between what is 'truly' Islamic and what is not. Although, theoretically, the *shari'a* should provide answers to all such questions, what happened in reality was different. Arab and Persian traditions generally came to symbolize authentic Islamic culture, especially in the Indian subcontinent; local traditions, including the languages, were generally dismissed as un-Islamic. Conformity to Perso–Arab cultural symbols, which included learning the two languages, was often sought by the devout even in Bengal. When it came to the question of genealogy, nothing short of a pure Arab origin, especially proximity to the Prophet, or his tribe, seemed acceptable. The social and cultural requirements of being a 'genuine' Muslim thus dictated that if you made such a claim you ought to have been ready to demonstrate your links to the 'Islamic' lands. Indo–Islamic scholars and theologians have often suggested that the 'original' intellectual and cultural background of Islam in Arabia, Persia, and, to a lesser extent, in Central Asia, gave Islamic culture its distinctive form and encouraged its adherents to consider themselves more as members of an Islamic *umma*, 'which extended far beyond the Indian frontiers',[19] than any particular Indian community. In a way, this was also related to a tendency among Muslims to differentiate themselves from people of other faiths, both religiously and culturally. Belief in Allah and His Prophet not only implied separation in religious terms from all others, but also meant that the cultural symbols separating a Muslim from a non-Muslim should be different and exclusive, which is one reason why sections of educated Bengali Muslims have historically been so keen to distance themselves from their Bengali roots.

Thus, appropriation of Arab or Persian cultural symbols, including language, dress, and social customs, and claims especially to an Arab ancestry, became integral to an authentic Islamic identity in the Indian subcontinent. Delhi, Agra, Lucknow, and Lahore, which emerged as imperial outposts of Indian Islam, promoted a particular form of Persian- and Urdu-based Islamic culture rejecting all local forms as un-Islamic: *mathnawi, ghazal, sam'a, qawwali, mushaira, qasida*—all in that tradition—came to be regarded as standard Islamic poetic forms. Similarly, the contributions of poets and authors like Rumi, Ghalib, Hali, and others who wrote in classical 'Islamic languages' were idealized and romanticized.[20] The Islamic languages included Arabic, Persian, and Urdu; while Indian languages like Tamil or Bengali, though the latter is spoken by the great majority of Indian Muslims, were excluded from the list principally because they were not written in the Arabic or Persian script. Feeble attempts made to Arabicize and Persianize some of these languages did not help much in elevating their status.[21] The result was the growth of a Perso–Arab, north India centred, imperial Islamic culture, which sought to standardize and define its social and cultural norms and behaviour by emphasizing specific symbols and traditions to the exclusion of those that came to be associated with regional Islam. To this day, this attitude prevails, both among scholars and theologians. On the question of an Islamic origin, those who had no way of making claims to Arab ancestry often opted for the second best, either a Central Asian, or, at the least, an Afghan (Pathan) parentage; they emulated the Delhi–Lucknow model of Islamic culture and sought to distance themselves from local culture in all possible ways. Thus, a contradictory trend came to symbolize Indo–Muslim cultural attitudes, which typically infected the educated middle classes in Bengal. Although 'commonality of belief and adherence to codes for conduct' (to borrow from Peter Bertocci) should ideally 'transcend the ties of blood' and create a cohesion among Muslims 'born of likeness in ideas, values, and normative commitment',[22] this ideal never translated itself into reality. The dichotomy in Bengali Islam is rooted in this historical fact.

A fundamental problem in conceptualizing the notion of an Islamic community based on the theory of 'likeness in ideas, values, and normative commitment' is posed by the question of linguistic and cultural diversity. Because of its proclaimed goal of proselytizing non-believers, Islam spread to peoples of diverse origins and backgrounds in different parts of the world making it inconceivable to promote a uniform cultural standard. Arabic may be the language of the Qur'an, but to expect that all Muslims, irrespective of their social and cultural backgrounds, would adopt the Arabic language is simply not practical. Thus, despite early hesitations on the part of the 'ulema, the Qur'an had to be translated into different languages to make its message comprehensible to Muslims in their own languages, including Bengali. This, in fact, implied a relaxation of the definition of what constitutes an Islamic language, although Arabic continued to retain its primacy. However, a far more complex problem in all newly converted Muslim societies, especially in the medieval and the early modern periods, was posed by the delicate question of how to integrate the masses of converts, with their own inherited ideas, traditions, and practices, within the framework of a single Muslim community. It was not easy. Asim Roy has argued that, in medieval Bengal, religious preachers, whom he describes as 'cultural mediators',[23] adopted a policy of compromise and concession in efforts to propagate the Islamic message. Like many early Jesuit missionaries, such as Matteo Ricci (1552–1610), who adopted and used Confucian idioms to propagate Christianity among the Chinese, these 'cultural mediators' too accepted some of the local cultural idioms and symbols to popularize Islamic themes among the Muslims of rural Bengal.[24] There was hardly any alternative: while not compromising the identity of Islam as a religion, what was considered an unchangeable and standardized system of beliefs and rituals had to be adjusted to the realities of life in deltaic Bengal.

2

Bengal, particularly the low-lying districts in the east and the southeast, comprising much of present-day Bangladesh, where Islam found most of its adherents, long remained largely insulated from the cultural influences of northern India. Even during the long years of Buddhist and Hindu political ascendancy in the territory, roughly from the third century BCE through the twelfth century CE, the low-lying districts were not closely integrated with the predominant Aryan culture of the upper-Gangetic north. The population was composed almost entirely of indigenous tribes, communities of scattered cultivators and, somewhat later, a dominant class of upper-caste Hindus who had begun migrating to the region ftom the north, especially since the third century BCE. Although some form of agriculture, including fishing, woodcutting, and boating, seems to have served the basic needs of those people who lived in these territories, large-scale organized cultivation did not develop until after the arrival of the Muslims in the fifteenth and sixteenth centuries.[25] While Brahmanical Hinduism increasingly became assertive and dominant in parts of Bengal by the eleventh century CE, Buddhist and native ideas and practices, especially those focusing on cults celebrating the forest goddess, still continued to shape the religious culture of ordinary people.

What the Muslim conquerors then encountered in eastern Bengal when they first arrived in the thirteenth century were cults of gods, goddesses, and spirits shaped by an overwhelming concern for survival. They did not immediately set about transforming the society; they neither had the time nor the zeal. Their principal goal was to consolidate their own political power in a territory which was almost entirely non-Muslim. Creation of an institutional infrastructure to solidify support for the new Muslim state was considered critical; they, thus, built mosques and *madrassas*, patronized Islamic scholars and preachers, gave support to Islamic religious endowments, appointed *qazi*s (Islamic judicial officers) who would promote Islamic ideals in addition to their juridical responsibilities, and encouraged immigration. These measures gradually contributed towards a slow process of expansion of the Muslim society, primarily through acculturation of new cultivating classes.

Under the protection of the Muslim rulers, but not necessarily with their support or approval, land-developers and pioneers, many of them later remembered as 'Sufis', settled in the Bengal countryside and participated in community building activity, including forest clearing and cultivation, thus winning the confidence especially of the cultivating classes from whose ranks most of the rural Muslim population came. Richard Eaton's argument (in chapter 1) on the relationship between an expanding agrarian frontier and the religious culture among the local population in eastern and south-eastern Bengal offers the most persuasive explanation to date of how the masses were increasingly Islamicized. The fact that the great majority of Bengal Muslims lived in the countryside until recently (only about 3 or 4 per cent of them lived in towns, as against a quarter of the total Muslim population in the North-Western Provinces, the seat of Muslim political power in the Indian subcontinent) and were engaged in the actual cultivation of land, mostly in the low-lying districts of Rajshahi, Dhaka, and Chittagong divisions, is suggestive of their agrarian background and, almost certainly, local origin. By no definition however were they members of the so-called 'ruling nation', nor were they associated with the immigrant cultural tradition.[26]

Those who claimed immigrant status, and considered themselves representatives of an authentic Islamic culture, formed a distinct social entity. From the early Muslim period they considered themselves different from, and in status superior to, the local Muslims. They harboured strong prejudices against the 'natives' and maintained a conscious distance from the latter. The social and cultural influences coming from outside Bengal remained restricted primarily to these classes, including the 'ulema, leaving local Muslims in the same situation where they had been in prior to their assimilation to Muslim society. The latter continued to live in their ancestral villages, were indistinguishable in occupation from neighbouring non-Muslims, and often participated in rituals and festivities long native to the delta. Even in the nineteenth century, and, in many instances, until recently, their lifestyle and world-views did not fundamentally change, nor did the attitude of the *ashraf* towards them. The real problem was one of acceptance and recognition: Bengali background and cultural symbols continued to be stigmatized, and neither the 'ulema nor the immigrant *ashraf* were keen on expanding the cultural boundaries of Islam. This, of course, does not imply that Indian rituals, practices, and symbols were uncommon to the *ashraf* society. Deprived of much direct contact with the Islamic 'heartland' and its culture, even the imperial aristocracy in northern India cultivated an essentially localized Indian version of Islam; the *ashraf* in Bengal were no different. What distinguished the latter from the local Muslims were their pretensions to what they regarded as an authentic Islamic culture. This was particularly evident during the Mughal period when a totally negative attitude towards the Bengali race and culture developed among Mughal offcials posted in Bengal and other immigrants. So great were their pretensions to a superior culture that they were not even keen to convert Bengalis to Islam.[27]

Thus, those who claimed immigrant status, and by implication the status of better Muslims, were separated from the Bengali converts by racial as well as cultural barriers. Either the latter must accept the cultural symbols introduced by the immigrants, or they must remain outside the accepted domain of Islam. This acceptance, however, did not mean that the social stigma attached to Bengali origin would cease to exist. In truth it never did. However, the immediate question confronting the religious preachers was: How to transmit the 'authentic' Islamic symbols to those who did not read the Arabic Qur'an or any other Islamic text, and had little or no contact with the larger world of Islam? How could the latter distance themselves from the land of their birth, its language and culture, and rise above the social environment in which they continued to live?

As indicated before, early efforts by medieval writers to transmit Islamic religious ideas and cultural symbols suffered from the immediate problem of finding the appropriate vocabulary and idiom in the local language. Much has been written on how local cultural mediums continued to play an important role in communicating with the masses. Many did not like this approach and resented the use of local cultural symbols, including the language, considered 'un-Islamic' in conveying the message of Allah and His Prophet. There were a few who reacted against such aspersions. Shah Abdul Hakim, a seventeenth-century Muslim poet, and author of several Bengali didactic works, thus wrote: 'Whatever language a people speak in a country, the Lord understands it. He understands all languages, whether it is Hinduani [Hindustani or Urdu?] or the language of Bengal, or any other'. He then went a step further in decrying those who had a negative attitude towards Bengali. 'Those who hate the Bengali language despite being born in Bengal', he wrote, 'cast doubt on their birth. The people, who have no liking for the language and the learning of their country, had better leave it and live abroad'.[28] Such radicalism however became increasingly marginal to the emerging trend that emphasized the non-Bengali character of Islamic culture and raised doubts about the appropriateness of Bengali as a medium of such a culture. Although the tension between the proponents and opponents of an extraterritorial identity continued to exist, which we notice even in the twentieth century (as pointed out by Shahadat Khan in chapter 7), desire for conformity with an Arab-oriented version of Islamic culture became the preferred goal of theologians as well as of the relatively affluent members of the society, including those who acknowledged their Bengali origins, though somewhat reluctantly. The state, the 'ulema, the aristocracy, as well as the religious institutions, such as the *madrassa*s, the *maktab*s, and the Sufi hospices and tomb–shrines, all patronized and promoted a version of Islamic culture consistent with their own definitions of authenticity, although they did not necessarily agree among themselves on its nature, scope, and ramifications.

When the British conquered Bengal in the eighteenth century, they encountered a Muslim population almost entirely rural in background, and not much different from their fellow Hindu neighbours in dress, manners, names, occupations, rituals, and practices. What they missed, however, was the growing sensitivity of the relatively articulate sections of the Muslim society, even in rural areas, towards a particular version of Islam. British rule did not hurt the Muslim peasantry of Bengal any more than it did the Hindu, but that rule created amongst Muslims a sense of deprivation that was uncommon to the Hindus. After all, they thought, the British had wrested power from 'them', as if to suggest that they had descended from ancestors who had ruled India long before the coming of the British! The eagerness with which scores of Bengali Muslims from remote areas of the territory joined the jihad in the North-West Frontier Province (led by the powerful nineteenth century Islamic 'revivalist' movements, notably the Tariqa-i-Muhammadiya, or the Wahabis of the British official records) is an extraordinary reminder of how things were changing. Hunter's account as well as the documents on the so-called Wahabi trials (1869–70), published some time ago, reveal fascinating stories of journeys from Bengal to the Frontier by many who chose to 'fight for Islam'.[29] They often came from humble rural backgrounds, had little formal education, and perhaps knew very little about the Islamic faith: to them, Islam was Allah's chosen Faith, an ideology of change that had been defiled and undermined by its enemies, and they were ready to fight for it.

What was particularly important about the Islamic revivalist movements of the nineteenth century—particularly the Tariqa-i-Muhammadiya, which organized the jihad in the North-West Frontier, and the Faraizis in Bengal[30]—was the demand for absolute conformity with an Arab-oriented Islam. Although apparently inspired by the eighteenth-century Wahabi movement in Arabia, whose message was brought home in different countries primarily by the Muslim pilgrims to Mecca, their rise was more directly linked to the social and political transformation produced by the dominant presence of colonial Europe in Asia and Africa. The economic and political reforms introduced by the colonial rulers often shattered and destroyed the foundations of older social orders and gave rise to new social classes and conditions. Decline of the older order consequently came to be linked to the notion of spiritual 'decadence', for which, in Muslim societies, the Muslims themselves were blamed. Going back to the ideals of the 'pure' Faith was seen as the only road back to political glory.[31] This was not however a uniquely Islamic phenomenon, as several Hindu reform movements, notably the Arya Dharm in northern India, also arose in response to British colonial presence.[32] Yet, for historical reasons, the sense of loss and decline was particularly felt by the Muslims.

Conformity with the idealized tradition was the stated goal of these movements. The new generation of Islamic reformers thus rejected all syncretic compromises outright. Rituals and practices that were linked to local culture were declared un-Islamic; they even challenged the popular *pir–muridi* relationship, which formed the core of traditionalist Islam in the subcontinent, and pushed for total 'purification', including dress and manners, rituals and practices, language and identity. There is an astonishing similarity between the uncompromising attitude of the nineteenth century 'revivalists' and the ideology of the Islamic 'fundamentalists' of our time insofar as they both promote the concept of an idealized Islamic community distinct from others and they both define the community in extraterritorial terms, rejecting all local variations of Islam. However, it is doubtful whether the modern-day movements, especially the Jama't-i-lslami in Bangladesh, which function more as political parties (as Enayetur Rahim points out in chapter 10), and pay little attention to ideological issues fit into the category of 'revivalist' movements. The social background of their participants, which is essentially middle- and lower-middle class and urban in character, and their direct involvement in state politics, contrary to their stated ideology (Enayetur Rahim's essay, chapter 10, provides useful hints about it), make their agenda wholly different from their 'precursors', despite a similar emphasis on 'authentic' Islam.

The determined push of the nineteenth century reformers for conformity increasingly led to a greater degree of systematization and standardization of Islamic cultural symbols in Bengal. Even the traditionalist 'ulema, who had opposed the revivalists on theological matters, took part in this effort. The debate and discussion that it occasioned gradually led to a greater sense of awareness among Muslims of all classes about their distinctiveness as 'Muslims'. It also promoted a certain degree of social mobility within the community, bringing the élite and the mass ethos closer to each other. Peter Bertocci argues (in chapter 3) that even the modern-day Bengali Muslim social organization in rural Bangladesh owes a great deal to the organizational structure popularized by the Islamic reformers, especially those associated with the nineteenth century Faraizi movement.

Among other things, this desire to conform to 'authentic' Islam also implied acceptance of an age-old argument that Bengali cultural symbols, including the language, were inconsistent with that ideology. Realistically however, Bengali could not be banished from the Muslim society of Bengal as it was the only language spoken by members of that society, but it could be lslamicized. Thus, through a conscious effort, large numbers of Arabic, Persian, and Urdu idioms and terms were incorporated into the language to make it as Arab-oriented as possible.

A massive quantity of literature, both didactic and fictional, was produced in this language, known as *Mussalmani Bangla*, and distributed widely in the countryside. At the same time, the study of Arabic, Persian, and Urdu by Muslims, even in secular schools, was particularly emphasized

This was truly an age of confusion for the Bengali-speaking Muslims; a determined effort was underway to try to cut them off ftom their local roots. When the educated Bengali Hindus, inspired by the spirit of the European Enlightenment, had begun their quest for a revitalized Bengali identity,[33] Bengali Muslims, both educated and uneducated, found themselves engaged in a futile search for their supposed extraterritorial roots. Even when a few of them, like Mir Mosharraf Hosain (1847–1911), felt impelled to participate in the intellectual deliberations of the time through the medium of 'Sanskritic' Bengali—which had by then developed into a highly artistic modern language, thanks to the interventions of the scholars of Fort William and subsequent Hindu authors—the themes chosen by them were often extraterritorial in content and character, as Clinton Seely points out in chapter 5. Both the *Mussalmani puthis* as well as works in modern Bengali by nineteenth and early twentieth century Muslim authors and poets helped popularize the notion of a community whose territorial and cultural boundaries extended beyond a specific territory. The realities of Muslim life in Bengal, however, made it difficult to conceive of a community identity entirely divorced from the territory of their birth, and hence the confusion that characterized most Bengali Muslim writings at this time.

Efforts to articulate Islamic cultural symbols roused Bengali Muslims' sensitivity to Islam and the Islamic world, but this could hardly bring about a total rupture with their Bengali cultural roots. A whole range of observances and ceremonies, like the celebrations of the Bengali New Year's day, elaborate marriage rituals in the Bengali tradition (common even today), and the festivities associated with the winter harvest, continued to persist. Even in matters of religious rituals and practices, similar contradictions persisted. A close observer of the Bengali Muslim social scene in eastern Bengal in the twentieth century thus discovered that 'popular rituals and beliefs . . . exercise no less influence on man's life and are not less important than "official Islam" itself'. 'Some of the rituals and beliefs', he added, 'verge on primitive animism'.[34] Despite the emphasis on an extraterritorial identity, Bengali Muslims could scarcely distance themselves from the socio–territorial reality of their life. The anthropologist Ralph Nicholas noticed it even in the 1960s and felt it necessary to point to this unique fact in his contribution to this volume. He writes: 'It is important to qualify Vaisnavism and Islam [in Bengal] with the adjective "Bengali" because some fundamental characteristics of these faiths are found uniquely in the delta of the Ganges and the Brahmaputra River' (see chapter 2). It was the juxtaposition of Islamic religious beliefs and local cultural conceptions that shaped the social and religious perceptions of the Bengali Muslims of Bangladesh.

Local environment and local culture thus continued to have a decisive influence on the life of Bengal's Muslims despite all attempts at conformity. There was also continued opposition to overzealous imitation of alien cultural symbols. Although in a minority, this opposition, by people like Shah Abdul Hakim in the seventeenth century, as mentioned above, kept alive the debate: 'Are we Bengalis or Muslims?' Shahadat Khan's essay (chapter 7) emphasizes the existence of continued tension in the early twentieth century, and introduces breathtakingly fresh material and argument about humanistic radicalism in Bengali Islam. Such a radical–secular trend, even in the heyday of religious antagonism between Hindus and Muslims, reinforces our argument about the persistence of an alternative ideology in Bengali Muslim society. This ideology, which Kazi Abdul Wadud and others propagated (as Shahadat Khan tells us), was rooted in Bengali culture and inspired by a concern for revitalizing Bengali identity. It was liberal and non-communal in orientation, and it favoured the construction of a community identity based on the historic heritage of Bengal.

These cross-currents in Bengali Muslim society inevitably produced a dichotomy between the 'Muslim' and the 'Bengali' contents of their culture. However, as their identification with Islamic idioms and symbols increasingly became more and more pronounced, progressively undermining their loyalties to aspects of Bengali culture—specifically those that were openly challenged by the Islamic reformers—the notion of an exclusive 'Muslim' identity gained ground and helped crystallize the boundaries of a self-conscious religious community, perhaps for the first time in their history. It was a process in which the colonial state equally participated. The British, especially since the 1870s, continually treated the Muslims as a separate political entity (indeed, treating the Muslims of the entire subcontinent almost like a monolithic community, as if Muslims of different regions, classes, and linguistic backgrounds, had similar cultural orientations, problems, and concerns!),[35] and, both through policies of state patronage and public as well as private rhetoric, encouraged, and even invited, them to organize separately. Peter Hardy argues that the 'very idiom of British rule after 1857 encouraged the development of political consciousness by religious communities'.[36] It was specifically so in the case of Muslims. Support for *madrassa* education, introduction of the teaching of Arabic, Persian, and Urdu languages in schools and colleges as 'Islamic languages', reservation of seats for them in jobs and municipalities, as well as various administrative and political decisions, including the decision to accept the principle of a separate electorate for Muslims in 1906, all but recognized that the Muslims of the subcontinent formed one distinct religious community (and, as such, deserved to be treated as a separate political community!). For the Muslims of Bengal, the decision in 1905 to redraw the boundaries of the province, giving them a solid majority in the eastern half and their 'leaders' a say in its running, proved equally decisive in accelerating the process of communal polarization. The measure not only created antipathy between Bengali Muslims and Bengali Hindus, who opposed it, but subsequent developments in the region including Hindu agitation against it and in general Muslim support for it, made the concept of a composite Bengali ethno–linguistic 'culture' increasingly meaningless. Between 1905 and 1947, the British pursued an uneven and often indecisive policy towards the Muslims, sometimes favouring them, sometimes not, but their actions and decisions did mobilize the latter as a distinct 'community' when Independence came in 1947.

We must not however underrate the importance of societal change, especially in the nineteenth and early twentieth century, in producing conditions for the construction of an Islam-oriented community in Bengal. Writing in 1871, W.W. Hunter (1840–1900) described the 'Musalmans' as in 'all respects . . . a race ruined under British rule'.[37] Hunter's remark did not apply to all of the subcontinent, but only to lower Bengal. What is important, however, is to remember how British policy in the period after the conquest of Bengal systematically eliminated the older aristocracy and gradually replaced it by newer people, who often happened to be high-caste Hindus. Although the British did not purposely eliminate the Muslims from positions of privilege, some of the critical measures, such as the Permanent Settlement of the land revenue system of 1793, the Resumption Proceedings after 1828, and the introduction of English as the official language in 1837, swept away the old structure of administration, seriously hurting the upper class Muslim society of Bengal more than anywhere else.

According to Hunter, 'Hundreds of ancient families were ruined, and the educational system of the Musalmans, which was almost entirely maintained by rent-free grants, received its death-blow'.[38]

So long as the Muslim aristocracy held positions of power and influence they did not care much about the local Muslims and sought to maintain their exclusive identity. Describing their social life and attitude towards the local population thus, Shaista Suhrawardy Ikramullah, herself a member of one such family, wrote: 'Families such as Nawab Syud Muhammad's [Shaista's grandfather] regarded themselves as custodians of the Mughal culture and guarded it jealously as a precious possession. This made them rather isolated from the rest of the people in the Province of Bengal and their social life was confined to a narrow circle, while for marriage they most often had to go to the families outside Bengal or to other enclaves of Muslim culture there, such as Murshidabad, Midnapur and Shaistabad . . .'[39] However, the loss of their privilege, and, consequently, their access to wealth and power, resulted in their gradual decline, and, ironically, in an end to their self-imposed social and cultural isolation. Forced to live in cosmopolitan settings like Calcutta and Dhaka, their ethos gradually underwent changes despite attempts by them to preserve the façade of an exclusive aristocratic culture, fondly portrayed by Shaista S. Ikramullah. She acknowledged that many of them 'lived by the values of a vanished age' and found it difticult to come to terms with the modern world but, like her grandfather Syud Muhammad, who was forced by circumstances 'to forsake this way of life at the age of twenty-two and come to Calcutta', many others had to follow suit.[40]

However, changes were taking place too at the other end of the Bengal Muslim society. Colonial conditions in the early twentieth century, including the rise in prices of crops (notably rice and jute), expansion of educational facilities and employment opportunities, and the decline of the dominant Hindu landholding classes, gradually led to the rise of new social classes among Bengal Muslims.[41] They were recruited both from the older aristocratic families as well as the rural gentry, generally the affluent farmers. Collaboration and social interaction between them increased as a result of the change in circumstances; this interaction included marriage ties, getting together under the umbrella of Muslim *anjuman*s (literary, cultural, and, eventually, political societies/associations), and living in the same locality in towns and cities. Increased competition with educated Hindus for available jobs and political developments after the 1905 Partition of Bengal intensified communal polarization. Communal riots, which became widespread during the early twentieth century,[42] furthered this process of collaboration and interaction between the declining Muslim aristocracy and the new bourgeoisie, and the urge to promote the interest of the Muslims by mobilizing them as 'Muslims'.

Contributing to this process were modern conditions, like the introduction of the printing press, which made possible the publication of inexpensive religious texts and books projecting the Islamic image of the community. Similarly, the growing number of Muslim newspapers in Bengali helped project the Muslim 'cause' and continually fed their readers with news and views of the Muslim world. Improvements in communication and transportation allowed greater opportunity to Islamic preachers to reach out to the common man. Equally, the state-supported modern *madrassas* produced better-trained individuals to propagate the Islamic ideal, while new forms of social and cultural organizations, like the *anjumans*, furthered this tendency towards religion-oriented community formation unmatched by similar developments favouring a composite culture.[43]

Ironically, the colonial state also created conditions that were responsible for the promotion of, inter alia, secular knowledge, secular thought, growing literacy among Muslims, and the growth of modern political institutions and ideologies. Among the beneficiaries of colonial reforms were women, many of whom were Muslims. Sonia Nishat Amin's essay (chapter 6) reflects the changes in Muslim social attitude towards female education in the early twentieth century. Muslim women's journey to modern schools was surely slow, partial, and painful, as Sonia Amin points out, but it was a movement inconsistent with the ideology propagated by the nineteenth century reformers (as well as the modern-day 'fundamentalists'!). In a sense, this demonstrates the limits of an exclusivist religious ideology in the social environment of Bengal.

The question now is: Did the emergence of Bangladesh, ostensibly on the basis of a linguistic–cultural identity, fundamentally transform the orientation and character of the Bengal Muslims? Although, theoretically, it meant a greater emphasis on Bengali cultural identity for those in Bangladesh, it is doubtful whether it signified a fundamental break with the earlier trend. Even Bangabandhu Sheikh Mujib (d. 1975), the architect of secular Bangladesh, could not ignore the Islamic content of Bengal Muslim culture and had to make concessions to Islamic symbols and institutions (*see* Enayetur Rahim in chapter 10). If anything, the independence of Bangladesh has reactivated the debate:

'What are we? Muslims or Bengalis?' The consequent tension is all too real, as indicated by Joseph O'Connell (in chapter 8).

The state in Bangladesh, like its colonial predecessors—the British and the Pakistani—has routinely attempted to manipulate choices of cultural and religious symbols, often for overt political reasons, contributing to the confusion and tension. Contradictory policies and programmes pursued by the state at different times, especially under successive military regimes, have particularly favoured the fundamentalist groups (as Enayetur Rahim points out in chapter 10), and, consequently, a greater emphasis on Islamic symbols than before. Shelley Feldman (in chapter 9) draws attention to this trend in recent years, explaining how the policies of these regimes have undermined democratic institutions and compromised women's rights, and made them vulnerable to religious extremism.

The role of the state in Bangladesh demonstrates the arbitrary nature of political control and manipulation of symbols by the post-colonial regimes. It also suggests that the historic process of systematization and articulation of cultural symbols, which had earlier played a critical role in defining and redefining the cultural boundaries of Bengali Islam, has increasingly been replaced by a highly politicized and limited agenda sponsored by authoritarian regimes and fundamentalist groups—and supported specifically by the Saudis and the Pakistanis—whose goal is to revive the exclusivist religious ideology and to isolate the Bengal Muslims from their cultural roots. This collection of essays should reveal the historic contradictions inherent in Bengal Muslim culture. It should also demonstrate that, although systematization and articulation of religiously-oriented cultural symbols have played a seminal role in the past in moulding the cultural boundaries of the community, the socio–territorial reality could never be ignored. Neither state intervention nor the determined efferts of the religious reformers were able to materially alter this dual trend.

Notes and References

1. *See* Benedict Anderson, *Imagined Communities: Reflections on the Origin and Spread of Nationalism* (London, New York: Verso, 1994 (rpt.)), 6.
2. However, I do not wish to be dogmatic about this argument; it has its limitations, particularly if we are talking about a nation or a political community. The Jewish nationalist movement which led to the creation of the state of Israel in 1948, for example, was led, and participated in by people

who 'had not had a common territory for many centuries', argues Karl Deutsch. *See* Karl W. Deutsch, *Nationalism and Social Communication: An Inquiry into the Foundations of Nationality* (Cambridge, Mass: The Technology Press of the MIT, and New York: John Wiley & Sons, London, Chapman & Hall, 1953), 4. It should be pointed out, however, that although dispersed for centuries in different parts of the world, the Jewish people did share a unique sense of history and destiny.

3. Anderson, 12–19.

4. Ibid., 15.

5. *See* Paul R. Brass, 'Elite Groups, Symbol Manipulation and Ethnic Identity among the Muslims of South Asia', in David Taylor and Malcolm Yapp (eds.), *Political Identity in South Asia* (London and Dublin: Curzon Press, 1979), 68. Although Paul Brass talks in terms of a 'distinct nation', the argument is equally valid for a self-conscious community.

6. *See* Asim Roy, *The Islamic Syncretistic Tradition in Bengal* (Princeton: Princeton University Press, 1983), esp. chap. 1.

7. See Muin-ud-Din Ahmad Khan (ed.), *Selections from Bengal Government Records on Wahhabi Trials, 1863–1870 (Documents on Wahhabi Trials*, henceforth, Khan (ed.)), (Dacca: Asiatic Society of Pakistan, 1961), esp. 52–94, 173–86; also Peter Robb, 'The Impact of British Rule on Religious Community: Reflections on the Trial of Maulvi Ahmadullah of Patna in 1865', unpublished conference paper, 11th Conference on Modern South Asian Studies, Amsterdam, July 1990 (panel 9).

8. Mukundaram, *Kavikankan Chandi* (Calcutta University, Calcutta: Bangabasi Karyalaya, 1926), 86; also Abdul Karim, *Social History of the Muslims in Bengal (Down to AD 1538)*, (Dacca: The Asiatic Society of Pakistan, 1959), esp. chaps. 4 and 5.

9. *See* Muhammad Abdul Wali, 'Ethnological Notes on the Muhammadan Castes of Bengal', in *The Journal of the Anthropological Society of Bombay*, vol. VII: 2, 101; *see also* 'A Letter from a Muslim', in *The Moslem Chronicle* (Calcutta), 25 April 1895.

10. Mukundaram, *Kavikankan Chandi*, 85–6.

11. J.N. Das Gupta, *Bengal in the Sixteenth Century AD* (Calcutta: The University of Calcutta, 1914), 93

12. Ibid., 86.

13. *See* James Wise, *Notes on the Races, Castes and Tribes of Eastern Bengal* (London: Asiatic Society, 1883); also Rafiuddin Ahmed, *The Bengal Muslims 1871–1906: A Quest for Identity* (Delhi: Oxford University Press, 1981 and 1988), chap. 1.

14. Khan (ed.), *Documents on Wahhabi Trials*, 52–96, 157–86.

15. Richard M. Eaton, *The Rise of Islam and the Bengal Frontier, 1204–1760* (Berkeley, Los Angeles, London: University of California Press, 1993), xxii.

16. Tamizuddin Khan, *The Test of Time: My Life and Days* (Dhaka: University Press, 1989), 2.

17. Abul Mansur Ahmad, *Atmakatha*, 4th edn (Dhaka: Abul Mansur Ahmad Smrity Sansad, 1988), 13.

18. Muhammad Abdur Rahim, *Social and Cultural History of Bengal*, vol. I, 1201–1576, (Karachi: Pakistan Historical Society, 1963), 56–70.

19. Aziz Ahmad, *Studies in Islamic Culture in the Indian Environment* (Oxford: Clarendon Press, 1969), 74.

20. *See* Shaista Suhrawardy Ikramullah, *From Purdah to Parliament* (Karachi: Oxford University Press, 1998 (first published 1963)), esp. 131–4. Shaista Ikramullah herself epitomizes this trend. Although born and brought up in Calcutta (Bengal) at a time when the celebrated Bengali poet, Tagore (also a resident of Calcutta), had attained world fame for his lyrics and literary works after winning the Nobel Prize for Literature in 1913, she never even mentions the poet or his work. On the other hand, she is almost ecstatic when she talks about *mushaira, qawwali*, and the little-known Urdu poets of Delhi.

21. Several attempts were made, especially in the nineteenth and early twentieth century, to write Bengali in the Arabic script. This was in addition to attempts at Islamicization of Bengali idioms and vocabulary in the nineteenth century, which gave rise to a new generation of Muslim poetic compositions in a language generally described as Mussalmani Bengali. However, none of these attempts helped in changing the Muslim attitude towards the language.

22. Peter J. Bertocci, *The Politics of Community and Culture in Bangladesh: Selected Essay* (Dhaka: Centre for Social Studies, 1996), 19.

23. Roy, *Islamic Syncretistic Tradition*, chap. 2

24. Ibid.

25. This argument is principally based on Eaton's recent study. *See* Eaton, *Rise of Islam and the Bengal Frontier*, esp. chap. 8.

26. *See* Peter Hardy, *The Muslims of British India* (Cambridge: Cambridge University Press, 1972), 2–11, for a useful discussion on the social composition of the Muslim population in different parts of British India.

27. Eaton, *Rise of Islam and the Bengal Frontier*, 167–79.

28. Shah Abdul Hakim, *Nur Namah*, in Muhammad Enamul Huq, *Muslim Bangla Sahitya,* 2nd edn (Dacca: Pakistan Publications, 1965), 205–6.

29. Khan (ed.), *Documents on Wahhabi Trial*, pp. 43–99, 156–86; W.W. Hunter, *The Indian Musalmans: Are They Bound in Conscience to Rebel Against the Queen?*, 2nd edn (London: Trubner, 1872), esp. chaps. 1 and 2.

30. *See* Ahmed, *Bengal Muslims 1871–1906*, chap. 2.

31. Clifford Geertz explains this phenomenon thus: 'In a curiously ironical way, intense involvement with the West moved religious faith closer to the centre of our peoples' self-definition than it had been before. Before, men had been Muslims as a matter of circumstance; now they were, increasingly, Muslims as a matter of policy. They were *oppositional* Muslims'. Clifford Geertz, *Islam Observed: Religious Development in Morocco and*

Indonesia (Chicago and London: The University of Chicago Press, 1971), 65. For an interesting discussion of some of the prominent movements, *see* William R. Roff, 'Islamic Movements: One or Many?', in William R. Roff (ed.), *Islam and the Political Economy of Meaning: Comparative Studies of Muslim Discourse* (Berkeley and Los Angeles: University of California Press, 1987), 31–52.

32. *See* Kenneth W. Jones, *Arya Dharm: Hindu Consciousness in 19th Century Punjab* (Delhi: Manohar, 1989), esp. the preface and chaps. 1 and 2.

33. For a somewhat idealized view of this trend in Bengali Hindu society, *see* Nirad C. Chaudhuri, *The Autobiography of an Unknown Indian* (Reading: Addison–Wesley, 1989), 179–217.

34. A.K. Nazmul Karim, 'Some Aspects of Popular Beliefs among Muslims of Bengal', in *The Eastern Anthropologist*, vol. 9:1 (1955), 29–40.

35. Read, for example, Hunter's *Indian Musalmans* (1871); although he begins with a caveat that his remarks applied only to lower Bengal, the rhetoric and the argument that he used gave the false impression that he was talking about the fate of Muslims throughout British India. In actuality, even in his own time, and, certainly, later, this is how his arguments were generally interpreted by British administrators and Muslim politicians.

36. Hardy, *Muslims of British India*, 116.

37. Hunter, *Indian Musalmans*, 149.

38. Ibid., 177.

39. Ikramullah, *Purdah to Parliament*, 4.

40. Ibid., 9, 5.

41. *See* Rafiuddin Ahmed (ed.), *Religion, Nationalism, and Politics in Bangladesh* (New Delhi: South Asian Publishers, 1990), 14–16.

42. Suranjan Das, *Communal Riots in Bengal 1905–1947* (Delhi: Oxford University Press, 1991), esp. chaps. 2–5.

43. For a detailed discussion on the role of the colonial state in defining the boundaries of South Asia's Muslim community, *see* Hardy, *Muslims of British India*, chaps. 5, 6.

1

Who are the Bengal Muslims?
Conversion and Islamization in Bengal

RICHARD M. EATON

A striking feature of Islam in pre-modern Bengal is the cleavage that emerged between a folk Bengali variant, which was built upon indigenous roots, and a variant practiced and patronized primarily by urban-dwelling, *ashraf* classes. This cleavage lay behind the nineteenth century reform movement and contributed to the twentieth century upheavals that led first to the inclusion of eastern Bengal in the state of Pakistan, and eventually to its secession from that state. This essay examines the evolution of the Bengal Muslims between the sixteenth century and eighteenth centuries, a period when evidence of the religious culture of both *ashraf* and non-*ashraf* communities is especially well-documented. It also explores why and how Islam became the dominant religious tradition in Bengal but not in upper India, the epicentre of Indo–Muslim political culture, and in the eastern portion of the Bengal delta but not the western.

In the Bengali context, the *ashraf* generally included those Muslims claiming descent from immigrants from beyond the Khyber, or at least from beyond Bengal, who cultivated a high Perso–Islamic civilization and its associated literatures in Arabic, Persian, and Urdu. Soon after the Turkish conquest of the delta in 1204, Muslim immigrants from points west settled in cities like Gaur, Pandua, Satgaon, Sonargaon, and Chittagong, principally as long-distance traders, administrators, soldiers, and literati. From 1342 to 1574, however, under the rule of a succession of independent Muslim dynasties, Bengal became isolated from north India and immigration from points west was largely curtailed. In the wake of the Mughal conquest of 1574, however, Muslim immigrants from north India once again settled the delta in such numbers that it was their understanding of Islam that came to define *ashraf* religious sensibilities in modern Bengali history.

Although the Mughals had originated in fifteenth century Central Asia, by the time they conquered Bengal in the late sixteenth century they had already assimilated the political traditions of north India, a process accelerated by Akbar's policy of admitting Rajputs into his ruling class. In fact, they had become virtual Rajputs themselves. In the early seventeenth century, for example, we already hear of Muslim officers in Bengal indulging in the Rajput practice of *juhar*, the destruction of women and children as an alternative to suffering their capture by an enemy.[1] The Mughals in Bengal also preferred Ayurvedic medical therapy to the Yunani system inherited by medieval Islamic civilization. Islam Khan, the first governor to establish permanent Mughal dominion in the delta, sent for an Indian physician when he fell terminally ill in 1613. As one was not available, the governor only reluctantly accepted the services of a Muslim *hakim* who was later blamed for having administered the wrong treatment and unnecessarily killing him.[2] Reliance on Indian systems of medical theory in the face of fatal illness, and on Rajput customs when faced with immanent annihilation in battle—both of them life-threatening situations—suggests the degree to which Indian, and especially Rajput, values had penetrated Mughal culture by the early seventeenth century.

Conversely, from the Mughal–Rajput perspective, Bengal was a distinctly alien land. Abu'l-fazl, Akbar's chief counsellor and ideologue, described the region as 'a house of turbulence' (*bulghak-khana*). As he wrote in 1579, shortly after Akbar's armies had seized the province from its Afghan rulers,

The country of Bengal is a land where, owing to the climate's favouring the base, the dust of dissension is always rising. From the wickedness of men families have decayed, and dominions ruined. Hence in old writings it was called Bulghak-khana (house of turbulence).[3]

In effect, we have here a theory of socio–political decay: an enervating climate corrupts men, corrupted men ruin sovereign domains and, implicitly, ruined domains pave the way for conquest by more virile, 'manly' races. In its linkage of Bengal's climate with the debased behaviour of the people exposed to it, Abu'l-fazl's theory of decay at once recalls similar views later adopted by British colonial officials.[4]

The Mughals' alienation from the land was accompanied by feelings of superiority or condescension toward its people. Especially in matters of language, dress, or diet, officials newly-arrived to the delta experienced profound differences from the north Indian culture to which they had been accustomed. The Bengali diet of fish and rice, for example, contrasted sharply with the wheat and meat diet of the Punjab and appears to have posed a special stumbling block for immigrants.[5] At the same time, Mughal officers associated Bengalis with fishing, a mode of life they despised. Around 1620 two Mughal officers, aiming to belittle the martial accomplishments of one of their comrades, challenged the latter with the words: 'Which of the rebels have you defeated except a band of fishermen who raised a stockade at Ghalwapara?' In reply, the other observed that even the Mughals' most formidable adversaries in Bengal, Isa Khan and Musa Khan, had been fishermen. 'Where shall I find a Dawud son of Sulayman Karrani to fight with, in order to please you?' he asked rhetorically, and with some annoyance, adding that it was his duty as an imperial officer to subdue all imperial enemies in Bengal; 'whether they are *Machwas* [fishermen] or Mughals or Afghans'.[6] Revealed in this exchange is the notion that the only opponents truly worthy of the imperial forces were Mughal rebels or Afghans like the recently-defeated Karranis; Bengalis, being fishermen, apparently occupied a separate category of less worthy adversaries.

Mughal officials thus saw themselves as the land's natural rulers, distinguished from Bengalis not only as tax-receivers as opposed to taxpayers, but as north Indian fighting men as opposed to docile fishermen. On one occasion governor Islam Khan's chief naval officer, Ihtimam Khan, expressed resentment that the governor had treated him and his son like 'natives'.[7] The idea that *ashraf* Muslims occupied a social category altogether separate from the 'natives' was echoed in the observation of an outside observer, Fray Sebastien Manrique, who in 1629 described Bengal's population as composed of three groups: 'the Portuguese, the Moors, and the natives of the country'.[8] According to this system of social classification, Muslims were, by definition, foreigners to the land. The idea that 'natives' could also be 'Moors', that is, that there could be Bengali Muslims, was, from the perspective of members of the urban Mughal ruling class whom Manrique met, conceptually impossible.

Regarding the religion of the Mughal *ashraf*, three features stand out: (a) a special link with the pan-Indian Chishti order, (b) a conceptual separation of religion and state, and (c) a disinclination to convert Bengalis to Islam. Most Muslims in the imperial corps brought to Bengal styles of Islamic piety that had already evolved in north India during the preceding century. We can glimpse a profile of this piety from the remarks of Mirza Nathan, a middle-level imperial officer whose unofficial memoir is filled with references to witchcraft, astrology, and notions of the paradisiac afterlife associated with Mughal soldiers he called *ghazis*. All of these elements were well integrated into his worldview.[9] Above all, Nathan's religion was characterized by a vivid sense in which Allah mediated his blessings to believers through the agency of saints. These, however, were not the village *pirs* who played such important roles in the world of rural Bengalis, but shaikhs belonging to the Chishti order of Sufism, the order most clearly associated with Mughal, and before that, Tughluq imperialism. This was also the most authentically Indian of Sufi brotherhoods, its wealth and power centred on the enormous cults based on the tomb–shrines of north Indian saints such as Muin al-Din Chishti (d. 1236) in Ajmer, Rajasthan; Nizam al-Din Auliya (d. 1325) in Delhi; or Farid al-Din Shakarganj (d. 1265) in Pakpattan, Punjab. Since the Tugluq period, this order enjoyed a very special status among Delhi's rulers, who lavishly patronized the descendants of the great Chishti shaikhs with magnificent tombs and considerable tax-free land. Mirza Nathan was himself a 'faithful disciple' (*murid-i bandagi*) of Farid al-Din Shakarganj, probably because the writer's ancestors had come from Punjab where Baba Farid's cult was especially prominent.[10] Moreover, Islam Khan, Bengal's first permanent governor (1608–13) and the man most responsible for consolidating Mughal rule in Bengal, was the grandson of Akbar's chief spiritual guide, Shaikh Salim Chishti. It was on this account that the governor on one occasion referred to Sufism as 'our ancestral profession' (*faqiri ki kasb-i buzurgan-i mast*).[11] One feature of *ashraf* piety, then, was a close and enduring connection with the Chishti order.

Second, *ashraf* Muslims conceptually distinguished religion and state, which was reflected, among other ways, in a functional specialization of their cities. As a provincial capital and administrative centre, Dhaka was primarily devoted to revenue collection, administration, politics, and military reviews. The city was also involved in considerable trade and money-making. Fray Manrique, who was there in 1640, wrote that merchants of Dhaka 'have raised the city to an eminence of wealth which is actually stupefying, especially when one sees and considers the large quantities of money which lie principally in the houses of the Cataris [Khatri], in such quantities indeed, that, being difficult to count, it is usually commonly to be weighed'.[12] In short, Dhaka was a secular city. Even its most imposing mosques, such as the Satgumbad Mosque (ca. 1664–76) or the mosques of Haji Khwaja Shahbaz (1679) and Khan Muhammad Mirza (1704), bear the stuccoed stamp of their north Indian patrons, and appear intended more to display imperial power than to inspire piety.

On the other hand, the ancient capitals of Gaur and Pandua, denied any political significance under the Mughals, emerged under their rule as Islamic sacred centres. The sanctity of Gaur focused in part on the Qadam Rasul, a reliquary established by Sultan 'Ala al-Din Husain Shah in 1503, containing a dais and black marble stone purporting to bear the impression of the Prophet's footprint.[13] However, the shrines most lavishly patronized by the Mughals were the older and more important ones in nearby Pandua: the tombs of Shaikh 'Ala al-Haq (d. 1398) and Shaikh Nur Qutb-i 'Alam (d. 1459). Both shaikhs were members of the Chishti order; they were indeed the most prominent Chishtis ever to have settled in Bengal. The shrine of Nur Qutbi 'Alam had been the object of state patronage ever since the son and successor of Sultan Jalal al-Din Muhammad (r. 1415–32), Sultan Ahmad (r. 1432–33), became a disciple of the famous shaikh. By the end of the fifteenth century it had become the focus of annual pilgrimages performed by Sultan 'Ala al-Din Husain Shah (r. 1493–1532).[14] A century later, in 1609, the Mughal officer Mirza Nathan went on a three-day pilgrimage to the shrine, having vowed to do so should his father recover from an illness.[15] Further, on the occasion of his own marriage, he went on a pilgrimage to Gaur's Qadam Rasul and Pandua's shrine of Shaikh 'Ala al-Haq.[16] Later, in 1624 when Shah Jahan was in Bengal, the future emperor distributed Rs 4,000 at Nur Qutb-i 'Alam's shrine, his largest cash contribution in all of Bengal.[17]

Thirdly, *ashraf* Muslims in Bengal adopted a strictly hands-off policy toward the non-Muslim society that everywhere surrounded them. Unlike the contemporary Ottoman empire where non-Muslim military recruits were converted to Islam as part of their assimilation into the ruling class, in India non-Muslims were given full admission into the Mughal officer corps as non-Muslims. What bonded together Mughal officers of diverse cultures was not a common religion, then, but the ideology of 'salt', the ritual eating of which served to bind people of unequal socio–political rank to mutual obligations: the higher-ranked person swore to protect the lower, in return for which the latter swore loyalty to the higher. Such bonds of loyalty among Mughal officers not only ran across religious or ethnic communities, but persisted over several generations.[18] At the same time, when making vows or swearing oaths, members of the imperial corps appealed to different deities according to their particular religious identities. On one occasion, a copy of the Qur'an and a black geode worshipped in the form of Vishnu (*salagram*) were brought to a mixed group of Mughal officers about to swear on oath. Placing their hand on the Qur'an, the Muslim officers took solemn oaths in the name of Allah; while the Hindu officers, placing their hand on the geode, did the same in the name of Vishnu.[19]

The invocation of a Hindu deity in this political ritual shows that unlike the early sultans of Bengal, Mughal officials did not patronize Islam as a state religion. Except for a brief episode of anti-Hindu persecution in the early 1680s,[20] Bengal's rulers maintained a strictly non-interventionist position in religious matters, despite pressure from local mullahs and Sufis to support Islam over other religions.[21] This point is seen most dramatically in the way local judges adjudicated disputes between Hindus and Muslims. In August 1640, a Bengali Muslim was brought before the judge (*shiqdar*) of Naraingarh in modern Midnapur District, having been accused of violating the religious sensibilities of nearby Hindu villagers by killing and eating a couple of peacocks. Turning to the accused, the judge, himself a Bengali Muslim, asked, 'Art thou not, as it seems, a Bengali and a Musalman . . . ? How then didst thou dare in a Hindu district to kill a living thing?' The judge then explained that sixty-six years earlier, when the Mughals conquered Bengal, Akbar had given his word 'that he and his successors would let [Bengalis] live under their own laws and customs: he [the judge] therefore allowed no breach of them'. With that, the judge ordered the accused to be whipped.[22] The larger point, of course, is that the Mughals were determined not to allow religion to interfere with their administration of Bengal.

One consequence of this hands-off policy was that Mughal officials refused to promote the conversion of Bengalis to Islam. Islam Khan is known to have discouraged the conversion of Bengalis, and on one occasion actually punished one of his officers for allowing it to happen. In 1609 when the governor's army was moving across the present Bogra region subduing hostile chieftains, one of his officers, Tuqmaq Khan, defeated Raja Ray, the zamindar of Shahzadpur. Shortly after this, Tuqmaq Khan employed the son of the defeated raja as his personal servant and at the same time converted him to Islam. This news deeply annoyed the governor, who punished Tuqmaq Khan by transferring him from his *jagir*.[23] Clearly, the governor did not view government service as a reward for conversion to Islam; to the contrary, in this instance the man responsible for causing the conversion was censured and transferred. Moreover, it was not only Islam Khan who opposed the conversion, but also 'the other officers of the State', suggesting that the hands-off policy was a general one.

This observation brings us to one of the great paradoxes of Bengali history, namely, that although Muslim regimes had ruled over Bengal since the early thirteenth century, a noticeable community of Muslim cultivators did not emerge there until the late sixteenth century, under a regime, the Mughals, that did nothing to encourage the conversion of Bengalis to Islam and in fact opposed such conversions. Communities of Muslim cultivators were first reported in the Dhaka region in 1599, at a time when the balance of power in that region was gradually shifting from powerful zamindars like 'Isa Khan and the other so-called 'twelve chieftains' (*bara bhuyan*), to Mughal imperial authorities.[24] Communities of Muslim cultivators were first reported in the Noakhali region in the 1630s, and in the Rangpur region in the 1660s.[25]

It is significant that the areas where communities of Muslim cultivators were first noticed—Dhaka, Noakhali, Rangpur—are located in the eastern half of the Bengal delta, and not the western delta. The reasons for this appear related to the extraordinary economic growth that the eastern delta was then experiencing relative to the west. Prior to the sixteenth century, eastern Bengal had been a heavily forested region that, being isolated from the principal centres of Brahmanic culture, had been only lightly touched by Indo–Aryan civilization. Archaeological data on the distribution and relative size of Bengal's ancient urban centres show that, between the Mauryan and Sena periods (4th c. BC–AD 12th c.), the western delta had become far more densely populated than had the east.[26] Greater urbanization suggests greater occupational specialization and social stratification. As a result, prior to the Turkish conquest of 1204, western Bengal had become far more deeply penetrated by Indo–Aryan civilization generally, and in particular by Brahman settlement and the diffusion of Brahmanic notions of hierarchical social organization and caste specialization. Around 1590, the poet Mukundaram, a native of Burdwan, described the highly elaborated caste society that by that time had appeared in western Bengal.[27] No such evidence exists for the east.

Two major obstacles inhibited the advance of Brahmanical society

into the eastern delta: heavy forestation, and lack of direct riverine contact with upper India. Today, West Bengal receives about 55″ of rain
annually, whereas central and eastern Bengal receive 60″ to 95″, with
the mouth of the Meghna receiving from 100″ to 120″ and eastern Sylhet about 150″.[28] Assuming this climatic pattern held in ancient times,
the density of vegetation in the delta's hinterland, formerly covered
with thick forests of sal,[29] would have increased dramatically as one
moved eastward. Cutting and clearing the land would have required
much more labour and organization, even with the aid of iron imple-
ments, than was the case in the less densely forested westerly regions.
The other obstacle to economic growth in the east was its isolation from
the great Ganges river system. In ancient times, the Ganges flowed
down the delta's western corridor through the present Bhagirata–
Hooghly channel, emptying into the Bay near Calcutta, where the river
is still known as the Adi-Ganga, 'original Ganges'. This left eastern
Bengal disconnected from the Ganges system. Due to continual
sedimentation, however, the Ganges in very early times began to spill
out of its former river-bed and find new channels to the east[30]—the
Bhairab, the Mathabhanga, the Garai–Madhumati, the Arialkhan—until
finally, in the late sixteenth century, it linked up with the Padma, enabling its principal course to flow directly into the heart of East Bengal.[31]
European maps dated 1548, 1615, 1660, and 1779 clearly show this
riverine movement.[32]

The implications of the Ganges's eastward migration, moreover,
were far-reaching. For one thing, it linked eastern Bengal's economy
with wider markets since it opened up a heavily forested and formerly
isolated region to direct commercial contact with upper India. More importantly, however, the great river's eastward migration carried with
it the epicentre of Bengali civilization, since its annual flooding
deposited the immense loads of silt that made possible the cultivation
of wet rice, which in turn could sustain ever larger concentrations of
population. Changes in the Mughal revenue demand between 1595 and
1659 reflect the changes in the relative fertility of different parts of the
delta, since such figures were based on the capacity of the land to
produce grain. Over the course of those sixty-four years, revenue
demand jumped by 117 per cent in the delta's most ecologically active
south-eastern region, and by 97 per cent in the northeast. On the other
hand, it increased by only 54 per cent in the less active southwest,
whereas in the ecologically moribund northwest it actually declined by
13 per cent.[33]

Moreover, the merger of the Ganges with the Padma occurred at the very moment that the whole of Bengal was absorbed into one of the largest imperial systems ever seen in South Asia: the Mughal empire under Akbar. Unlike earlier Muslim rulers of Bengal, who situated their capitals in the northwestern delta (i.e. Gaur, Pandua, Tanda), the Mughals in the early seventeenth century planted their provincial capital in the heart of the eastern delta, Dhaka. This meant that for the first time ever, eastern Bengal, formerly an underdeveloped, inaccessible, and heavily forested hinterland, became the focus of concerted and rapid political and economic development. Indeed, already by the late sixteenth century Bengal was producing so much surplus grain that rice emerged as an important export crop, which had never before happened. From two principal seaports, Chittagong in the east and Satgaon in the west, rice was exported throughout the Indian Ocean to points as far west as Goa and as far east as the Moluccas in Southeast Asia.[34] Although the eastward export of rice declined after about 1670, in lower Bengal it remained cheap and abundant throughout the seventeenth century and well into the eighteenth. In this respect, rice now joined cotton textiles, the delta's principal export commodity since at least the late fifteenth century, and a major one since at least the tenth. It was the delta's textile industry, of course, that attracted Portuguese, Dutch, and English merchants, and by the end of the seventeenth century, Bengal had emerged as Europe's single most important supplier of goods in Asia as a whole.[35] In exchange for manufactured textiles, both European and Asian merchants poured into the delta substantial amounts of silver which, minted into currency, fuelled the booming agrarian frontier by monetizing the local economy.[36]

In the ecologically active portions of the delta, and more particularly on the cutting edge of East Bengal's agrarian frontier, the pivotal figure was the forest pioneer, tied economically to the land and politically to the expanding Mughal state. Concerned with bringing stability to their turbulent and undeveloped eastern frontier, the Mughals did more than plant their provincial capital in the heart of the eastern delta. They also granted favourable or even tax-free tenures of land to industrious individuals who were expected to clear and bring into cultivation undeveloped forest tracts. The policy was intended to promote the emergence of local communities that would be both economically productive and politically loyal. Every recipient of such grants, Hindu or Muslim, was required to support his dependent clients and to pray for the long life of the Mughal state.[37] Hundreds of Mughal records dating from the mid-seventeenth century down to the advent of British power in 1760 document these pioneers' steady push into virgin jungle and their recruitment of local peoples to clear the jungle and bring the land into rice cultivation.[38] Because they mobilized local labour for these purposes, these men played decisive roles in the socio–economic development of the eastern delta. Through their agency, much of this region witnessed either the introduction or an intensification of wet rice cultivation, while local communities formerly engaged primarily in hunting, fishing, or shifting agriculture began devoting more time to full-time wet-rice peasant agriculture.

These pioneers also played decisive roles in the religious development of the region, as one of the conditions for obtaining a grant was to build on the land a mosque or temple, to be supported in perpetuity out of the wealth produced on site. Grants made out to Hindu institutions (e.g. *brahmottar, devottar, vishnottar, sivottar*) tended to integrate local communities into a Hindu-ordered cultural universe, whereas grants authorizing the establishment of mosques or shrines tended to integrate such communities into an Islamic-ordered cultural universe. Subsequent demographic patterns evolved from these earlier processes.[39] As most of the pioneers were Muslims, however, mosques comprised the majority of institutions established, with the result that the dominant mode of piety that evolved on East Bengal's economic frontier was Islamic. To be sure, the mosques themselves were not architecturally comparable with the great stone or brick religious monuments that the Mughals built in the cities. They were, rather, humble structures built of thatching and bamboo.

Nonetheless, such simple structures exercised considerable influence among the indigenous peoples of the eastern delta. For one thing, long after the founding pioneer died, the mosque he had built would continue to diffuse Islamic religious ideals amongst local communities, since Qur'an readers, callers to prayer, and preachers were also supported in perpetuity according to terms specified in the foundational grants. Furthermore, by the Mughal period the peoples of rural eastern Bengal, unlike those of the more Hinduized western delta, had not yet been integrated into a rigidly-structured caste society informed by Brahmanical notions of hierarchy and order. That is, they were not yet 'Hindu', meaning that in much of the eastern delta rice agriculture and Islam were introduced simultaneously and grew together, both of them focused on these humble mosques. In consequence, many pioneers who had obtained the land grants, mobilized labour, and founded these institutions passed into subsequent memory as powerful saints (*pirs*). In several cases, tomb cults grew up on their gravesites.

The religious authority possessed by the hundreds of tiny mosques and shrines that sprang up along the eastern frontier was further enhanced by the simultaneous diffusion of paper-making technology.[40] Traceable to the fifteenth century and unmistakably identified with Islamic civilization—the ordinary Bengali for 'paper' (*kagaj*) and 'pen' (*kalam*) are both Perso–Arabic loan words—the new technology fostered attitudes that endowed the written word with an authority qualitatively different from oral authority. With the proliferation of books and the religious gentry in the countryside, a 'culture of literacy' began to spread far beyond the Mughal state's bureaucratic sector or the delta's urban centres. Contemporary government documents confirm that Qur'an readers were attached to rural mosques and shrines as part of their endowments,[41] while Bengali sources dating from the fifteenth century refer to the magical power popularly attributed to the Qur'an.[42] In particular, the culture of literacy endowed the cult of Allah with a kind of authority—that of the unchangeable written word—which the delta's preliterate forest cults had until then lacked. That was because, apart from those areas along the older river valleys where Hindu civilization had already made inroads among indigenous peoples, most of the eastern hinterland was populated by communities lightly touched, if touched at all, by Hindu civilization and its own 'culture of literacy'. In the east, then, Islam came to be understood as a religion, not only of the axe and the plough, but also of the book.

Thus, although the Mughal government does not appear to have intended to Islamize the East Bengal countryside, such an outcome nonetheless resulted from its land policies. Seen from a global perspective, moreover, at the very time that the region became integrated politically with the Mughal Empire, that is, from 1574, it was also becoming integrated economically with the whole world, as silver originally mined in South or Central America and shipped to Spain eventually ended up fuelling the eastward push of Bengal's economic frontier. This occurred when silver imported to pay for Bengal's textile exports was coined into Mughal currency and locally invested, as when Hindu financiers advanced capital to Muslim pioneers, who in turn organized local labour to cut forested regions and founded mosques around which new agrarian communities coalesced.[43] All of this fostered a kind of cultural authority that was in the first instance

Mughal, but eventually Islamic. Ironically, Europe's early modern economic expansion in the 'New World' contributed to the growth of Islam in the 'Old World' and especially in Bengal, which by the end of the seventeenth century had become one of the most dynamic economic zones in all Eurasia.

It is true, of course, that deltaic peoples had been transforming forested lands to rice fields long before the Mughal age. What was new from at least the sixteenth century on, however, was that this process had become particularly associated with Muslim holy men, or perhaps more accurately, with industrious and capable forest pioneers subsequently identified as holy men. In popular memory, some of these men swelled into vivid mythico–historical figures, saints whose lives served as metaphors for the expansion of both religion and agriculture. They have endured precisely because, in the collective folk memory, their careers captured and telescoped a complex historical socio–religious process whereby a land originally forested and non-Muslim became arable and predominantly Muslim. For this reason, one finds evidence of medieval Bengal's socio–economic and religious transformations not only in Mughal revenue documents, but also in contemporary Bengali literature.

For example, the *Candi-Mangala* composed around 1590 by the poet Mukundaram, celebrates the goddess Chandi and her human agent, the hunter Kalaketu. In this poem the goddess entrusts Kalaketu with temporal sovereignty over her forest kingdom on the condition that he, as king, renounce the violent career of hunting and bring peace on earth by promoting her cult. To this end, Kalaketu is enjoined to oversee the clearing of the jungle and to establish there an ideal city whose population will cultivate the land and worship the king's benefactor, Chandi. The poem can thus be seen as a grand epic dramatizing the process of civilization-building in the Bengal delta, and more concretely, the push of rice-cultivating civilization into virgin forest. It is true that the model of royal authority that informs Mukundaram's *Candi-Mangala* is unambiguously Hindu. The king, Kalaketu, is both a devotee of the forest goddess Chandi and a raja in the classical Indian sense, while the peasant cultivators in the poem show their solidarity with the king by accepting betel-nut from his mouth, an act drawing directly on the Hindu ritual of devotion performed for a deity, that is, puja. Yet the principal pioneers responsible for clearing the forest, the men who made it possible for both the city and its rice fields to flourish, were

Muslims. 'The Great Hero [Kalaketu] is clearing the forest', the poet proclaimed,

> Hearing the news, outsiders came from various lands.
> The hero then bought and distributed among them
> > Heavy knives (*kath-da*), axes (*kuthar*), battle-axes *(tangi)*, and pikes (*ban*).
> From the North came the Das (people),
> > One hundred of them advanced.
> They were struck with wonder on seeing the Hero,
> > Who distributed betel-nut to each of them.
> From the South came the harvesters,
> > Five hundred of them came under one organizer.
> From the West came Zafar Mian,
> > Together with twenty-two thousand men.
> Sulaimani beads in their hands,
> > They chanted the names of their *pir* and the Prophet.
> Having cleared the forest
> > They established markets.
> Hundreds and hundreds of foreigners
> > Ate and entered the forest.
> Hearing the sound of the axe,
> > The tiger became apprehensive and ran away, roaring.[44]

Muslim pioneers in this poem are associated with three interrelated themes: (a) subduing a tiger, that is, taming Bengal's untamed wilderness, (b) clearing the jungle, thus preparing the land for the cultivation of rice, and (c) establishing markets, that is, introducing commerce and a cash economy into a hitherto undeveloped hinterland. Moreover, these men are said to have come from the west, suggesting origins in upper India or beyond, in contrast to the aboriginals who came from the north and the harvesters who came from the south, that is, from within the delta. In point of numbers, the twenty-two thousand Muslims far surpassed the other pioneers. We also see that the Muslims were led by a single man, 'Zafar Mian', evidently the chieftain or organizer of the Muslim workmen. Finally, these men practiced a style of Islamic piety that focused on chanting the name of a *pir*, who quite possibly was Zafar Mian himself.[45] Although the narrative cannot be understood as an eyewitness account, it probably had some basis in what was happening in Mukundaram's own day. Even had there been no historical 'Zafar Mian', the poet was clearly familiar with the theme of thousands of Muslims entering and transforming the forests under the leadership of capable chieftains or charismatic *pir*s.

Similar themes are seen in the legend of Shaikh Jalal al-Din Tabrizi, found in another sixteenth century text, the *Sekasubhodaya*.[46] Although the events described in Mukundaram's poem take place in a 'time-out-of-time', those described in the *Sekasubhodaya* are set in the period just prior to the Turkish conquest; indeed, its author purports to have been the minister of Lakshmana Sena, the Hindu king defeated by the Turks in 1204. Both poems belong to a genre of pre-modern Bengali literature, the *mangala-kavya*, which typically glorified a particular deity and promised the deity's followers bountiful auspiciousness in return for their devotion. However, the hero of the *Sekasubhodaya* is not a traditional Bengali deity, but Shaikh Jalal al-Din Tabrizi, a figure said to have come from somewhere west of Bengal. He was instructed by *Pradhanpurusa* ('Great Person', i.e. God) to go to 'the eastern country', where he would meet Raja Lakshmana Sena, in whose kingdom he would build a 'house of God' (*devasadana*), or mosque. Shaikh Tabrizi did as he was told. Walking on the Ganges river with his magical shoes, Shaikh Tabrizi reached the Senas' capital at Pandua, and upon meeting Raja Lakshmana Sena he challenged the king to cause a nearby heron to release a fish caught in its bill. When Lakshmana Sena declined, the shaikh merely glanced at the bird, which at once dropped the fish. Seeing this, the astonished king asked for the shaikh's grace (*prasad*) and vowed to remain his steadfast devotee.

Shaikh Tabrizi then set about building the mosque. After Lakshmana Sena donated some forest land for the purpose, the holy man prepared the site by clearing the area of demons and offering handfuls of holy water to *Pradhanpurusa*, to the Himalayas, and to various other personages. This done, Shaikh Tabrizi 'invited people from the country and had them settled in that land'. Here we see a clear division of labour between the Hindu monarch and the Muslim holy man: the former donates forest land for the mosque while the latter performs the ritual feats necessary to establish the institution and invites local people to settle a formerly forested land. The shaikh issued formal documents of settlement to these men, who now cultivated the fields the income from which would be used to support the mosque.[47]

As with 'Zafar Mian' in Mukundaram's poem, we should not hope to recover in this text the historical 'Shaikh Tabrizi'. Rather, both men represent metaphors for changes experienced by people all over the delta, and in particular, the gradual cultural shift, well under way by the sixteenth century, from a Bengali Hindu world to a Bengali Muslim world. The *Sekasubhodaya* accomplished this by presenting the new in the guise of the familiar: Shaikh Tabrizi radiated a 'glow of penance' or *tapahprabhab*, the power acquired through the practice of ascetic austerities; the 'grace' he gave to the king was *prasad*, the food a Hindu deity gives a devotee; the shaikh's consecration of the mosque followed a ritual programme consistent with that of a temple, and the shaikh's patron deity, 'Allah', was given the generic and hence portable name *Pradhanpurusa*, 'Great Person'. Shorn of its fabulous embellishments, the text presents us with a model of patronage—a mosque linked economically with the hinterland and politically with the state—that was fundamental to the historical expansion of Muslim agrarian civilization throughout the delta. The *Sekasubhodaya* and the *Candi-Mangala* thus present us with literary versions of a process of socio–economic and cultural change that confirm the evidence of such change found in administrative documents of the period.

A more complex and self-consciously 'Islamic' work is Saiyid Sultan's great epic poem *Nabi-Bamsa*. Composed in the Chittagong region and also dating to the late sixteenth century, this ambitious work seeks to carve out a theological space for Islam amidst the various religious traditions already nested in the Bengal delta. For example, the work treats the major deities of the Hindu pantheon, including Brahma, Vishnu, Siva, Rama, and Krishna, as successive prophets of God, followed in turn by Adam, Noah, Abraham, Moses, Jesus, and Muhammad. By commenting in this way on Vedic, Vaishnava, and Saiva divinities, in addition to biblical figures, *Nabi-Bamsa* fostered the claim that Islam was the heir, not only to Judaism and Christianity, but also to the religious traditions of pre-Muslim Bengal. In this way, rather than repudiating those older religious traditions, Saiyid Sultan's epic served to *connect* Islam with Bengal's socio–religious past, or at least with that part of it represented in the high textual tradition of the Brahmans. But it would be wrong to characterize the work as merely 'syncretic'; on fundamental points of theology, the poet clearly drew on Judeo–Islamic and not on Indic thought. For example, although the author freely interchanges the Arabic term *nabi* with the Sanskrit *avatara*, his meaning is not the Indic conception of repeated incarnations of the divine, but rather the Judeo–Islamic 'once-only' conception of prophethood. Similarly, the epic did not subscribe to a view of cosmic time as oscillating between ages of splendour and ages of ruin in the cyclical manner characteristic of classical Indian thought. Rather, as religion in the time of each *nabi/avatara* became corrupt, God sent down later prophets with a view to propagating belief in one god, culminating in the last and most perfect one, Muhammad. Already in the four Vedas, the poet states, God ('Kartar') had given witness to the certain coming of Muhammad's prophetic mission.[48]

It is in its characterizations of Adam and Abraham, however, that the epic poem's agrarian dimension comes through most clearly. Adam, for his part, made his first earthly appearance on Sondwip island, off Bengal's southeastern coast. There the angel Gabriel instructed him to go to Arabia, where at Mecca he would construct the original Ka'aba.[49] When this was accomplished, Gabriel gave Adam a plough, a yoke, two bulls, and seed, addressing him with the words, 'Niranjan [God] has commanded that agriculture will be your destiny'. Adam then planted the seeds, harvested the crop, ground the grain, and made bread.[50] Similar ideas are found in the poet's treatment of Abraham, the supreme patriarch of Judeo–Christian–Islamic civilization. Born and raised in a forest, Abraham is said to have travelled to Palestine, where he attracted tribes from nearby lands, mobilized local labour to cut down the forest, and built a holy place, Jerusalem's Temple, where prayers were offered to Niranjan.[51] Clearly, the principal themes of Abraham's life as presented here—His sylvan origins, his recruitment of nearby tribesmen, his leadership in clearing the forest, and his building a house of prayer—mirrored quite precisely the careers of the hundreds of pioneers who, during the sixteenth to eighteenth centuries, had been given state land-grants for the purpose of mobilizing local clients in the Bengali countryside for just such activities.

Here, then, was a remarkable fit between social reality and religious thought. To be a good Muslim, so it was believed, one must cultivate the earth, as Adam did. Present-day Muslim cultivators attach a similar significance to Adam's career. Cultivators of Pabna district identify the earth's soil, from which Adam was made, as the source of Adam's power and of his ability to cultivate the earth. In their view, farming the earth successfully is the fundamental task of all mankind, not only because they themselves have also come from (i.e. were nurtured by the fruit of) the soil, but because it was God's command to Adam that he reduce the earth to the plough. It was by farming the earth that Adam obeyed God, thereby articulating his identity as the first man and as the first Muslim. Hence all men descended from Adam, in this view, can most fully demonstrate their obedience to God, and indeed, their humanity, by cultivating the earth.[52] A 1913 village survey in Dhaka district noted that Muslims there 'entirely fall upon agriculture as their only source of income, and unless driven to the last stage of starvation they never hire themselves for any kind of service, which is looked upon with contempt on their part'.[53] In 1908 the gazetteer for Khulna district noted that the Muslim masses 'are descendants of semi-Hinduized aborigines, principally Chandals and Pods, and of low caste Hindus, who were converted to Islam . . . . [They] do not, however, know or admit that they are the descendants of converts to Islam; according to them they are the tillers of the soil, while the Ashraf do not cultivate the land with their own hands'.[54]

The last phrase in this passage takes us back to the socio–religious cleavage referred to at the outset of this essay. I have argued that what defined *ashraf* identity was the cultivation of high Perso–Islamic civilization and a claimed descent from immigrants from west of Bengal. This however fails to go far enough. What served most profoundly to distinguish Bengali Muslim cultivators from *ashraf* classes, as the evidence cited above suggests, was the plough. Whereas cultivators defined their Muslim identity around cultivating the soil, the *ashraf* disdained the plough and refused to touch it. A 1901 survey among the Muslims of Nadia district found that 'the Ashrafs will not adopt cultivation for their living. They consider cultivation to be a degraded occupation and they shun it for that reason'.[55] Also, in the Census for the same year H. H. Risley wrote that 'like the higher Hindu castes, the Ashraf consider it degrading to accept menial service or to handle the plough'.[56] After all, the bulk of the Turks, Afghans, Iranians, or Arabs who had migrated to India from the eleventh century onward no more saw themselves taking up agriculture than did English servants of the East India Company. Like the British, foreign-born Muslims saw themselves as having come to India to administer a vast empire whose wealth they would appropriate, and not to participate with Indians as fellow cultivators.

Conclusion

Over the past fifteen centuries Islam has been continuously redefined, reinterpreted, and contested, as competing social groups have risen or fallen in prominence and influence. To the historian, the challenge is to identify those groups and, by situating them in their unique historical contexts, to determine how they constructed the religion in the particular way they did. From this perspective, it becomes unproductive, or simply wrong, to speak of one group's understanding of Islam as 'orthodox' and another's as 'unorthodox' or of one variant as 'fundamentalist' and another as 'syncretic', or whatever. Such rhetorical labels may help in identifying and sorting out competing social classes in a given historical situation, or in determining who is on whose side in a particular debate. However, as analytical tools they are quite useless.

In the same way, it would be wrong to view Islam as a monolithic essence that simply 'expanded' across space, time, and social class, in the process assimilating great numbers of people into a single framework of piety. In Bengal, as elsewhere, Islam was continuously reinterpreted as different social classes in different periods became its dominant carriers, spokesmen, or representatives. Thus, in the thirteenth century, Islam had been associated with the ruling ethos of the delta's Turkish conquerors, and in the cities, at least, such an association persisted for several centuries, sustained especially by Sufi shaikhs of the Chishti order. Later, the Mughal conquest permitted an influx of a new élite class of *ashraf* Muslims, immigrants from points west of the delta, or their descendants, who were typically administrators, soldiers, mystics, scholars, or long-distance merchants. For them, a rich tradition of Persian art and literature served to mediate and inform Islamic piety, which most of them subordinated to the secular ethos of Mughal imperialism. In particular, the *ashraf* classes refused to engage in agricultural operations, and some Mughal officers even opposed the Islamization of native Bengalis who did. By the seventeenth and eighteenth centuries, however, owing principally to phenomenal levels of agrarian and demographic expansion in East Bengal, the dominant carriers of Islamic civilization in the delta were no longer the urban *ashraf*, but peasant cultivators of the eastern frontier, who in extraordinary ways had assimilated Islam to their agrarian worldview.

What made this possible was that in the Mughal period, Bengal's agrarian and political frontiers had collapsed into one. From Sylhet through Chittagong, the government fused the political goal of deepening its authority among dependent clients rooted on the land with the economic goal of expanding the state's arable land area. This was achieved by issuing grants aiming at the agricultural development of the forested hinterland, most of whose recipients were petty mullahs, pilgrims returned from Mecca, preachers, charismatic *pir*s, and local chieftains seeking tax-free land. These men oversaw, or undertook to oversee, the clearing of forest and the construction of mosques or shrines, which in turn became the nuclei for the diffusion of Islamic ideals along the agrarian frontier.

Above all, the local communities that fell under the economic and religious influence of these institutions do not appear to have perceived Islam as alien, or as a closed, exclusive system to be accepted or rejected as a whole. Although today one habitually thinks of world religions as self-contained and complete systems with well-defined borders, such a static or fixed understanding does not apply to Bengal's pre-modern frontier, a fluid context in which Islamic superhuman agencies, typically identified with local superhuman agencies, gradually seeped into local cosmologies that were themselves dynamic. This 'seepage' occurred over such a long period of time that one can at no point identify a specific moment of 'conversion', or any single moment when peoples saw themselves as having made a dramatic break with the past.[57] Islam in Bengal absorbed so much local culture and became so profoundly identified with the delta's long-term process of agrarian expansion, that the cultivating classes never seem to have regarded it as 'foreign'—even though some Muslim and Hindu literati and foreign observers did, and still do.[58]

In the context of pre-modern Bengal, then, it would seem inappropriate to speak of the 'conversion' of 'Hindus' to Islam. What one finds, rather, is an expanding agrarian civilization whose cultural counterpart was the growth of the cult of Allah. This larger movement was composed of several interwoven processes: (a) the eastward movement and settlement of colonizers from points west, (b) the incorporation of frontier tribal peoples into the expanding agrarian civilization, and (c) the natural population growth that accompanied the diffusion or the intensification of wet rice agriculture and the production of surplus food grains. Because this growth process combined natural, political, economic, and cultural forces, we find in eastern Bengal a remarkable congruence between a socio–economic system geared to the production of wet rice and a religious ideology that conferred special meaning on agrarian life. It is a testimony to the vitality of Islam, and one of the clues to its success as a world religion, that its adherents in Bengal were so creative in accommodating local sociocultural realities with the norms of the religion.

Notes and References

1. Mirza Nathan, *Baharistan-i Ghaybi*, Persian MS (Paris: Bibliothèque Nationale, Pers. Sup. 252, fols. 203b-204a), trans. M.I. Borah, *Baharistan-i Ghaybi*, 2 vols. (Gauhati: Government of Assam, 1936), 1:440. Mirza

Nathan, the author of one of the most important literary sources for early seventeenth century Bengal, was a junior officer who accompanied Bengal's first governor, Islam Khan Chishti (1608–13), out to Bengal in 1608 and participated in many, if not, most of the political and military engagements that marked Bengal's consolidation into the Empire during the years 1608–18. During this time, Nathan maintained a careful account of his operations in Bengal, as well as those of his colleagues and adversaries. The *Baharistan* is especially valuable for our present purposes since its author, a Punjabi Muslim, saw Bengal from both a north Indian and an imperial perspective.

2. Mirza Nathan, *Baharistan*, text fol. 140b; tr., 1:256.

3. H. Beveridge, tr., *The Akbar Nama of Abul-Fazl*, 3 vols, 2nd rept (Delhi: Ess Ess Publications, 1977), 3:427; text, 3:290.

4. Typical were those of Robert Orme, written in 1763: 'The abundance of advantages peculiar to this country', he wrote, 'through a long course of generations, have concurred with a languor peculiar to the unelastic atmosphere of the climate, to debase all the essential qualities of the human race, and notwithstanding the general effeminacy of character which is visible in all the Indians throughout the [Mughal] empire, the natives of Bengal are still of weaker frame and more enervated disposition than those of any other province'. Robert Orme, *History of the Military Transactions of the British Nation in Indostan* (rept, Madras: Pharaoh, 1861), 2:4–5.

5. Written in 1786, the *Riyaz al-salatin* reads almost like a colonial British manual on how to survive 'amongst the natives': 'And the food of the natives of that kingdom, from the high to the low, are fish, rice, mustard oil and curd and fruits and sweetmeats. They also eat plenty of red chilly and salt. In some parts of this country, salt is scarce. The natives of this country are of shabby tastes, shabby habits and shabby modes of dress. They do not eat breads of wheat and barley at all. Meat of goats and fowls and clarified butter do not agree with their systems'. Ghulam Husain Salim, *Riyazu-s-Salatin: a History of Bengal*, trans. Abdus Salam (rept Delhi: Idarah-i Adabiyat-i Delli, 1975), 21.

6. Mirza Nathan, *Baharistan* text, fol. 278b; trans. 2:650–1.

7. Ibid., text fol. 18a; trans. 1:51. Since the Persian term used here, *ahl-i Hind*, means simply 'Indian', one might expect to find it used only by those members of the ruling class who had immigrated from beyond India, however, Ihtimam Khan was himself an Indian Muslim from Punjab; hence his use of the term '*ahl-i Hind*' in a pejorative sense suggests that he had adopted *ashraf* attitudes as a result of serving in a power structure in which such attitudes were dominant.

8. Fray Sebastien Manrique, *Travels of Fray Sebastien Manrique, 1629–1643*, trans. E. Luard and H. Hosten, 2 vols. (Oxford: Hakluyt Society, 1927), 1:40.

9. Thus he remarked on the efficacy of witchcraft, as in the ability of Muslim practitioners to cause blood to spontaneously appear from the throats and stomachs of victims. Both Muslim and Hindu astrologers counselled Mughal commanders against inauspicious activities such as moving armies northward on Tuesdays or Wednesdays. Reflecting his understanding of the afterlife, Nathan wrote the following in describing a particularly bloody battle in which many Muslim warriors died: 'The houris of the highest heaven were waiting with the cups of heavenly drink in their hands watching which of the brave heroes, with their eyes fixed on the Unique and the Incomparable God, will make his journey to the heavenly kingdom in the most glorious way so that they might embrace him and satiate him with a drink of the pure wine from the reservoir of *Kawsar* [the river of paradise]'. *Baharistan*, text fols. 286a, 180a, 190a; trans. 2:671–2, 1:367, 397–8.

10. Ibid., text, fol. 302b; trans. 2:716.

11. Ibid., text fol. 60a; trans. 1:152.

12. Manrique, *Travels*, 1:44.

13. Shamsud-Din Ahmed, (ed. and trans.), *Inscriptions of Bengal*, vol. 4 (Rajshahi: Varendra Research Museum, 1960), 163. In 1609 Mirza Nathan, while in the midst of Mughal military operations in northwestern Bengal, paid his respects at this shrine, noting that the marble footprint had been purchased and brought from Arabia by one of the sultans 'so that the people of Bengal and everybody else, who were destined to come there, might attain eternal blessing by kissing the holy footprint'. Mirza Nathan, *Baharistan*, text fol. 58a; trans. 1:146.

14. 'Abd al-Rahman Chishti, *Mirat al-asrar*, Persian MS, composed 1654, copied 1806 (Patna: Khuda Bakhsh Library, Pers. MS no. 204), fol. 517b; Khwajah Nizamuddin Ahmad, *Tabaqat-i-Akbari*, trans. Brajendranath De, ed. Baini Prashad, 3 vols. (1939; rept Delhi: Low Price Publications, 1992), 3:443.

15. Mirza Nathan, *Baharistan*, text fol. 15a–b, trans. 1:42–3.

16. Ibid., text. fol. 58a, trans. 1:145.

17. Ibid., text fol. 299b; trans. 2:707.

18. When Mirza Nathan donned the garb of the Sufi in his protest against Governor Islam Khan, several Hindu offcers obstinately stood by Nathan and even suffered imprisonment and flogging for their loyalty to him. When brought before the governor to explain their behaviour, one of the Hindus, Baikuntha Das, was interrogated with the words, ' "You are a Hindu; why did you join this rebellion?" He replied, "God forbid! No rebellion will ever be raised either by Ihtimam Khan or his son [Mirza Nathan]. But as from my childhood, my father, at the request of his father, has given me to serve him and as 1 have been equally sharing his prosperity and adversity from my early life, so I cannot leave his company" '. *Baharistan*, text fol. 60b; trans. 1:153.

19. Ibid., text fol. 219b; trans. 2:476–7.

20. In 1679 Emperor Aurangzeb (r. 1658–1707), the most controversial of Mughal emperors, imposed the religion-sanctioned *jizya* tax on all non-Muslims of the empire. Theoretically required of all non-Muslims in return for state protection, the *jizya* had never previously been imposed or collected in Bengal. However, in early 1681 Dutch observers noted that imperial officials had begun collecting the *jizya* from the Hindus of Dhaka 'ever so strictly'. *Dagh-Register gehouden int Casteel Batavia vant passerende daer ter plaetse als over geheel Nederlandts-India* (Batavia: C. Kolff, 1928), 1680:121. In Qasimbazar, at that time the centre of Bengal's flourishing textile industry, officials forcibly demanded the *jizya* from Hindu silk workers, which disrupted the local textile production business and drove the city's 'little people' into the interior. Bengal's *diwan* or chief revenue officer, demanded that even resident European officials of the Dutch East India Company, as non-Muslims, pay the tax. *Generale missiven van gouverneurs-generaal en raden aan Heren XVII der Verenigde Oostindische Compagnie* (The Hague: Martinus Nijhoff, 1960), 4:391, 445, 564.

21. Fray Manrique, who was in Dhaka in 1640, wrote that mullahs and Sufis, that is, members of both the official and unofficial Muslim establishments, had urged the Mughal government in Dhaka to prosecute European Christian missionaries on grounds that they had been encouraging Muslims to break Islamic injunctions against taking pork and wine. However, both Shah Jahan and the Governor rejected these appeals. 'These attempts at persecution', he observed, 'would have succeeded had the [Christian] Brethren not obtained the support of the Emperor and consequently of the Nababo [governor]'. Manrique, *Travels*, 1:46–7.

22. Ibid., 2:95–115.

23. Mirza Nathan, *Baharistan*, text fol. 10b; trans. 1:32.

24. H. Hosten, 'Jesuit Letters from Bengal, Arakan and Burma (1599–1600)', *Bengal Past and Present*, 30 (1925), 59.

25. S.H. Askeri, 'The Mughal–Magh relations down to the time of Islam Khan Mashhadi', *Indian History Congress, Proceedings*, 22nd session (1959), 210. Kazim b. Muhammad Munshi Amin, *'Alamgir-nama*, ed. Khadim Husain and 'Abd al-Hai (Calcutta: Asiatic Society of Bengal, 1868), 677.

26. Barrie Morrison has made comparative calculations of the total area in square feet of ancient Bengal's six principal royal palaces: Pundranagara, 22,555,000; Pandua, 13,186,800; Gaur, 10,000,000; Kotivarasha, 2,700,000; Vikrampur, 810,000; and Devaparvata (at Lalmai), 360,000. The four largest of these were located in cities in Varendra, or north-western Bengal, whereas Vikrampur and Devaparvata, located in the east and southeast respectively, were many times smaller than the others. *See* Barrie Morrison, *Lalmai, a Cultural Center of Early Bengal: An*

Archaeological Report and Historical Analysis (Seattle: University of Washington Press, 1974), 124.

27. Mukundaram gives detailed lists of Hindu communities, divided into four tiers of occupationally differentiated endogamous groups, or jatis. The first tier included Brahmans, Kayasthas, and Baidyas. The second included productive classes such as cultivators, herders, iron smiths, potters, weavers, gardeners, barbers, candy makers, spice merchants, brass smiths, gold merchants, and so on. The third tier comprised ritually less pure castes: fishermen, oilpressers, woodcutters, launderers, tailors, molasses makers, carpenters, ferrymen, and beggars. At the end of the list, compelled to live outside the poet's imaginary city, were the grasscutters, leatherworkers, prostitutes, and Dom tribals who were scavengers and sweepers. Mukundaram, *Kavikankana Candi*, ed. Srikumar Bandyopadhyaya and Visvapati Chaudhuri (Calcutta: University of Calcutta, 1974), 355–61.

28. O.H.K. Spate and A.T.A. Learmonth, *India and Pakistan: A General and Regional Geography*, 3rd edn (London: Methuen, 1967), 575.

29. Anil Rawat, 'Life, Forests and Plant Sciences in Ancient India', in *History of Forestry in India,* ed. Ajay S. Rawat (New Delhi: Indus Publishing Co., 1991), 246.

30. *See* R.K. Mukerjee, *The Changing Face of Bengal: A Study of Riverine Economy* (Calcutta: University of Calcutta, 1938), 3–10; S.C. Majumdar, *Rivers of the Bengal Delta* (Calcutta: University of Calcutta, 1942), 65–72; Kanangopal Bagchi, *The Ganges Delta* (Calcutta: University of Calcutta, 1944), 33, 58. N.D. Bhattacharya, 'Changing Course of the Padma and Human Settlements', *National Geographic Journal of India.* 24/1–2 (March–June 1978), 63–5.

31. Already in 1567, the Venetian traveller Cesare Federici noted that ships were unable to sail north of Satgaon (near modern Calcutta) on the old Ganges, and seven years later Abu'l-fazl, Akbar's principal ideologue, recorded that the Ganges had divided into two branches at Tanda, with one branch following south to Satgaon and the other following east toward Sonargaon and Chittagong. By 1666, the deterioration of the former Ganges had progressed to the point that it had become altogether unnavigable. Cesare Federici, 'Extracts of Master Caesar Frederike his Eighteene Yeeres Indian Observations', in Samuel Purchas, *Hakluytus Posthumus, or Purchas his Pilgrimes* (1625; rept Glasgow: James MacLehose & Sons, 1905), 10:113; Abu'l-fazl 'Allami, *A'in-i Akbari*, vol. 3, trans. H.S. Jarrett, ed. Jadunath Sarkar, 2nd edn (1927; rept New Delhi: Oriental Books Reprint Corp., 1977–8), 3: 153, Jean-Baptice Tavernier, *Travels in India*, ed. V. Ball (1889; rept Lahore: al-Biruni, 1976), 1: 125.

32. *See* Richard M. Eaton, *The Rise of Islam and the Bengal Frontier, 1204–1760* (New Delhi: Oxford University Press, 1994), 196–7.

33. Eaton, *Rise of Islam*, 198–9.

34. François Pyrard, *The Voyage of François Pyrard of Laval to the East Inde, the Maldives, the Moluccas and Brazil*, ed. and trans. Albert Gray (Hakluyt Society, 1st ser., nos. 76, 77, 80, 1887–90; rept New York: Burt Franklin, n.d.), 2:327.

35. Om Prakash, *The Dutch East India Company and the Economy of Bengal, 1630–1720* (Princeton: Princeton University Press, 1985), 75. The notion that the influx of silver was primarily a European and maritime phenomenon has been vastly overstated in the literature. Even as late as the mid-eighteenth century, Asian traders, especially Gujaratis, Armenians, and Punjabis, played a more important role in Bengal's commercial economy than did Europeans. *See* Sushil Chaudhury, *From Prosperity to Decline: Eighteenth Century Bengal* (New Delhi: Manohar, 1995), esp. chaps seven and eight.

36. Eaton, *Rise of Islam*, 200–7.

37. The earliest of such grants issued from Chittagong, dated 2 September 1666, transferred to a certain Shah Zain al-'Abidin 166.4 acres of jungle land which he was required to bring into cultivation. The order issuing the grant also stipulated that 'he must assiduously pray for the survival of the powerful state. Chittagong District Collectorate Record Room, 'Kanun Daimer Nathi', no. 1, bundle 59, case no. 3863.

38. *See* Eaton, *Rise of Islam*, ch. 9.

39. In 1898, a time when the colonization of some of the Sylhet forests was still within living memory, a Muslim gentleman of northern Sylhet recalled that whenever a new village was founded, a temple to the goddess Kali was built if the founding landlord were a Sakta Hindu, and a temple to Vishnu if he were a Vaishnava. If a majority of the village were Vaishnava, they would build a shrine (*akhra*) to Radha and Krishna. If the area were infested with snakes, the patron deity was the snake goddess Manasa and if the village were founded by Muslims, a shrine to some Muslim *pir* would be established. P.N. Bhattacharjee, 'Folkcustom and Folklore of the Sylhet District of India', *Man in India*, 10/1 (Jan.–March, 1930), 133.

40. Jeremiah P. Losty, *The Art of the Book in India* (London: British Library, 1982), 10–12, 113; W.W. Rockhill, 'Notes on the Relations and Trade of China with the Eastern Archipelago and the Coast of the Indian Ocean during the Fourteenth Century', *T'oung Pao*, 16/2 (1915), 440.

41. 'Qur'an readers' were entitled *Qur'an-khwani* or *tilawat. See* 'Kanun Daimer Nathi', Chittagong District Collectorate Record Room, no. 65, bundle 73, case no. 4677; no. 72, bundle 63, case no. 4100; no. 113, bundle 35, case no. 2296.

42. Writing in 1494 in the Barisal region, Vijaya Gupta speaks of 'a teacher of the Qadi named Khalas . . . who always engaged himself in the study of the Qur'an and other religious books. . . . He said, if you ask me, I say, why are you afraid of demons [*bhut*], when you have got the religious books. Write [extracts] from the book and hang it down the neck. If then

also the demons [implying snakes] bite, I shall be held responsible'. Abdul Karim, *Social History of the Muslims of Bengal (down to* AD *1538)*, trans. Karim (Dacca: Asiatic Society of Pakistan, 1959), 171. Cf. Vijaya Gupta, *Padma Purana* (Calcutta: University of Calcutta, 1962), 140.

43. Already in the late sixteenth century, the poet Mukundaram had linked mobile cash with the process of forest clearing and agricultural operations. In the *Candi-Mangala*, the goddess Chandi orders the poem's hero, Kalaketu, to sell a valuable ring and use the money thus obtained to clear the forest so that a city may be built in her honour. Once the land was prepared for agriculture, Kalaketu was to advance his men rice, seeds, and cash, thereby facilitating their establishment on newly claimed lands. Mukundaram, *Kavikankana Candi*, ed. Srikumar Bandyopadhyay and Visvapati Chaudhuri (Calcutta: University of Calcutta, 1974), 290, 295–6, 354–5.

44. Ibid., 299–300.

45. It is possible that this Zafar Mian represents a hazy memory of Zafar Khan, the historical pioneer who in 1298 patronized the constructions of a *madrasa* at Tribeni, not distant from Mukundaram's home in Burdwan. *See* Shamsuddin Ahmed (ed. and trans.), *Inscriptions of Bengal*, 4 vols. (Rajshahi: Varendra Research Museum, 1960), 4:18–21.

46. Sukumar Sen (ed. and trans.), *Sekasubhodaya of Halayudha Misra* (Calcutta: Asiatic Society, 1963), ix–xi.

47. Ibid., 135–7, 179, 217–18, 220, 222–4.

48. Saiyid Sultan, *Nabi-Bamsa*, ed. Ahmed Sharif, 2 vols. (Dhaka: Bangla Academy, 1978), 1:24–5.

49. Ibid., 1:88, 98, 103.

50. Ibid., 1:107–9.

51. Ibid., 1:348, 420–1.

52. John P. Thorp, 'Masters of Earth: Conceptions of "Power" among Muslims of Rural Bangladesh', Ph.D. dissertation, University of Chicago, 1978, 40–54.

53. Dhaka District Collectorate, Record Room, Mauza Notes, Rupganj, vol. 1, Agla, no. 1063.

54. L.S.S. O'Malley, *Bengal District Gazetteers: Khulna* (Calcutta, 1908), 65.

55. 'Reports on the Religious and Social Divisions amongst the Mahomedans of Bengal', London: India Office Library, Risley Collection, Eur. MSS E 295, 9:88.

56. E.A. Gait, 'Muhammadan Castes and Tribes', in *Census of India, 1901*, vol. 6, 'The Lower Provinces of Bengal and their Feudatories', pt. 1, Report, 439. These turn of the century observations are echoed in more modern studies of Bengali Muslim Society. In 1960, a village study conducted in Comilla District by the Pakistan Academy for Rural Development found that 'the Muhuri Bari claimed greater respect because of their [Pathan] ancestry in the village . . . . For them, working in the field was

considered beneath one's dignity, as was true with the Khondkars, the Mirs and others who received formal education . . . . The Khondkars who are a sort of religious leaders are held in respect. Cultivation with their own hands is considered taboo. . . the "Mirs" whose title generally signifies dignity of a great lineage came to this village three generations ago. Apparently the first to settle had little land. Cultivation was repugnant to this family, too. It initially thrived on trade and service'. S.A. Qadir, *Village Dhanishwar: Three Generations of Man–Land Adjustment in an East Pakistan Village* (Comilla: Pakistan Academy for Rural Development, 1960), 52–4.

57. As late as the early twentieth century, Muslim cultivators retained indigenous names like Chand, Pal, and Dutt. J. E. Webster, *Eastern Bengal and Assam District Gazetteers: Noakhali* (Allahabad: Pioneer Press, 1911), 39.

58. In 1629, when Sebastien Manrique divided Bengal's population into three groups, 'the Portuguese, the Moors, and the natives of the country', he anticipated by several centuries the thinking of later observers who, informed like Manrique by normative understandings of what constitutes proper Islam, had difficulty understanding how Bengal's 'natives' could also be 'Moors'. In particular, during the nineteenth and twentieth centuries, British imperialists and both Hindu and Muslim reformers, each for their own reasons, stressed Islam's 'foreignness', which further contributed to the notion that there was a certain tension between being Bengali and being Muslim. For further discussion, *see* Joya Chatterji, 'The Bengali Muslim: A Contradiction in Terms? An Overview of the Debate on Bengali Muslim Identity', *Comparative Studies of South Asia, Africa, and the Middle East,* 16/2 (1996), 16–24.

2

Islam and Vaishnavism in the Environment of Rural Bengal

RALPH W. NICHOLAS

Introduction

Ordinary people in rural Bengal pay primary allegiance to one of two religions: Bengali Vaishnavism or Bengali Islam. It is important to qualify Vaishnavism and Islam with the adjective 'Bengali' because some fundamental characteristics of these faiths are found uniquely in the delta of the Ganges and Brahmaputra rivers. I shall argue that the distinctiveness of these religions is a product of some unique features of Bengali rural society, and that religious distinctiveness has, in its turn, contributed to Bengal's distinctive identity. In addition, I shall put forward some ideas that I cannot defend in detail but may be worth further exploration.

Background

In 1960, after a short visit to Delhi with Bengali friends to spend the Durga puja holidays, I took up residence in a small village in Midnapur district in West Bengal. I had read and heard a great deal about Bengali religion: I was, thus, alert to the importance of the Shaktis and Lord Shiva. I had a notion that elements of Tantric Buddhism might be readily visible if I kept my eyes open. My expectations were not unfulfilled. The villagers maintain temples for Shiva and Shitala, the powerful goddess controlling contagious diseases, particularly smallpox. They make offerings to Manasa, the snake goddess. Besides, almost every family has promised, at one time or another, to sacrifice a goat to the

Pancanana (five-faced Siva) of a nearby village if a family member is restored to health. Barren women perform fertility rituals during the annual Poush Baruni Mela at the Barga Bhima (Tara) temple in Tamluk town. Even the Muslims have a kind of Shakti in Olabibi, who is thought by some villagers to be the consort of Allah, just as Durga is the consort of Shiva, and who, like Shitala, is believed to be responsible for contagious diseases, particularly cholera.

As I began to more greatly appreciate the significance of daily activities and make more of the religious symbolism present in ordinary affairs, it became increasingly apparent that the predominant orientation of the Hindu villagers is not toward Shiva and the Shaktis, but toward Lord Krshna and his beloved Radha. Every household in the village has a *tulasi manca*, an altar on which a small basil plant, a symbol of Visnu, is grown. In prosperous houses, the altar is sometimes made of cement, and perhaps adorned with a bas-relief of Radha and Krshna in the embracing *yugalmurti*. In the homes of the poor the *tulasi manca* might be no more than a mud pillar, but in every Hindu household, just after the sun sets, a woman waters the *tulasi* plant in the *manca*, places a lighted lamp before it, sounds the conch three times to drive away malign spirits, and then bows reverentially before the *manca*. Some devout Vaishnavas cultivate small gardens of *tulasi*; the leaves are used in pujas, and beads are made from the stems. Very few Hindu villagers of the high and middle castes go without a tight-fitting necklace of *tulasi* beads.

On the night of the full moon (*purnima*), as soon as the moon begins to rise, the sound of the Vaishnava drum (*shri khol*) and cries of '*Haribol*' are heard throughout the village. There are two bands of Vaishnava singers in the village. On *purnima* they perform all night: they begin to sing slowly, the leader of the *dal* telling a story of Krshna's exploits in Brndaban. As the mood develops, the *khol*-players begin to finger out well-kown rhythms; the small brass cymbals (*kartal*) begin to ring. All the members of the *dal* begin to repeat the choruses in adoration of Lord Krshna. The leader dances with his arms raised straight above his head in the posture of the ecstatic Nityananda. His voice soars above the others, fervently repeating the name 'Hari'.

When I saw this demonstration of genuine religious emotion for the first time, I began to appreciate the fact that while these villagers *respect* Shiva and the Shaktis, they are devoted to Krshna and Radha. If Kali arouses in a high-caste Calcutta Hindu what Clifford Geertz would call the 'powerful, pervasive, and long-lasting moods and motivations of religion',[1] it is Radha and Krshna who do it for Hindu villagers. While I know much less about Islam in rural Bengal, I am impressed by a similar devotional quality that appears in it and which suggests that the kind of analysis proposed here is applicable to it too.

The mutual interchange of religious symbols and practices between Hinduism and Islam in Bengal is well known. In the recent past, Hindus and Muslims participated jointly in Muharram processions and in the veneration of Muslim saints (*pir*). Bengali Islam has an elaborate ritual life that certainly did not originate in Arabia or Persia. A systematic survey of religious beliefs and practices in rural Bengal could produce volumes on the syncretism of Hinduism and Islam. There are two reasons why I shall not take up this fascinating phenomenon.

First, religion, like any other component of a culture, is an orderly system of symbols.[2] Because symbols in a religious system have unique and complex relations to one another, these elementary constituents cannot be randomly rearranged. Nor can they be taken arbitrarily from one religious system and appended to another. Symbol-borrowing will not take place simply because practitioners of two religions happen to live near one another, or because conversion from one to the other was 'incomplete'. Rites and symbols are to be understood not by the discovery of their origins, but by the discovery of (a) their meanings to the faithful (meanings that may have nothing whatever to do with their origins), and (b) their functions in the systems of which they are parts.

Second, although the phenomenon of religious synthesis, by which I mean the building up of an orderly set of religious symbols somehow 'satisfactory' to a particular human group, would make for exciting study, there is more to be gained at the moment by analysis. This means taking apart the categories 'Hinduism' and 'Islam', 'Vaishnavism' and 'Shaktism', 'Sufi' and 'Orthodox', to see what kinds of systems these are. It lies beyond my present undertaking to try to say what kinds of symbolic systems they are. However, I think I can set forth some general ideas about connections between Bengali religions and Bengali society.

Society in the Bengal Delta

Like every other region in the world, Bengal is unique because it is located on a specific portion of the earth's surface, and no two portions are exactly alike. However, of the various kinds of natural features over which individual regions are distributed—deserts, mountains, plains, valleys—the river delta is a comparatively rare form. Besides, there is no other delta on earth the size of the Bengal delta. The Ganges, carrying the water from the southern slopes of the Himalayas, and the Brahmaputra, originating in the drainage of the Tibetan slopes of the same mountains, both find their way to the sea through Bengal. The heaviest rainfall in the world occurs in the north-eastern portion of the South Asian subcontinent, so that even the local rivers of Bengal discharge enormous volumes of water. Each of these mighty rivers carries with it a load of silt. Over some millenia, each year's deposit of silt has contributed to the building of the delta, raising the level of the land and extending it a little fiurther southward until today there is a 50,000 square mile deltaic plain. This delta, together with the fringe of non-alluvial raised land that forms a kind of horseshoe around it, is physical Bengal.

Until quite recently, the Bengal delta was technically a frontier area. There are several common meanings of the word 'frontier'. There is the modern European notion of a line on the surface of the earth that precisely demarcates one nation from another. The exactitude of these political frontiers is clearly indicated by the contemporary habit of erecting walls or fences along them. Another current conception of 'frontier', that of the 'ethnic frontier', is vaguer. People who speak the same language, practice the same way of life, and respond to the same cultural symbols are frequently found not only on both sides of a political frontier but also mixed among members of one or more different groups.[3] Most Americans, however, are likely to associate 'frontier' with the great American West in the nineteenth century. Many of us even have a vague idea about Frederick Jackson Turner's 'Frontier Hypothesis', which holds that unique features of American democracy are an outgrowth of the inherently democratic society of the frontier. However, there is more to be gained from the analysis of the case at hand than from analogy with another case.

Briefly, the conditions for continuous, frontier-type settlement were created in rural Bengal by changes in the courses of major rivers.[4] The Ganges originally flowed down into the Bay of Bengal through a channel on the westernmost side of the delta while the Brahmaputra once flowed down the eastern side. Where these great rivers reached the deltaic plain, the swiftness with which they were flowing before they entered Bengal was greatly decreased. A slow-moving river cannot carry as large a silt load as a swift river can, so much silt is deposited near the place where the rate of flow is reduced. Thus, the Bengal rivers gradually clogged their own courses, which caused them to shift to new, lower-lying stream-beds. As a consequence, the most important channel of the Ganges has shifted gradually and systematically toward the east, while the Brahmaputra has cut off its easternmost loop. These two rivers now flow the last hundred miles down to the sea along a united course.

The best agricultural land in Bengal is found in the areas where the rivers are most active. Thus, the location of the most productive soil has been changing over the centuries from the northern and western portions of the delta toward the eastern and southern portions. There is much evidence to indicate that the agriculturists moved with the rivers, out of the north and west into east and south. The fact that new land lay in the lower delta, waiting to be reclaimed, created a kind of longstanding frontier situation in Bengal.

Undoubtedly, a number of factors have conspired to produce what I call the 'ethnic homogeneity of the active delta'. The most frontier-like portions of the delta are simplest in their (Hindu) caste composition. In the areas of the deepest annual floods and the richest soils, single castes tend to predominate over large expanses of territory. Members of the caste-like group of Muslim agriculturists, often known as *shekhs*, predominate in all the rural districts of East Bengal. The Hindu pioneers of the delta are primarily Mahishya, Pod, and Namashudra. Mahishyas predominate in the southwestern portion of the delta: Midnapur, Howrah, Hooghly, and 24-Parganas; Pods are found primarily in areas near the sea in 24-Paraganas and Khulna, as well as in Jessore district; Namasudras are most numerous in the southeastern portion of the delta: Barisal, Faridpur, Khulna, and Jessore.[5] The Shekhs, Mahishyas, Pods, and Namashudras constitute the great bulk of the population of undivided Bengal. Their techniques as housebuilders, boatmen, fishermen, and 'deep water' cultivators are precisely adapted to the requirements of life in the delta.

These groups have non-Aryan origins: perhaps they are indigenous to Bengal or were perhaps driven, by the movement of the Aryans down the Ganges plain, into this land beyond the pale of Aryan civilization. No records suggest that they were ever elaborately divided into specialized caste groups, or that they were profoundly affected by Hindu conceptions of 'proper' social organization. As Hunter has put it: 'No one can study minutely the local monuments and traditions of the Lower Valley without coming to the conviction that the Hindu creed, as laid down in Manu and the Brahmanas, is a comparatively modern importation from the north, and that Buddhism was the first form of

elaborated religious belief which the Bengali people received'.[6] Super-
imposed over the relatively simple and unstratified society of delta
pioneers is a heterogeneous 'foreign' aristocracy, holding ideas about
both religion and society that are quite different from those of ordinary
villagers.

Sect and Social Statification

A careful examination of the evidence would reveal that until recently
the religion of the rural masses of Bengal has always been different
from that of their rulers. In the recent past, since about the end of the
eighteenth century, the effective rulers of rural Bengal have been
zamindars, mostly members of one of the various sections of three
highest-ranking castes in Bengal: Brahman, Baidya, and Kayastha. The
eighteenth and nineteenth centuries, during which the deposition of the
Muslims and the Permanent Settlement strengthened the positions of
the Hindu zamindars, constituted 'a period of great Sakta revival over
Bengal'.[7] My impression, based upon unsystematic observation of
members of these castes in the countryside, in Calcutta, and outside
Bengal, is that their primary religious orientation is toward the manifestations of Shakti and, to a lesser extent, toward Shiva. There is not any
sense of exclusiveness in what I call their 'orientation'; many a good
Calcutta Brahman wife is known to be a Baishnabi in daily practice.
Such Vaishnava temples as receive regular priestly service receive it
from Brahmans. I suspect, however, that if an all-Bengal survey of
temple priests were conducted, most would turn out to be Brahmans
serving in Shiva and Shakti temples. Among urban and middle-class
Bengalis, Durga puja would certainly be chosen the pre-eminent festival
of the annual cycle, and it is probable that a great majority of nomina-
tions for the most important temple in Calcutta would go to the Kali
temple at Kalighat. The nearest Vaishnava temple of importance comparable to that of Katighat is at Puri in Orissa.

People in Radhanagar, the small Midnapur village where I learned
about the importance of Vaishnavism in rural life, paradoxically choose
Shib gajan as the most significant festival in their annual cycle.[8] This
would appear to contradict the argument that deities of the Vaishnava
pantheon occupy the place of pride in their religious orientation. However, the villages are more catholic in their religion than high caste
people and city dwellers; they are not prone to ignore powerful deities.
They gladly accept the protection of the two Shiva lingas housed in the

Radhanagar temple, though they were installed there not at the villagers' initiative, but by former zamindars—high-caste men who must have worried about the 'imperfect' religion of the people of Radhanagar.

The inhabitants of Radhanagar join residents of nearby villages in attendance at a Durga puja which is held in the nearest *hat* (bi-weekly market). This puja was begun recently by the *hat's* owners, a Brahman family of Tamluk, who bear half the cost of the ceremony. The remaining expenses are paid by prosperous betel merchants of the market who can ill-afford to offend their landlords.

For Bengalis in Delhi, Durga puja is an important social event: members of the community meet one another and ritually affirm their identity in the alien context of north India. In Punjab and the UP too, Durga is a symbol of Bengali identity. Of course, another symbol might serve equally well, but the fact that most of the Delhi Bengalis are high-caste people with some connection to Calcutta was undoubtedly of great importance in the selection of their central symbols.

Residents of Chandipur, a village in Murshidabad district, were complaining, when I arrived to do research there, that village unity no longer existed. Located in one of the oldest portions of the Bengal delta, Chandipur is no longer inhabited primarily, as it once must have been, by one of the castes of delta pioneers. A complex and differentiated society, made up of nineteen different caste groups, has grown up in the village. At the top of the hierarchy are Bhumihar Brahmans who took over as landlords when the last of the indigo planters who had owned the village died.[9] Although not originally a Bengali caste, the Chandipur Bhumihars are now thoroughly Bengali. Also, although their claim to Brahmanhood is not old, they regard themselves and are treated by other villagers as Brahmans. The Bhumihars were never zamindari tax-collectors; even prior to Independence they owned their agricultural lands outright. Many Muslim cultivators and members of middle- and low-ranking Hindu castes are either share-croppers on Bhumihar land, or work as servants under the supervision of the proprietors, who are forbidden by caste rules to work in the field themselves.

The time of great prosperity in the village is early autumn, when the proceeds from important cash crops, including sugar-cane, jute, and vegetables, are all in hand. Before Independence, it was the custom of the Bhumihars to stage an elaborate Kali puja, during which annual payments were made to servants and gifts of cloth were distributed to dependents, both Hindu and Muslim. Increased population density, especially in the post-Partition period, and land ceiling legislation have resulted in a greatly reduced expenditure on the Kali puja. As an aside, it seems to me significant that the Bhumihars, non-Bengali newcomers to the local scene at the beginning of the twentieth century, took control of village society previously dominated by a British indigo planter, in part by establishing their ritual superiority and then by ceasing to make the 'traditional' prestations that symbolized their superordination. All this occurred within the lifetimes of some residents of the village. One cannot be too careful about applying the terms 'traditional' and 'modern' to features of Indian village society.

The important point here is that Kali is the preferred deity of the Bhumihar Brahmans of Chandipur, as well as the Barendra Shreni Brahmans who are landlords in the neighbouring village, and Brahmans and Kayastha groups all over southern Murshidabad and eastern Bengal districts. She and her sisters are the principal deities of the high castes throughout the older portions of the Bengal delta.

As in Radhanagar, religious activity in Chandipur is by no means confined to elaborate seasonal ceremonies, or to the Shaktis. On the contrary, a group of young Chandipur men from middle ranking castes gather almost nightly for Krshna kirtan. As a measure of the nonexclusiveness of cults, it is a Bhumihar Brahman who leads the group, but it is the middle-ranking castes—Barbers, Potters, Cowherds, Weavers, Garland-makers—that provide the most active participants, and whose members most often wear the Vaishnava *tulasi mala*.

Relatively elaborate Kali pujas are still held annually in the *paras* of Chandipur inhabited by the low-ranking Hari scavengers and Muci leather-workers. Castes in the lower ranks of society appear to be oriented to the Shaktis perhaps even more exclusively than the Brahman. In the case of certain low castes, such as Bagdis, whose relatively recent origin from hill tribes can be demonstrated, it may be argued that devotion to Shiva and the Shaktis represents the well-known phenomenon of merging the identities of tribal deities with those of deities in a larger system. However, Haris, Mucis, and Doms have been playing their unenviable roles in caste society for many generations.

In Radhanagar, there is no *para* of untouchables comparable to that of the Chandipur Mucis. In the village just west of Radhanagar, however, there is a neighbourhood of Kaora Haris, who work as toddy-tappers, labourers, and midwives. Like all other Hindus in the village, they grow a little *tulasi* plant on a humble earthen altar, but they are not Vaishnava oriented in the same sense as the majority of other villagers.

Members of their caste resident in a number of villages meet annually for a Kali puja, which is alleged to be a wildly drunken affair. One member of the group described this occasion as Manasa puja, suggesting that the exact identity of their caste goddess is not fully resolved.

Although I have spoken primarily about some villages which I am well-acquainted with, the general pattern of caste stratification and loose sectarian identification is quite widespread. In East Bengal, before 1947, a general picture of society would show small groups of Brahman, Kayastha, and Baidya zamindars dominant over large groups of Muslim and Hindu Namasudra cultivators and fishermen. Most of the middle-ranking artisan and service castes, Potters, Blacksmiths, and Barbers, among others, were Hindu. At the bottom of the system was a stratum of menial castes, nominally Hindu, but largely isolated in their religious life from the remainder of society. Throughout the east, but particularly in the less fertile tracts north of the Padma, were villages of Santal tribesmen, recent immigrants not yet absorbed into the caste hierarchy. Since Partition, most of the Hindu zamindars left East Bengal, and more of the Namashudras and others moved to India after each outbreak of communal rioting. The artisan and service castes, however, continued to be, and still are, to an extent, important in the rural economy of East Bengal, now Bangladesh.

In West Bengal, the position of the high caste zamindars was affected by zamindari abolition, land ceiling legislation, and subsequent socio–economic changes. In the north-western portion of the delta and in the Rarh country, some Brahmans and Kayasthas remained in the countryside, continuing to exercise dominance over middle- and low-ranking dependents. This pattern prevails in the Chandipur area, where Muslims constitute a majority of the local population and stand in the same relation to the dominant caste as they did before Partition and modern land reform legislation. In Radhanagar, and in the active deltaic areas generally, the influence of high castes upon village society was always more intermittent and less intense than in areas with relatively large, resident, high-ranking dominant castes.

Taking a very general view of Bengali rural society, particularly prior to 1947, it seems useful to envision it as composed of three tiers: At the top stand the *bhadralok*, mostly Brahmans, Kayasthas, and Baidyas, primarily devoted to the Shaktis and to Shiva. The middle stratum, by far the largest and least differerntiated of the three, is composed primarily of a few large groups of cultivators together with artisan and service castes, predominantly either Muslim or Vaisnava in religious orientation. The lowest-ranking groups of menial and labour-ing castes are primarily Shakti worshippers, though the basis of their religious commitment is surely different from that of the highest castes.

This very broad picture of Bengal rural society, which omits much of the detail that social anthropologists so dearly love, suggests three lines of further enquiry about Vaishnavism and Islam. The first of these is suitable for investigation by a social anthropologist: The fact that Vaish-navas and Muslims occupy the same general structural position in Bengali rural society suggests that their religions perform the same kind of functions in that society. The second line of enquiry deals with the symbolic systems that lie at the centre of belief and practice in these religions. If Vaishnavism and Islam serve the same general functions for groups in similar structural positions, then there are probably significant similarities between their religious ideas. A third line of investigation, essentially historical, would examine whether there are significant similarities between the methods by which Vaishnavism and Islam were succesfully propagated in the Bengal countryside.

The Social Organization of Islam and Vaishnavism in Rural Bengal

One of the most significant similarities between Vaishnavism and Islam, from the point of view of a social anthropologist, is the parallel sets of religious roles that they encapsulate. Perhaps the first of these sets of roles that strikes the outsider is the *bairagi*–fakir pair. Hardly a day goes by in a village without a visit from a Muslim or Vaishnava mendicant begging for a little food. Though both *bairagi*s and fakirs are supposed to have given up anything that would attach them to this world, and though they may travel great distances to attend important *mela*s (fairs), where they sit in long rows to receive alms from the devout, all the mendicants I knew maintained village homes and received their regular support from villagers in a fixed territory. Hindu villagers customarily give a little rice, or perhaps rice mixed with lentils, whether they are addressed by a *bairagi* or a fakir. Unfortunately, I never witnessed alms-giving in a Muslim neighbourhood, and cannot tell whether Muslims respond in the same way, though I believe they do. The merging of the *bairagi* and fakir roles is virtually complete in the *baul*, a religious mendicant whose attire, song, and speech all consciously mix symbols from Vaishnavism and Islam.

The role of the *bairagi* or fakir, implying detachment from the world, is held in relation to the general public which must, of course, remain attached if the mendicant is to get a living. The role of guru or *murshid* is defined in relation to the *cela* or *murid*. Guru is a general term with a number of specialized synonyms: the disciple of a particular Vaisnava guru, for example, may address him as *babaji* and refer to him as *gosvai*. A good *bairagi* friend in Murshidabad told me:

> *thakurer thakur amar baishnab gosvain*
> *e kali bhave toraite ar keha nai*
>
> [Lord of lords is my Vaishnava master,
> In this troubled world, there is no one else to deliver me.]

The *murshid*, the Sufi master, is said to hold much the same relationship to the initiate *murid*. The task of the murshid or guru (and guru is, in my experience, the most common term for both Hindu and Muslim religious teachers) is to initiate the *cela* or *murid* into the mystical knowledge of profound religious experience or religious ecstasy. Although some of the initiates become *bairagis* or fakirs, most are mature men with families who remain householding cultivators and constitute the principal sources of material support for their preceptors. The teacher may also instruct the disciple in curing illnesses, magical arts, or other important forms of ritual, but I have the impression that this is highly variable and incidental to the central task.

While most villagers to whom I talked about religious affairs were not particularly respectful toward the teachers (guru or *murshid*) who lived nearby and were well-known to them, most had the idea that there were teachers who lived a little distance away or were now dead who did have a more profound capacity. Thus, the local guru or *murshid* might become a *gosvain* or *pir*, as his reputation passed by the usual processes of rumour through the countryside. There is probably no village in Bengal that does not have the shrine of a *pir* (*dargah*), the tomb of a *gosvain* (*samadhi*), or both. The death anniversary of a renowned *gosvain* or *pir* is the occasion of a *kirtan* or '*urs*. Initially, the occasion probably attracts only villagers who were attached to the teacher during his lifetime. Then, however it appears likely that social process takes control over the rise in the reputation of some and the decline of others. A guru who died in the middle of the agricultural season will not attract many devotees, since there is no rest on the following day for those who would sing *kirtan* all night, and since supplies for a large feast are not so plentiful. [There are other factors, such as myths and miracles associated with the life of a departed guru, the extent of support received by him from well-to-do families in the village, etc. which equally contribute toward the rise and decline in reputation of a daceased guru. *Editor.*] Thus, since the group is smaller, there is less prospect that one of the participants will have a unique religious experience that will add stature to the cult. On the other hand, the renown of a teacher who dies shortly after the winter harvest may well increase over a period of years, and the size of his following may be greater in death than it was in life. (It is possible for the date of celebration of an important death anniversary to be changed to suit the agricultural calendar.)

To summarize what I have said about the parallel sets of roles that are created by Vaishnavism and Islam in rural Bengal, there are three important components of the society in its religious posture: the teacher, the disciple, and the village public. The man who is a disciple in the eyes of his teacher, is a *bairagi* or fakir in the eyes of the public. The man who is teacher to his disciple, is a guru or *murshid* to the public. However, there is nothing distinctively Bengali in this set of relations. Throughout southern Asia there are religious mendicants who rely upon charity for their existence and upon personal instruction for their enlightenment. The guru–*cela* relation might be seen as a special form of the patron–client relation upon which the caste system is built, and thus, as one of the most characteristic forms of social relation, not only in Bengal, but throughout South Asia. Yet, there are forms of social organization within the village public, whether Hindu or Muslim, that are uniquely Bengali. Both the forms of organization that I shall discuss are related to the peculiar structure of caste in the Bengal delta.

Vaishnava and Sufi 'Castes'

When I first went from house to house making my acquaintance with villagers of Radhanagar, I invariably asked people to what caste they belonged. Most people—over 75 per cent of the population—were Mahishyas, one of the castes of delta pioneers. A surprisingly large group, however, of 11 per cent, reported themselves as 'Baishtam'. I had not previously been aware that ordinary, settled families of agriculturists and labourers could have Vaishnavism as their only caste affiliation. On being questioned closely, they invariably asserted that they were '*asal jaṭiya* Baishnab', 'original' or 'pure caste Vaishnava'. Knowledgable men of the village, asked about the 'identity' of the Vaishnavas of the village, replied in a similar vein that everyone was a

Vaisnava. What about the man who was leader of the *samkirtan dal* in the east neighbourhood? Oh, he is a 'widow Vaishnava' (*bidhaba* Baishnab, locally pronounced *bedo* Baishtam). His mother was a Mahishya woman, but she became pregnant when she was a widow. When this happens, the villagers compel the widow to call in a *gosvain* for a reading of the *Bhagavata* (*Bhagabatpath*) in her house. Through *Bhagabatpath*, she becomes a Vaishnavi, and this is the caste of her child. With whom do such children marry? Only other such Vaishnavas.

The complexities that exist within the group that reported their caste as Vaishnava are not often easily understood. For example, those whose illegitimate ancestry is far enough in the past to be forgotten will not marry those whose origin is recent enough to be known. Not all who say they are *jatiya* Baishnab are descendants of widows; my next-door neighbour was a convert and, although he reported himself and his wife as Baishnabs, he said his children were Mahishyas and his son was married to a Mahishya girl from a thoroughly respectable family. The watchman in the adjacent village of Govindapur said he was *jatiya* Baishnab, but other villagers said he had been a member of a low-ranking Hindu weaver caste before he moved to the village.

The majority of *jatiya* Baishnabs are known as *bidhaba* Baishtams. Articulate villagers even proposed that the distinction between the rustic term Baishtam and the more literary form Baishnab describes the difference between the descendants of widows and the true devotees who have forsaken a respectable caste. Although most of the *jatiya* Baishnabs, like most other villagers, depend upon agriculture for their livelihoods, most of them have no agricultural land, since the paternal ancestor from whom they might have inherited was not a legitimate ancestor. Thus, most of them work as agricultural labourers, although they regard ploughing as demeaning and will not undertake it.

Criteria that are very important in caste ranking—respectability or origin and wealth—are against the *jatiya* Baishnabs being accorded a very high position in the village caste hierarchy. Yet the men whom I interviewed about the relative standings of village castes almost invariably ranked Baishnabs very high: as high as the dominant, respectable Mahishyas. Vaishnavism legitimates the illegitimate in the microcosm of the village, just as it did for so many members of morally dubious Buddhist sect in the early days of the Caitanya movement.[10]

There is a longstanding joke in Bengal about the proclivity of rural Muslims to rearrange their descent according to their fortunes. A village leader may claim descent from a Mughal or Afghan, and style himself

'Khan'. If his crops are good and his landholding increases, he may dis-cover that he is directly descended from the Prophet and become a 'Syed'. The great majority of ordinary Muslim villagers in Bengal, however, call themselves Shekh and respond with this term when asked for their 'caste'. To the linguistic sophisticates, *shekh* refers to descen-dants of Arabs, and, since it is clear that the Muslim cultivators of rural Bengal have little to do with Arabia, their apparent claim to Arabic de-scent is treated with derision. Too much attention has been paid to etymology, and to the meaning of the Arabic term from which Bengali *shekh* is derived. The important question to ask is: What is the associa-tion which people in rural Bengal have with the term *shekh*? Their earliest and most important experience with *shekh*s was their contact with Sufi preachers, who were almost invariably called *shekh*. Pious converts perhaps modelled themselves after those admirable holy men, just as the later Vaisnavas patterned themselves in the image of Nityananda. In order to understand why every Muslim villager I met in Bengal said he was a *shekh* it is much more important to understand that there is probably no village in Bengal that was not touched by Sufi preachers,[11] than to know all about the meaning of *shaykh* in Arabic.

The Muslim Weavers in Radhanagar village are known to other vil-lagers as Jola *tanti*, a term that has connotations of foolishness. They reported their 'caste' as Nur Musalman. *Nur* is an Arabic word meaning 'light', although it is sometimes used derisively by Bengali Hindus to refer to the beard of a Muslim. My informants, however, explained that they were called Nur Musalman because they earned their living through *nuri kam*, which they understood to be the Urdu equivalent of *tanti kaj*, 'weaver work'. In rural Bengal, the 'light of Islam' (*nur-ul-Islam*) has become a loom. It is appropriate that words of great symbolic importance should be attached to things of great symbolic importance

Every man in Radhanagar Tanti *para* preceded his name with the title *shekh* when I took his household census. They are quite clear that they are not *jatiya shekh* like the cultivating Muslims who live in an adjacent village, as the following incident, related by the *para* Malik illustrates:

Seven or eight years ago, people from Mirabar village came to our *para* for a religious talk by our guru [sic]. An *ashraf* girl from Mirabar asked my daughter-in-law for a drink of water, and when my daughter-in-law began to pour it for her, she said she could not take water from the hand of a *nurikam*. My daughter-in-law complained to me, and I told the guru. He told the *ashraf* people that they must not maintain distinctions of high and low during religious occasions. The food which is prepared during these occasions is the sacred *sinni*, and it must be eaten by all, lest they become *kafir*. Then he asked the girl who has refused to drink: 'Are these Christians whose water you will not accept'?

Although the caste of the Radhanagar Tantis is low, and they could never marry *ashraf* cultivators of Mirabar, the two groups have in common a guru, a creed, and an identification, however dimly it may be realized nowadays, with the Sufi preachers who brought Islam to the Bengali countryside.

Vaishnavism and Islam intersect the structure of the caste system in several important ways. Perhaps, the most important connection between the two is, unfortunately, the one about which, at present, I know least.

Mandali and Millat in Frontier Society

Earlier I suggested that the Bengal delta might usefully be treated as a kind of slowly opening frontier which was gradually settled by ethnically homogeneous groups of pioneers. Social order is a serious problem in frontier society everywhere. The people of the lower delta are known to be tough and independent. They are famous for their skill with the lathi (a long bamboo staff, seasoned, hardened and polished to make it an effective weapon), which is often the only means of establishing a claim to a plot after a flood has changed the location of agricultural land, or new plots (*char*) have appeared along the banks of rivers, either because of changes in the course of rivers, or due to the accumulation of heavy silt during the monsoon months. For centuries, in the lower delta, authority was poorly organized; centres of officialdom were few and widely scattered. It seems likely that Islam and Vaishnavism functioned to provide authority in an anarchic frontier society, and that they did so through loosely constituted religious organizations. The Vaishnava form of this organization was called a *mandali* (circle, congregation); it was organized around a particular guru, who may have been called a *gosvain* by his followers, and was frequently constituted of persons from more than one village. The Muslim organization was called by some variant of the Arabic *millat* (sect, party, religious group/community) or simply *samaj* (society); it was organized around a particular mullah, who may have been called a *pir* by his followers. There seems to have been a considerable range in the sizes and territorial extents of individual organizations. Fellow members had closer contacts with one another, both ceremonially and informally, than with non-members.

I do not have any personal experience with *millat* organizations among Bengali Muslims, but a paper by Robert Glasse,[12] which describes 'mallot' groups in western Comilla district, and Peter Bertocci's research, which involves *samaj* groups in eastern Comilla district,[13] reveal striking similarities to the *mandali* organizations of Vaishnavas in eastern Midnapur district. Besides meeting for worship and to hear the teachings of the leader, *mandali* and *millat* organizations exercise over their members social comrol of a kind that has been very important in Bengal's frontier days, when distinct village authority systems had yet to develop.

Radhanager men are mostly members of a *mandali* which includes men from about six other villages. They met, while I was living in the village, on the death anniversary of their *gosvain*, who had lived in the village north of Radhanagar. The deceased *gosvain's* son presided over the congregation. His father's samadhi had been washed with fresh mud and sprinkled with *tulasi* leaves for the occasion; his photograph was hung from a nearby tree. The meeting was begun the night before I came. Members of *kirtan dal*s from constituent villages had sung the praises of Lord Krshna throughout the night, one *dal* taking over when its predecessor was exhausted. Thus, while the singing was constant, most of the men had an opportunity to talk with one another and, especially, to bring up problems that might suitably be settled under the auspices of the *mandali*.

Rules of inter-caste behaviour are specifically different for *mandali* feasts than for those of the village. In the *mandali*, all men eat at the same time, seated on the ground. Members of low and untouchable castes, such as Fishermen and Doms, sit a little apart from Mahisyas and *jatiya* Baishnabs, but they are fed at the same time as other castes. In the village, a Fisherman, if he were invited to a feast, would not get his meal until the Mahishyas and Baishnabs had finished theirs. A Dom would be fed only as a beggar, taking whatever food was left and eating outside the walls of the house.

The *mandali* may have been formerly responsible for a wider sphere of social control than it is at present (i.e. in the 1960s when I undertook my research in Radhanagar). The *millat* in East Bengal appears to exercise much greater authority than the *mandali* that I saw in action. Much more field research will be required before the basic forms and variations that may exist among these organizations are understood.

Meanwhile, it is worth noting, once again, that Islam and Vaishnavism in rural Bengal serve very similar social functions through very similar forms of organization.

Conclusion

It is possible to identify Bengal by a list of the unique properties of its language and literature, its culture and social structure, its history, and even such elemental characteristics as its physical geography and the biological peculiarities of its inhabitants. The encyclopaedic approach to the definition of a 'culture area' was typical of American anthropology in the 1930s. Nowadays, most of us do not assemble trait lists of this kind, both because we do not get much intellectual satisfaction from it and because it does not answer any of the questions that we have. Trait lists and the study of religious syncretism have a good deal in common: both assume that cultures or societies can be seen as series of discrete elements that are 'explained' by discovering the origin of each bit in a different, prior 'culture'.

There is an alternative assumption, for which the founders of modern social anthropology argued: Cultures and societies are systems, the components of which function together for the maintenance of the whole. Some contemporary social anthropologists, most notably Claude Lévi-Strauss, even hold that each system has a key that reveals the ideal form of all sets of relations within it. While I have worked under the assumption that society in rural Bengal can best be understood as a system, I have not attempted to find a single key to all its parts.

Perhaps, the organizing principles of Bengali society and culture will become apparent as we continue our particular investigations. At this time, it seems impossible to attribute the formation of Bengali regional identity to a single cause or a unique set of causes. To give primacy to language is to ignore the larger culture of which language is a vehicle, and to avoid the question of why the languages of Bengal and Bihar, for example, became distinct rather than remaining the same, or why linguistic nationalism developed in East Bengal, leading to the creation of Bangladesh, and not in West Bengal. The accounts of historians must begin and end somewhere in time. Histories can tell a segment of the story of the development of regional uniqueness; but each segment is ultimately connected, through the relentlessness of chronology, to earlier uniqueness. The peculiarities of Bengali tastes in literature are just the well-known differences between Bengalis and other people set in a literary context. An exhaustive ethnographic catalogue of customs and traits through which Bengalis identify one another would be nothing more than a list of diverse symbolic singularities without a clue to the unitary structure of ideas that may underlie them.

Where can we begin to break into the mass of elements that contribute to regional identity? The emergence of Bangladesh in 1971, makes the question all the more complex though not incomprehensible. There is, in every discipline, some method that allows the analyst to synthesize; to see a structural order in the chaos of facts. The method that I have sought to use here is crude: After analysing some features of rural society and religion, I have sought to see how they are related. There are some important connections between the organization of society in general and the particular organization of religious roles and groups. Vaishnavism and Islam prove to be similar in organizational and social location, which leads me to surmise that perhaps they perform many of the same social functions. Their organizational similarity is at least as striking as their apparent symbolic differences.

Notes and References

1. Clifford Geertz, 'Religion as a Cultural System', in *Anthropological Approaches to the Study of Religion*, Association of Social Anthropologists, Monograph no. 3 (London: Tavistock; New York: Praeger 1965), 4.

2. Ibid.

3. *See* E.R. Leach, 'The Frontiers of Burma', in *Comparative Studies in Society and History*, vol. 3 (1960), 49–68.

4. For details, *see* Ralph W. Nicholas, *Villages of the Bengal Delta: A Study of Ecology and Peasant Society*, Ph.D. dissertation, University of Chicago, 1962.

5. The demographic character especially of the eastern Bengal districts, has since changed substantially because of subsequent political developments in the region leading to mass migrations of Hindus to western Bengal districts. (Editor.)

6. W.W. Hunter, *Annals of Rural Bengal*, 7th edn (London: Smith, Elder, & Co., 1897), 99.

7. *See* Melville T. Kennedy, *The Chaitanya Movement: A Study of the Vaisnavism of Bengal* (Calcutta: The Association Press, 1925), 77.

8. *See* Ralph W. Nicholas, 'Ritual hierarchy and Social Relations in Rural Bengal', *Contributions to Indian Sociology*, n.s., no. 1, 1967, 63–71.

9. For details, *see* Ralph W. Nicholas, 'Structures of Politics in the Villages of Southern Asia', in Milton Singer and Bernard S. Cohn (eds), *Structure*

and Change in Indian Society, Viking Fund Publications in Anthropology no. 47 (Chicago: Aldine Publishing Company, 1968).

10. *See* Dinesh Chandra Sen, *History of Bengali Language and Literature*, 2nd edn (Calcutta: University of Calcutta, 1954), 351.

11. Abdul Karim, *Social History of the Muslims of Bengal (Down to AD 1538)* (Dacca: The Asiatic Society of Pakistan, 1959), 124.

12. Robert Glasse, *La Societe musalmane dans le Pakistan rural de l'Est: etude preliminaire.* Etudes Rurales, nos. 22–3–24, 1966, 202–4.

13. *See* Peter J. Bertocci, *Elusive Villages: Social Structure and Community Organization in Rural East Pakistan*, Ph.D. dissertation, Michigan State University, 1970.

3

Islam and the Social Construction of the Bangladesh Countryside

PETER J. BERTOCCI

Introduction

This essay suggests some of the ways in which indigenous Bengali Muslim interpretations of Islam help to shape the social institutions of the Bangladesh countryside. This is not a topic that has received much treatment despite the twenty-five years of progress we have made in understanding the social organization of rural Bangladeshi communities and the general condition of the Bangladesh peasantry. The basic community groupings of rural Bangladesh have been well described, and their link to the agrarian political economy and problems of inequality of wealth have been well analysed. We have largely missed, however, giving a full account of, or, for that matter, full credit to, the functioning of indigenous Islamic ideology and symbols in the construction and practical operation of rural social institutions and the elaboration of social rank. More often than not, religion in general and Islam in particular is not discussed in great detail if at all. Where it does find description, it is treated either as a kind of background, almost superfluous variable of little or, in the writings of some, pernicious influence, or as a dependent variable whose expression is wholly a function of other factors.[1] In consequence, I submit, our appreciation of peasant society and culture in Bangladesh is less complete and less nuanced than it could and should be. This is not to say that religious culture has received no attention in rural Bangladesh studies. Ellickson is the first I know of to focus a study on the religion of Muslim peasants; the work of Thorp takes as its major thrust the link between indigenous Muslim ideology and social institutions on the ground, as does the fascinating, more recently published study by Kotalovà, which focuses especially on the situation of Muslim women in rural Bangladesh.[2] In this essay, I will rely especially on these pioneering efforts. I also draw heavily from earlier papers, published in 1980 and 1981, in which some of these ideas were first sketched out.

Jati: The Social Differentiation of the Countryside

When first encountering the rural culture of Comilla district in Bangladesh in the mid-1960s, I was astonished to be asked by Muslim peasants, to whom I had barely been introduced, to identify my *jati*. My sole earlier experience with Bengali people had been with Hindu *bhadralok* during a year in Calcutta, and my initiatives in learning Bengali both there and while a graduate student at Michigan State University had exposed me only to the 'standard' dialect spoken and written by the members of that class. Thus, I recognized the word *jati* as denoting a Hindu caste, and I failed to see how anyone could remotely associate me as a sahib, an apellation which I had become accustomed to being applied to me in Calcutta and which, I would soon learn, East Bengali rural people tended to attach to any non-Indic foreigner with any *jati* category. Patiently my new Bangladeshi acquaintances clarified their question. Was I, they wanted to know, a member of the *kristiyan*, *ihudi*, *hindu*, or their own *musalman jati*, which was to ask whether I belonged to the Christian, Jewish, Hindu or Muslim community. I, thus, came to learn that they comprise distinct human communities, distinguished not by birth, as in the Hindu notion of *jati*, but with primary reference to the god(s) each recognizes and the moral code each faith community requires its adherents to observe. For the Bangladeshi Muslims I was meeting, then, the initial differentiation to be made among human beings was that of religious belief and code, or dharma.[3] What distinguishes the musalman *jati* from others, I would later be told, was that Muslims possess the sharia, that their community is based on guidance by the law of Allah as set forth by the Qur'an and in the life and teaching of the Prophet. 'So what is the difference', I some time later inquired of a local imam friend of mine, 'between you Muslims and the Hindus?' He thought briefly, perhaps wondering how I could ask so elementary a question, and then replied: '*Tader sariyat nay*' (they do not have the sharia).

Thus, for rural Bengali Muslims the social world is divided into different *jati*s based on belief and code. That, however, is not the end of the social distinctions they are prepared to make. Indeed, they are aware that Hindus themselves make myriad distinctions by birth and that within the Hindu community there are many 'birth groups' to which Hindus apply the term *jati*. The fact that similar groups exist within the Muslim community—endogamous subgroups they call *jat* or *jati*—is also readily acknowledged. In Comilla in the 1960s, I was told that barbers specializing in circumcision, *hajjams*, were '*ekta jat*', a community unto themselves[4], and that no one would marry into it *(tader sate keha biye dibe na)*. The same was said of butchers *(kasai)*, and in Rajshahi District years later, I came across the first members of the famous *jola* weaver community I had ever met. Despite their having long abandoned weaving as their principal trade and living side by side with the ordinary farmers from whom they were indistinguishable, they retained the custom of marrying only into patrilines bearing the same weaver surname *(karikor)*. In that same area, a group of itinerant snake-catchers *(sharpuriya)* maintained their home base, a neighbourhood of houses on upright poles near the edge of the Atrai river, also largely endogamous and segregated, but related, it was said, to the *thandar*, travelling bangle sellers, and both groups were said to be part of the larger *bede* or *bediya* community of 'gypsies' mentioned for many parts of Bangladesh. Despite their symbolic or real occupational separateness, reinforced by marital segregation, members of these communities considered themselves to be part of the larger Muslim fold, and they were acknowledged as such by the farmer majority. Thorp, in fact, found his Pabna informants reluctant to admit the persistence of such low-ranked endogamous subgroups within their local Muslim communities, but his work eliciting a local myth of origin helps greatly in understanding at least the current ideational rationale for the distinctions on which this differentiation is based[5]. As he relates in fascinating detail, Bengali Muslim peasants consider farming the quintessential human preoccupation, from Adam on down to the present.

Allah created Adam out of the earth in order that he might possess the earth and be its master or *malik*. In the [rural Bengali Muslim] version of creation, Adam exercised his mastery of the earth by farming it. All the *jati*s of men descended from Adam are also considered to have farmed the land. The farmers . . . see themselves as immediate descendants of Adam, possessed of land, and farming it as they were created to do. To be a master of the earth, a *malik*, has a special significance . . . , and to become and remain a *malik* in the fullest sense possible is [thought of as] the goal of every adult male . . .[6]

Thorp goes on to relate how mastery of all aspects of farming, both agronomic and economic, is crucially related to becoming a successful *malik*, which equates to following the *sariyat* (as *sharia* is locally known) of Allah not only by adhering to the law, but in the more fundamental sense of becoming a proper and successful householder, the basis of which is found in the ownership or control of land. This in turn is tied to success in his political sphere, that is, becoming a local man of consequence (*baralok*). It follows from this that those who do not farm, or do not have origins as farming people and retain some control over land regardless of their present occupation, are automatically a kind of 'other', and if they claim to be Muslims, so they may be, but of a lower, residual category or *atraph*.

Thus, the rural Bengali Muslim society is thought of by its male members, at least, as being characterized by a dominant farming majority and a non-farming minority further subdivided into a variety of endogamous occupational groups. The latter would appear to correspond to the *atraph* section of Muslim society commonly discussed in social histories as ranked beneath the *asraph* classes, the proverbial *sayad*s, *sekh*s, pathans, and mughals. The utility of these categories, however, in bearing any serious relationship to understanding the ideology of social rank in today's Muslim Bengal has long been suspect. Occasional forays I have conducted into the historical censuses of Bengal have startlingly shown that the vast majority of Bengali Muslims reported themselves as *sekh* for almost as long as data on 'caste' was collected; so much so that it might seem that as long ago as that being classed as *sekh* was becoming embedded in Bengali Muslim national identity. Thorpe's work suggests that more relevant to social differentiation among rural Bengali Muslims is the farmer/landowner vs non-farmer distinction alluded to above, at the upper echelons of which one finds a vast majority who think of themselves as farming *sekh*s and a symbolically subordinate group of non-farming endogamous groups corresponding to the historical *atraph*. Among the farming *sekh*s, a variety of titles are commonly attached to their patrilines (*bamsa*): titles related to land control, harking back to Mughal times, such as *chaudhuri*, *majumdar*, and *talukdar*, titles related to traditional religious office, such as *khandakar* and *kaji*, and titles bespeaking long family association with village leadership, e.g. *mandal* and *pramanik*.[7] These titles are further associated with the wealthier families among the cultivating *sekh*s as group, and so, tend to be found among lineages whose members claim local status as *baralok,* men of influence, in local community affairs, who are also usually the owners of larger amounts

of land. It is perhaps obvious that the cultivating *sekh*s who see themselves as *maliks* or 'masters of the earth' as Thorp describes them,
constitute a kind of intermarrying yeomanry, ranked above the non-
farming, specialized *jat* or *quam*. In this manner, the Bengali Muslim
myth of creation, which focuses on Adam the farmer and his local descendants, sets the backdrop for the social construction of the
countryside into a variety of *jati*.

In a more formal way, one might suggest that a rural Bengali Muslim
map of the social world and those who people it might read something
like that charted below.[8]

Humanity (*manabjati*)			
Muslims (*musalman jati*)		Non-Muslims	
Par Excellence	Residual	People of the Book	Idolaters
(*malik*)	(*jat*)	(*kitabi*)	(*kapher*)

In this conception, Humanity (*manabjati*) may be first divided into
those who are Muslims (*musalman jati*) and non-Muslim 'others' (*hindu
jati, kristiyan jati,* and the like), which is to distinguish between human
groups primarily on the basis of belief and code (i.e. dharma).[9] That this
corresponds to a classically Islamic dichotomy between the world of
Islam (*dar ul-Islam*) and the world of potentially hostile non-Muslim
'others' (the *dar ul-harb*), should be readily apparent. Moreover, Bengali Muslims would, I think, follow the further conventional Islamic
division of non-Muslims into People of the Book (*kitabi*), Christians
and Jews of which peoples they have little experience, and 'idolaters'
(*kapher*), Hindus whom they know quite well. The *musalman jati*
would appear to be bifurcated further into what we might call par excellence Muslims, the farming *sekh*s, who see themselves as living in
accordance with the *sharia* by following the way of life passed on by
Adam, the first *malik,* and residual Muslims, members of endogamous
non-farmer groups following specialized occupations. Some of these
obviously resemble low-ranked Hindu *jati* engaged in defiling tasks,
e.g. the Muslim hajjam or *kasai*. These groups may have their origins
among the apparently many Hindu artisan and service *jati* recruited
wholesale to Islam during the period of medieval Bengal,[10] but
prevented from full integration into a fully homogeneous Islamic community by an emerging myth of origin that privileged farming as the
quintessential Muslim occupation par excellence. In any event, viewed

in cultural terms from the perspective of the 'masterful *maliks*' whom Thorp describes, the Bangladesh countryside is dominated by a host of cultivating *sekh*s among whom a diverse collection of 'other' Hindu and Muslim *jati*s subordinate in status and power.

Samaj: The Local Expression of the Umma

Nearly everywhere in rural Bangladesh, I have analytically argued,[11] peasants organize themselves in localized religious corporate groups of the sort postulated by Weber, which appear to have been widespread in many parts of the world before the rise of the modern industrial state and appear to persist in places like rural Bangladesh where the latter has not yet penetrated with all its force. In the Bangladesh case, these groups are *religious* in the first instance and provide the social venue for collective worship as also the observance of important Islamic festivals. Their memberships often overlap with the congregations of local mosques, although this need not be the case. These groups are *corporate* in the classic Weberian sense that they limit admission to co-religionists, and Muslim *samaj* groups stipulate allegiance to Islamic codes of conduct as interpreted by their leadership. They are entirely indigenous, having no formal connection to or the sanction of either the official state institutions of 'local government' or ecclesiastical bureaucracies (which in any event are rare in Islam). Thus, they may be considered *autonomous* in Weber's terms, as well as 'self-led' or *autocephalous*, to use the somewhat cumbersome term of Weber's English translators, in that their leaders act in some combination of their own charismatic empowerment and that vested in them by the group as a whole. These 'religious corporations' are most conspicuous in their efforts at enforcement of social control and mediation of disputes. Leadership decisions are enforced, once again in Weber's terms, in a *hierocratic* manner, involving what he described as ' "psychic coercion" through the distribution and denial of religious benefits'[12] as well as the modification of behaviour by way of threats to personal honour (*izzat*) and evoking fear of shame.

In such conclaves, rural Bengali Muslims most commonly act out what is morally and ritually meaningful as community, celebrating important public religious festivals (e.g. the Ids, Ramadan, Muharram, as well as Sabe Miraj), coming together in prayer on critical days of atonement (especially Sabe Barat), the major family rites associated with birth, male circumcision, marriage and death, and also reinforcing as deemed necessary the normative standards to which all are enjoined to adhere.[13] It is especially significant that these religious corporate groups are most commonly referred to by the term *samaj*, which of course is the generic term for 'society' in Bengali as well as other Indic languages. However, as Kotalovà,[14] following Ronald Inden, points out, *samaj* 'reflects the notion of "going together" ', and thus, the performance of ritual and sharing of food within the local *samaj* a sense of what she perceptively calls dharmic belonging[15]. In some parts of Bangladesh, these groups are also known as *reyai*[16], a word derived perhaps from the Arabic *ra'iyya* and connoting the idea of 'follower' or 'citizen', and by extension implies the protection afforded to 'those who submit'. The social bond that ties *samaj* members together is often described as tantamount to kinship; indeed, so impressed was Thorp[17] by the quasi-kinship quality that these groups exhibit that he consistently alludes to the Bangladeshi Muslim peasant *samaj* as a 'residential brotherhood'. Muslims the world over, of course, are taught to think of themselves as such a brotherhood, and, indeed, for the Muslim peasants of rural Bangladesh their *samaj* groups might be seen as the local expressions of the *umma*, the universal Muslim community, in which they live lives guided by the sharia (or, *sariyat*, as it is usually called in their local dialects).

It may be useful at this juncture to sketch out how these groups are formed. Throughout the densely populated, low-lying deltaic plain that dominate the topography of Bangladesh, sudden monsoon flooding is the constant nemesis of the works of men and the toils of women. Human settlement, for that reason, defies concentration, and scattered peasant homesteads cluster on whatever offers itself by way of elevation—a mound of earth, an embankment—producing, to paraphrase the opening lines of Jasimuddin's *Field of the Embroidered Quilt*, 'a hamlet here, a hamlet there, with broad fields in between' (*Ei ek [para], oi ek [para]/madhye dhu dhu math*). Such hamlets, my rendering of the Bengali term *para*, are what constitute the first level of community infrastructure above the level of the peasant homestead (*bari*) and its resident patrilineal kin groups (*gusthi*). Where the proximity of hamlets facilitates neighbourly interaction and regular personal contact among their residents, those living within such loosely tied constellations often come to see themselves as members of a discrete and distinct local community. Sometimes such communities may call themselves villages (*gram* or *gaon* are the usual Bengali terms), in which instance the terms bestow consensus on 'villages' as socially defined. In rare instances, socially defined villages may even coincide with one of the official '43,000 villages' alluded to by government pronouncements, even though this term alludes primarily to the historic *mauja*, which were tax revenue units first created in Mughal times and ever since then officially designated as 'villages' by successive governments of Bengal. Nonetheless, the term *samaj*, and thus the religious corporate group that I have described above, is equally applicable, and thus *samaj* can be eoterminous with *gram/gaon* or 'village' as locally recognized. Several or even numerous *samaj* groups may be found in a single *mauja*,[18] but more often they cross-cut *mauja* boundaries.[19] Thorp's 1978 study focused on a single union ward of the then functioning local government set-up in (the historic) Pabna district, encompassing less than three miles in area, but in which he counted seventeen Muslim *samaj* groups along with four Hindu ones.

With respect to their ritual functions, one may speak of a 'minimal *samaj*' a concrete worshipping congregation whose members may attend a common mosque or at least collectively celebrate the major feast days such as Id ul-Fitr or Korbani Id (Feast of the Sacrifice), and hold special observances during Ramadan. Within the *samaj*, too, life cycle rites are carried out;[20] an often important function of these groups lies in the control of marriage alliances, it being commonly the case that the *samaj* seeks to restrict marriages to its own members. Local *samaj* groups also act to regulate conduct and arbitrate disputes among their members. One may, however, also speak of a 'maximal *samaj*' because, if the nature of a dispute requires it, the leaders of disparate, but adjoining *samaj* units may come together to adjudicate the case. This may occur among the *samaj* groups of a single *mauja*, or an effective maximal *samaj* unit may incorporate several smaller ones over a much wider area. In south-easterly Comilla district, where I initially worked, I found that minimal *samaj* groups could expand to a maximal *samaj* encompassing eight *mauja* or 'official villages' covering a square mile containing some 1,800 people. By contrast, in north-western Rajshahi district, in which I did subsequent field-work, minimal *samaj* groups could combine over as many as twenty-two *mauja*, an arrangement so fixed by tradition as to have acquired its own name, *baisi*, or 'group of twenty-two'. Studies from nearly everywhere in rural Bangladesh describe peasant organization in ways evoking this same theme, in which a multiplicity of localized religious corporate groups expand and contract their kinship, ritual, and quasi-governmental relations and activities.

One should not imagine rural Bangladeshi *samaj* groups as stable, enduring social units; indeed they are not. Nearly every extended account of the *samaj* emphasizes its faction-ridden nature, often describing in some detail the split and recombination of *samaj* groups over time,[21] and the domination of these groups by local élites, with resulting injustices in the generation and application of *samaj* decisions, is everywhere evident in the literature. Of interest for this essay, however, is the fact that, however beleaguered, no matter how often dismembered by wrangling and disputation, a *samaj* seems to re-emerge in a similar form, once again to find use for good or ill, the actions of its members continually justified in terms of Muslim brotherhood and the maintenance of Islamic norms. Thus, for example, there have been widespread recent reports of *salisi*—rural courts of judgment traditionally made up of *samaj* elders (variously called *sardar*, *matabbar*, *mandal*, or *pramanik*, to name the principal titles)—called up to chastize women and members of non-governmental development organizations thought to have violated some Islamist groups' notions of proper conduct for Muslim women. Despiriting though these reports may be, they give current testimony to the persistence of *samaj* forms and practices, despite counter evidence of the *samaj*'s demise.[22]

It is tempting to link the possible origins of the *samaj* system to the well-known Fara'idi Movement of the last century, most definitively studied to date by Muin-ud-Din Ahmed Khan.[23] The Fara'idis were, it will be recalled, Muslim reformers who militantly advocated the abandonment by Bengali Muslims of such practices as saint worship (*pir*ism) as well as the eschewal of what they considered Hindu customs, and they sought to impose on their benighted Bengali co-religionists their perceptions of Islamic orthodoxy and insisted that belief and behaviour be shaped in conformity with the Five Pillars. Following Rafiuddin Ahmed,[24] I believe that the Farai'dis and other revivalist purification movements of the nineteenth century not only deepened Islamic consciousness in Bengal, but also played an immeasurably important role in shaping present-day Bengali Muslim customs and institutions. In that connection, then, I submit that the rural Bangladeshi *samaj* may well be derived from Fara'idi political organization.

Consider Khan's observations regarding the Comilla district countryside,[25] where, he claimed, as late as 1958, one could find remnants of a Fara'idi local court system in which villages had been organized in 'blocks' each headed by a '*khalifa*' whose role it was to act as 'superintendents' of Fara'idi villages, providing political leadership as well as legal administration. Of particular note is Khan's assertion that the Fara'idis 'were organized in small *samaj*, consisting of about 40 families or more'. Each *samaj*, moreover, 'had five *Matbars* [Elders], with whose help the *khalifa* administered justice to the people'.[26] Khan went on to claim that even at the time of his research, 'the *Fara'idi khalifah* exercise[d] considerable control in the social and religious sphere of [rural Bengali Muslim] society, "controlling marriage arrangements, mediating disputes and sanctioning misconduct" ',[27] all well documented traditional functions of the traditional *samaj* system as described in the presently abundant ethnograpic and village studies writings on rural Bangladesh. Alas, however, nowhere in that literature do we find reference to 'khalifa' and Khan may well have seen more in the contemporary Comilla countryside than warranted in supporting his historical thesis. It does not however strain credulity to speculate that he may have well been seeing in the workings of the *samaj* system the remnants of Fara'idi efforts to organize the countryside, and I would urge some aspiring social historian of rural Bengal to investigate these possible connections. If it is accepted that Fara'idi and other Islamic revivalist models of the last century exercised great formative influence over the intellectual and emotive expression of modern Bengali Islam, then it seems not far fetched to hypothesize a similar impact on rural social and political institutions as well.

Des: Kinship Alliances and Micro-regional Integration

As Imtiaz Ahmad's classic collection readily illustrated some years ago, patterns of kinship and marriage among the Muslims of South Asia are nothing if not varied, and this holds especially true with regard to norms of endogamy and exogamy as strategic guidelines for the establishment of kinship ties.[28] Whereas kin group endogamy is commonly the norm in many parts of the Islamic world, the Muslims of rural Bangladesh show a definite preference for contracting marriages not only outside their existing kinship networks, but also beyond the reach of their immediate localities.[29]

Quantitative studies available rarely show a statistically impressive number of cousin marriages, for example, although cousin marriage does appear to be more regularly associated with relatively high social rank, a natural result of wealthier families tending to choose each other as sources for mates.[30] Furthermore, marriage out of one's village community appears to be highly preferred. Aziz has nicely summarized this point:

... Marriage relations are most frequently sought outside the village, since this will bring new people into the domain of [one's] kinsmen. A new lineage other than one's own may have highly respected and well placed members. Important kinsmen who are distantly related are also taken into consideration at the time of settling a marriage since they might be able to provide certain favours in future. With a wider circle of kinsmen a family can enhance its social and economic power. .... Marriage within the village does not help in extending the circle of acquaintances, because all the people in a village already know each other. But the forming of such matches to people in different villages widens a family's circle of acquaintances.[31]

In contrast to people in other Islamic cultures, then, it is the extension of social ties through marital alliance with non-kin that is crucial to rural Bengali Muslims' strategies of making their way in the world. Of particular interest to this discussion, however, is that these strategies appear to be embedded in indigenous Bengali Muslim conceptions of *takdir*, the Islamic notion of life's struggle in dealing with one's personal destiny, and striving to realize one's full potential (i.e. *tadbir*). '[T]he *malik* does not carry out his life's task or fulfill his destiny (*tadbir*) in autonomous void', Thorp notes; rather, he 'is firmly enmeshed within an intricate and extensive network of social relationships'.[32]

While the rhetoric of *takdir* sometimes misleadingly laces Bengali Muslim peasant discourse with the taint of resignation and fatalism, actually that concept of personal destiny bespeaks no more than a realistic acceptance of the limits that Allah bestows upon each life. As played out daily, people's lives just as often display all manner of individualistic impulse for achievement and success, whether through economic improvement, political advantage and attainment of social prestige, all of which, if acquired in an ethical way, are quite consistent with moral virtue. Indeed, all this constitutes the stuff of *tadbir*. For Bengali Muslim farmers, this ties into the myth of the masterful *malik* that Thorp has elucidated and 'translates into the ownership and/or control of land, ... the mastery of the cultivation techniques required to make it fruitful, ... and the social relationships of agricultural production ... necessary to the accomplishment of this task'.[33]

The food grown from the land not only feeds a man and his dependents, which is central to *tadbir* as an obligatory self-actualization process, but any surpluses he can extract from his land are essential to the contributions he can make to the rituals which create larger solidarities and by which he gradually establishes a larger network of dependents and allies who are crucial to the promotion of his influence in wider community affairs.[34]

Kinship extensions are central to this process. One's kinspeople are, for example, important as lenders of land and money, and the first resort as sources of employment. They are one's most immediate potential allies in factional conflict and constitute the likely core of the network of patron–client relationships that permeate economic and political activity in rural Bangladesh.

The extension of marriage ties and their reinforcing link to the overlapping of *samaj* and village institutions builds, I further suggest, into the identification of rural people with their 'local country' or *desh*. This latter term, among Bengalis as well as other Indic peoples, has a variety of potential referents, but none have greater centrality to their culture than that which denotes and connotes the idea of one's 'ancestral village' or 'home region'. The local *desh*, moreover, acquires sociological reality from the concrete extension of kinship and other social ties across space. I have tried to demonstrate[35] that the preponderance of social, political, and economic ties that hold the Bangladesh peasantry together tend to cluster around rural markets and their hinterlands, loosely unifying an otherwise dispersed plethora of local villages and *samaj* groupings into what one might call 'micro-regions'. This notion has further led me to propose that these market-centred micro-regions constitute the geographic locus of the microcosmic *desh* that is the building block of Bangladeshi cultural identity.[36]

As evidence for the role of marriage ties in this regard, one can cite data from a variety of studies showing a tendency of families to seek marital connections outside their local 'village communities' (however these may be defined), most commonly within areas varying from five to fifteen square miles.[37] Overall, then, marriage data confirm the importance of micro-regional areas containing the critical mass of daily interactions between rural people of different villages and *samaj* groups, 'as they meet to trade in local markets, as they frequent the government centres often located at market sites, . . . and as they travel to attend multifarious religious gatherings'.[38] Thus, the local *desh* derives sociological underpinning from the clustering of multiple ties across space, and marital alliances are among the more important of such human connections. These same extensions link the *samaj* units discussed above, and thus they help reinforce the notion I have also advanced that the *samaj* system may be seen as a microcosm of the Muslim *umma* as a community of the faithful and a brotherhood of believers.

Concepts such as *umma*, *samaj* and *desh* represent, let us hasten to add, culturally constructed orders, 'thought of' models of solidarity, in which the metaphors of kinship buttress the ideals of social cohesion. These, of course, contrast sharply with the 'lived in' order of social structure, where *hingsa* (greed, envy, malice) and *daladali* (factionalism) are the everyday terms by which rural Bangladeshis describe the quality of interpersonal relations and group life that they commonly experience despite the use of kinship metaphors to evoke ideal codes of conduct. Here, however, we stress the use of kinship ties in the extension of the 'dyadic solidarities which assist people in managing their relationships in the social world writ large and its structure of power',[39] and wish to suggest the links to Islamic ideology that sustain these processes.

On the Relevance of Islam: Final Note

This essay has sought to suggest some of the ways indigenous Bengali Islam has shaped the social order of the Bangladesh countryside. I hope, the effort will not be seen as an exercise in reification or 'essentialism'. Rather, what one would like to see is a greater appreciation of the role of Islamic religious ideation in configuring the way rural Bangladeshis respond to their world. Much of the literature on rural Bangladesh has stressed the social cleavages, economic inequalities, and political oppression that permeate people's lives there. Attention to all that is valid. What one would hope to see more of is the way in which the discourse of Islam shapes all those dynamic processes and provides the rhetoric and the 'vocabularies of motive' that frame contestation and struggle.[40] It is to that end that this contribution has been made.

Notes and References

1. See, e.g., Peter J. Bertocci, *Elusive Villages: Social Structure and Community Organization in Rural East Pakistan*, Ph.D. dissertation, Michigan State University, 1970; Jenneke Arens and Jos van Beurden, *Jhagrapur: Poor Peasants and Women in a Village in Bangladesh* (Birmingham, UK: Third World Publications, 1977); Eirik G. Jansen, *Rural Bangladesh: Competition for Scarce Resources* (Dhaka: University Press Ltd, 1987); Willem Van Schendel, *Peasant Mobility: The Odds of Life in Rural Bangladesh* (Assen, Netherlands: Van Gorcum, 1981); and Geoffrey D. Wood, 'Class Differentiation and Power in Bandakgram: the Minifundist Case', in *Exploitation and the Rural Poor: A Working Paper on the Rural*

Power Structure in Bangladesh, ed. M. Ameerul Haque (Comilla: Bangladesh Academy for Rural Development, 1976), to name a few of the better known studies.

2. Jean Ellickson, *A Believer among Believers: The Religious Beliefs, Practices and Meanings in a Village in Bangladesh*, Ph.D. dissertation, Michigan State University, 1972; John P. Thorp, *Power Among the Farmers of Daripalla: A Bangladesh Village Study* (Dhaka: Caritas Bangladesh, 1978); Jitka Kotalova, *Belonging to Others: Cultural Constructions of Womanhood among Muslims in a Village in Bangladesh*, Uppsala Studies in Cultural Anthropology, volume 19 (Uppsala: Acta Universitatis Upsaliensis, 1993).

3. *See also* Thorp, op.cit., and Kotalova, op. cit., 44–7, 58–61, and elsewhere.

4. *See also* Ellickson, op. cit., 124.

5. *See* Thorp, op. cit., 16–20.

6. Ibid., 21; *see also* Thorp essay in this volume.

7. Bertocci, *Elusive Villages*, op. cit.; Thorp, op. cit., 16.

8. My use here of the terms 'par excellence' and 'residual' is inspired and borrowed admiringly from the Inden and Nicholas' discussion of Bengali kinship. *See* Ronald B. Inden and Ralph W. Nicholas, *Marriage and Rank in Bengali Culture* (Berkeley: University of California Press, 1976).

9. *See also* Kotalova, op. cit., passim.

10. *See* Richard M. Eaton, *The Rise of Islam and the Bengal Frontier, 1204-1760* (Berkeley: University of California Press, 1993), 97–102.

11. Bertocci, 'Models of Solidarity, Structures of Power: The Politics of Community in Rural Bangladesh', in *Ideology and Interest: The Dialectics of Politics, Political Anthropology Yearbook* 1, ed. Myron J. Aronoff (New Brunswick, NJ: Rutgers University Press, 1980).

12. As quoted in ibid., 100.

13. *See* Ellickson, op. cit., 72–107; Thorp, op. cit., 47–77; Kotalova, op. cit., 87–110.

14. Kotalova, op. cit., 88.

15. Ibid., 110.

16. Bertocci, *Elusive Villages,* op. cit.; and Ellickson, op. cit.

17. Thorp, op. cit.

18. Ellickson, op. cit.

19. Bertocci, *Elusive Villages*, op. cit.

20. For an extended discussion, *see* Kotalova, op. cit., 87ff.

21. *See*, e.g., Arens and van Beurden, op. cit, 147–54; Bertocci, *Elusive Villages*, op. cit.; Jansen, op. cit., 85–91; Kirsten Westergaard, *The Relationship Between State and Rural Society in Bangladesh*, Institute of Political Studies (Copenhagen: University of Copenhagen, 1979), 178–213; and M.Q. Zaman, *The Socioeconomic and Political Dynamics of Adjustment to Riverbank Erosion Hazard and Population Resettlement in the*

Brahmhaputra–Jamuna Floodplain, Ph.D. dissertation, University of Manitoba, 1988, 105–27.

22. On the current use of *salisi* for this purpose, *see* M. Rashiduzzaman, 'The Liberals and Religious Right in Bangladesh', *Asian Survey*, 34 (1994), 974–90.

23. Muin-ud-Din Ahmad Khan, *History of the Fara'idi Movement in Bengal, 1818–1906* (Karachi: Pakistan Historical Society, 1965).

24. Rafiuddin Ahmed, *The Bengal Muslims, 1871–1906: A Quest for Identity* (Delhi: Oxford University Press, 1981, 1988).

25. Muin-ud-Din Ahmad Khan, op. cit., 131–7.

26. Ibid., 133.

27. Ibid., 134.

28. Imtiaz Ahmad, *Family, Kinship and Marriage among the Muslims in India* (Columbia, Missouri: South Asia Books, 1976).

29. K.M. Ashraful Aziz, *Kinship in Bangladesh* (Dhaka: International Centre for Diarroeal Disease Research, 1979), 127–30; Ellickson, op. cit., 47; Thorp, op. cit., 79.

30. Bertocci, 'Marriage Alliance and Dyadic Solidarity in Rural Bangladesh', in *Asian Thought and Society*, 4 (17 & 18) (1981), 104–21.

31. Ashraful Aziz, op. cit., 127; *see also* Thorp, op. cit., 79.

32. Thorp, op. cit., 29.

33. Bertocci, 'Marriage Alliance and Dyadic Solidarity in Rural Bangladesh', 116–17.

34. Ibid.

35. Bertocci, 'Microregion, Market Area and Muslim Community in Rural Bangladesh', *Bangladesh Development Studies*, 3 (1975), 349–66.

36. *See* Bertocci, 'Marriage Alliance and Dyadic Solidarity in Bangladesh', for the extended argument.

37. *See* Ibid., 114, Table 1; also Ashraful Aziz, op. cit., 129.

38. Bertocci, 'Marriage Alliance and Dyadic Solidarity in Bangladesh', 115.

39. Ibid., 115–6.

40. *See* Bertocci, 'Models of Solidarity, Structures of Power', op. cit., for a beginning in this regard.

4

The Bengal Muslims and the World of Islam: Pan-Islamic Trends in Colonial Bengal as Reflected in the Press

MOHAMMAD SHAH

Background

Pan-Islamism[1] in Bengal, as elsewhere in the Indian subcontinent, in the later nineteenth and early twentieth centuries was, in part, a reaction against European aggression on the territorial integrity of the Turkish *khilafat*. The *khilafat*, long held by the Turkish sultan, was regarded by most Sunni Muslims as a sacred institution, and any challenge to its existence was viewed by them with the utmost concern. The connection of the subcontinent's Muslims with the sultan of Turkey was purely symbolic; the sultan, who was also the acknowledged caliph (*khalifa*) of the Sunni Muslims, did not have any meaningful contact with, or concern for, the former. However, after a long period of political setbacks suffered by Muslims all over the world in the eighteenth and nineteenth centuries, which included the Muslims of the Indian subcontinent, Turkey had come to be considered the only remaining land of Muslim refuge by many in the subcontinent, and any threat to its integrity and stability was considered a serious matter by the latter.[2]

There was a growing concern among Bengal Muslims during the nineteenth century, though initially not within the framework of any organized pan-Islamic movement, about the fate of the Ottoman empire. In one instance, as early as the 1860s, contributions were openly made in several villages in Malda district in West Bengal for a *jihad* for the restoration of Muslim rule in India by driving out the British. Several persons were arrested. One Nazir Sardar was the leader of this movement. He had taken an active and prominent part in organizing this movement, inducing others to join the *mujahid*s at Malka and Sittan in the North-West frontier. He and his agents collected contributions from Muslims on account of *jihad*.[3]

Pan-Islamic movements in Bengal, in the sense of an organized movement to fight against European aggression on Muslim territories, may be traced specifically to the Russo–Turkish war of 1877–8, which created a general sense of frustration among Muslims everywhere about the steadily narrowing boundaries of Islam. For the same reason, Turkish successes in that war were celebrated in Bengal (as in northern India), and money was collected and sent to Turkey. An urge to support the Turks became a dominant theme among Bengal Muslims at this time, and this was clearly reflected in public discussions and deliberations in Muslim newspapers and periodicals. Theoretically, pan-Islamism in Bengal inculcated the same principle of support for Turkey amongst Muslims in northern India; Turkey had become a symbol of Sunni Muslim hope at this point in time: defending Turkey had become synonymous with defending Islam. Muslims generally believed that the British were committed to an anti-Muslim policy in pursuit of their imperial dreams and that they (the British) were determined to extinguish the last visible symbol of Muslim temporal and spiritual authority, which was combined in the *khilafat*.

Syed Jamal-al-din al-Afghani (1838–97) was the prophet of the pan-Islamic ideal. His writings on the subject were quite popular among educated Muslims in Bengal and northern India in the later nineteenth century. Articles from *Al-Urwa al-Wuthqa* ('The Indissoluble Link'), which called for unity and common action amongst all Muslims against European imperialism, were routinely translated and published in the *Dar al-Saltanat* in Calcutta, and the *Mushir-i Qaisar* in Lucknow. In the *Al-Urwa al-Wuthqa* one finds those basic ideas which were later developed by the leaders of the Indian Khilafat movement. The Muslims of Calcutta professed for al-Afghani a sense of affection and loyalty which bordered on 'something like worship'. During his visit to Calcutta in 1879, he was welcomed as a hero, and he soon became the idol of the pan-Islamists.

The Muslim press, too, played its part in triggering off pan-Islamic sentiments amongst Bengal Muslims. British officials, especially

Gladstone, were portrayed as enemies of Islam who wished to destroy Muslim power lest Muslims should triumph over the Christians.[4] On one occasion, when addressing a public meeting, Gladstone was alleged to have violently struck his hand against a copy of the Qur'an and suggested that unless that book was destroyed, peace and civilization could not spread over the world.[5] With like disrespect for Islam, it was said, a mosque in Rajmahal was converted into a dispensary; similarly, a British government official had caused a mosque, which was close to a government office, to be demolished simply because the *azan* (or the call to prayer) was reportedly offensive to him.[6] Christian missionaries in Bengal wrote some highly provocative tracts against the Islamic religion and the Prophet of Islam. Munshi Mohammad Meherullah (1861–1907), a well-known Islamic preacher in Bengal, wrote in *Mihir o Sudhakar* in 1899 alleging that some Roman Catholic missionaries of Jessore had written a book entitled *Satya Dharma Nirupan* ('Finding the true religion') in which, the Prophet of Islam's character was questioned and he was assailed for all sorts of deception, theft, robbery, adultery, child abuse, and every other sinful act that could be committed in the world. Meherullah appealed to the Muslims to unite and seek a remedy against the writer of the book.[7]

Taking his cue from Meherullah, one of his closest disciples, Shaikh Zamiruddin (1870–1937), better known as John Zamiruddin, who had earlier converted to Christianity but subsequently reconverted to Islam, wrote in the *Mihir o Sudhakar* in 1899 that the Christian author of the book *Satya Dharma Nirupan* was so abusive to the Prophet of Islam that it became incumbent upon every Muslim to exert himself to stop the printing and circulation of it. Other leading Muslims of Jessore district formed a committee to stop the printing and publication of the book and decided to take legal action against the author. They appealed to Muslims all over the world to join and help the movement.[8]

Similar complaints about Western/Christian antipathy towards Islam were routinely reported in the Muslim newsmedia from all around the country. A correspondent of the *Roznama-i Muqaddas Hablul Matin* thus observed that after the European powers had compelled the sultan of Turkey to evacuate Crete and appointed Prince George, the heir apparent of Greece, the governor of that island, almost half the Cretan Muslims were compelled to emigrate to the dominions of the sultan of Turkey to escape oppression; the remaining Cretan Muslims were allegedly slaughtered by their Christian neighbours. The Greek and Cretan Christians, it was pointed out, had surpassed the Spanish Chris-

tians in oppressing and killing Muslims.[9] Referring to the forcible evic-
tion of Muslims from Crete, Bulgaria, and Serbia by the European
powers, the *Roznama-i Muqaddas Hablul Matin* argued that it was their
zeal for the Cross that had induced Christian Europe to force the sultan
to cede all those territories. Muslims were, therefore, urged to unite;
otherwise, it was warned, some day, the cradle of their faith would be
conquered by the Christians of Europe.[10]

The European Powers were accused of purposely undermining the
Turkish *khilafat* by inciting the Arabs to take up positions hostile to the
sultan. In consequence, the *khilafat* declined and disintegrated. To
remedy the situation, Muslims everywhere were urged to rise against
the occupation of Islamic territories (absorbing thus, the little remnants
of the Muslim empires) by the Christian powers. It was feared by many
that there was no escape from the doom that otherwise awaited
them.[11] Referring to the Balkans, the *Soltan* argued that the European
powers would not be satisfied until they saw Bulgaria, which was of
their 'own nationality', independent.[12] It feared the risk of loss of Muslim superiority in the Turkish empire if Turkey were to become a
republic under the new constitution of 1924 promulgated under the
leadership of Mustafa Kemal Ataturk (1881–1938) declaring Turkey a
secular state. Under that constitution, the voice of the people of different faiths in the country would be in proportion to their numerical
strength; as such, the Christians would be no less a factor than Muslims
in governing Turkey. Thus far, the Muslims were dominant in Turkey,
but under the altered circumstances Muslims would no longer possess
sole power and authority in that country. This was seen as an impending
calamity for the Muslims.[13]

Similarly, the European powers were portrayed as being all too eager
to obliterate all traces of the Turkish empire from Europe because of
its Islamic character. They were blamed for having incited the party
of Young Turks to dethrone Sultan Abdul Hamid (1876–1909), and
thus put an end to the solidarity of the Ottoman empire, which had
ever been held sacred by Sunni Muslims. The establishment of a
republic in Turkey, with a Christian president at its head, was also
apprehended.[14]

In a similar vein, the *Mohammadi* alleged that the Western powers
constantly endeavoured to sweep away the last vestiges of the Muslim
empire from the face of the earth. Those 'incarnations of peace' in
Europe did not care whether Muslim sovereign power was threatened
with destruction as a result of 'Christian high-handedness', and whether

any part of the Ottoman empire ran the risk of falling into the hands of a Christian power. However, when, far from annexing any foreign territory, a Muslim state sought to assert its authority over its own rebellious subjects, anger was vociferously expressed in Europe. The political changes in Turkey (initiated by the Young Turks in 1908) and Iran in the early twentieth century were seen as manifestations of European designs to alter the balance of power against Islam. The sixty million Muslims of India, the paper asserted, were extremely alarmed and aggrieved at the news that, in deference to the decision of an international convention, England would remain neutral over Turkey.[15]

The reverses of Turkey in Tripoli at the hands of Italy had aroused amongst Indian Muslims a sense of unity inspired by a necessity for self-preservation.[16] Dwelling on the decay that had overtaken Muslim countries all over the world, the *Mohammadi* asked Muslims to learn a lesson from history, bury all their mutual differences, and unite as brethren.[17] The weekly suggested that Muslims should freely help Turkey by sending contributions for the wounded Turkish soldiers.[18] It supported a proposal made by Muslim students of the Edinburgh University that all Muslims of the world should contribute to a common fund to purchase the British-made warship *Dreadnought* for Turkey, which would increase the latter's naval strength.[19] It repeated its appeal to Muslims to help the Turks with money and material, as the Turks were shedding their blood in Tripoli for the 'sake of Islam' and 'national' honour. It also appealed to them to boycott Italian goods.[20]

The Italian invasion of Tripoli was regarded as a very serious phenomenon, especially because the bishop of Italy had supposedly given a religious colour to this war.[21] Calling the silence of the great powers 'ominous', the *Mussalman* of 3 November 1911 described the Turko-Italian war as virtually a trial of strength between Islam and Christianity; a Crusade against Islam. The paper suggested that the defeat of Turkey would mean the annihilation of Islam.[22] Maulana Shibli Numani (d. 1916) called the Turko–Italian war of 1911 another Christian crusade against Muslims. The *Rojnama-i-Muqaddas Hablul Matin* reported that the Pope of Rome had handed over a photo (rosary) to the Italian admiral as a blessing and good omen; this was to be exhibited to his soldiers and sailors to encourage them to fight against the Muslims. The bishops of Italy were reportedly inciting Christians against Muslims, and an Italian gentleman in London had expressed the view that Muslims should be expelled from Europe. The European powers looked on placidly while Christian Italy was murdering the old and infirm, the women and children of the other faith in cold blood simply because, those attacked and murdered were Muslims. The moral that was drawn from this position was that if the Muslim countries did not join hands their fate could be sealed and they were certain to be deprived of hearth and home by the Christian powers. The salvation of Muslims thus lay in the unity of Muslims all over the word.[23]

Referring to the reported threat by Italy to blow up the Kaaba, or 'the House of God' in Mecca, the *Mohammadi* warned that if the *ghelab* (curtain covering the Kaaba) of the Kaaba was set on fire by the Italians, that fire would spread and the entire Muslim world would gladly throw itself into its flames as, it was argued, there was still some Islamic spirit smouldering in the hearts of that people which could never be extinguished.[24]

The *Moslem Hitaishi*, an influential Calcutta Muslim periodical in Bengali, described the Balkan wars as a religious war (Christian priests had said the same thing about it!), and asserted that the war was meant only to turn Muslims out of Europe.[25] European threats against Turkey on various occasions gave Muslims the impression that the Allies had declared a crusade against Islam, and that they would go to any lengths to damage Islam.[26]

Similar sentiments were expressed by most educated Muslims in Bengal, especially in Calcutta. Agha Maidul Islam and Abdullah al-Mamun Suhrawardy, two influential Muslim leaders of the city, addressed a letter to Muslims in March 1913 suggesting that the Balkan war was gradually being transformed into a war between races and religions; thus, efforts were being made to stir up Christian fanaticism by Christian priests and orators. St Petersburg talked of placing the Cross on the dome of the mosque of St Sophia, and the king of Greece dubbed it as a new Crusade. The war would, it was felt, eventually determine the fate of Islam as a whole and not that in Turkey alone.[27]

There was thus, a growing sentiment of support among Bengal's educated Muslims in favour of pan-Islamc unity. Christianity and Europe were perceived as enemies of Islam, and Muslims all over were repeatedly urged to fight back against European Christian aggression. This was the overwhelming tone in all Muslim-edited newspapers and periodicals of this time.

The Call for Unity

By the First World War, many members of the new Muslim 'middle class' in Bengal, who were educated and vocal, were dissatisfied with British policy towards Indian Muslims.[28] Many had turned against the conservative politics of the traditional Muslim leaders, who favoured cooperation with the British, and leant towards the pan-Islamists led by Maulana Mohammad Ali (1878–1931).

As explained earlier, the Muslim press in Bengal took a leading role in popularizing pan-Islamic thoughts and ideas by writing leaders, publishing reports of their correspondents, and articles by the Muslim intelligentsia about the Pan-Islamic activities of Muslim leaders and Muslim organizations. The press, particularly, focused on how the religion of Islam was construed as a threat by the European powers, and how that threat was being used to mobilize public opinion against Muslims. The Urdu daily *Safir*, for example, published an article in August 1915 entitled 'Pan-Islamism', alleging that European newspapers, their correspondents, and travellers who had visited Islamic countries frightened the Christian nations of Europe by conjuring up the ghost of pan-Islamism. They warned their brethren against the rise of a progressive movement in Islam that aimed at bringing together the different sects and groups, inspiring them with one grand ideal of life and character. This progressive movement had its headquarters in Egypt and had adherents in India. The supposed leader of this movement was the sultan of Turkey and its object was to rouse the Islamic nations against the European powers, with a view to preventing them from invading Turkey. The writer resented the fact that these Europeans considered any attempt to unite Muslims on the basis of one religion as reprehensible, and yet attempts of the Europeans to translate the Bible into 400 different languages, distribute, and broadcast it in all countries, establish Christian missions in every city, and bring the whole world under the umbrella of their ideals were thought fair and logical.[29]

The appeal for Muslim unity was made, mostly through the Muslim press of Bengal, as early as 1853, when Russia tried to wrest a portion of Turkey's dominion by openly resorting to a policy of 'might is right'. Disunity amongst Muslims was identified as the principal cause of ruin of Muslim kingdoms in the past. Thus, it was often suggested that when the British East India Company wrested India from its Muslim rulers, the other Muslim rulers of Asia and elsewhere did not even raise a finger to help the latter. Again, when Russia declared war against Persia, no Muslim power came forward to assist her. Then, when the Ottoman empire came to be surrounded by hostile Christian powers, Muslims everywhere, were mere onlookers. The *Hablul Matin* wrote that unless Muslims united there could be no hope of their deliverance from the hands of their enemies. It argued that nothing could check the progress of Islam so long as there was unity amongst its followers.[30] The *Darussaltanat and Urdu Guide* voiced a similar concern, and explained that it was only in consequence of the folly and indifference of Muslims that the Christian powers were able to 'make a mountain of a molehill' in dealing with the so-called Armenian 'atrocities'. Had Muslims strongly protested against the actions of the European powers, the matter would possibly have ended there![31]

Muslims were similarly reminded of how the Prophet of Islam had turned the 'wild' Arab tribes (who, before his coming, were wont to thrust their daggers into each other's hearts without remorse) into a 'nation of brothers' by preaching the holy doctrine of the brotherhood of man. The *Sudhakar* stressed that the only way out of the degrading condition of the Muslims of colonial Bengal was to abide by the dictates of Islam.[32] The *Mohammadi* emphasized that Muslims must, on the one hand, demonstrate that their loyalty to the British government had not been affected by external circumstances (such as their support of Turkey and the *khilafat*) and, on the other, they must represent their communal grievances with a persistence and emphasis that would command the attention of the government. There must be a unity of thought and voice in regard to public questions amongst Muslims all over Bengal. They will not be able to attain success through mere loyalty until with it they are able to convulse the entire country through intense agitation. They must also show that Muslims all over the world are a single community, undivided by territorial or national distinctions.[33]

Muslims of India had a tendency to emphasize their own importance by insisting on the homogeneous character of the community. The editor of *Hablul Matin*, though a Shia, publicly owed spiritual allegiance to the sultan of Turkey, and he was never taken to task for this by the Shi'ite mullahs. The congratulations showered by the Shias of Persia and India (particularly of Bombay) upon the sultan on his successes against the Greeks showed that they were the well-wishers of the sultan as the protector of the holy places of Islam.[34] The *Hablul Matin* stressed that Islam teaches Muslims (irrespective of sect: Shia or Sunni) to be united, and that they should not quarrel with one another.[35] The *Roznama-i Muqaddas Hablul Matin* urged Muslims, both Sunnis and Shias, to help the Turkish government with money for the construction of the proposed Damascus–Hejaz railway, which was to be built for the benefit of Muslim pilgrims.[36] It was glad that the Shias of Bombay had celebrated the Silver Jubilee of Sultan Abdul Hamid (on 31 August 1900) on a grand scale. The paper was also glad that the shah of Persia had made donations to the Damascus–Hejaz Railway Fund, and that cordial amity between the shah and the sultan was demonstrated during the former's stay at Istanbul.[37]

The Muslim community was showing strong sympathies with their coreligionists in Turkey in their struggle against Italy. This feeling was manifest primarily in Calcutta where meetings were held and prayers offered for the success of the Turks. The most important of the meetings was one inaugurated by the Red Crescent Society on 22 October 1911 and held at the Federation Hall grounds at which thousands of Muslims were present. All Muslim shops were closed for the day. A resolution was passed urging all Muslims to give a practical demonstration of their sympathy for Turkey by boycotting Italian goods. Efforts were also made by the Red Crescent Society, of which Abdul Jalal, the editor of the *Hablul Matin*, Dr Suhrawardy, and Ghulam Hussain Arif were the organizers, to collect funds to assist the Turkish cause.[38]

The unease, caused by the war between Italy and Turkey, also spread beyond Calcutta. Ordinary Muslims in the countryside were excited by the appeals made to them to hold meetings to pray for the success of the Turks. Attempts to stage a boycott of Italian goods had likewise led in some districts to an idea that it was the duty of all good Muslims to boycott European goods of whatever nationality. However, Nawab Sir Salimullah of Dhaka, who was pro-British in his political orientation, opposed this boycott and was greatly successful in preventing it from becoming widely popular.

The Turko–Italian war however contined to be of interest to the Muslims of Bengal. Several meetings were held in Calcutta in December 1911 to protest against Italy's action in seizing control of Tripoli, and to raise funds on behalf of wounded Turks. The most important of these meetings were those held under the auspices of the Indian Red Crescent Society. The Persian language newspaper, *Nama-i-Muqaddas Hablul Matin*, formerly published as a weekly, became a daily recounting the progress of the war and commanded an extensive sale.[39]

Convinced that unity was critical to safeguard the interest of Muslims, the *Nama-i-Muqaddas Hablul Matin* proposed 'formulae' for the achievement of such unity, which included, inter alia, (a) the 'removal' of the germs of dissension from the minds of the people, (b) the formation of an association consisting of Shi'ite mullahs and the Shaikh-ul Islam of Istanbul (on behalf of the Sunnis) to draw up a programme of action and inviting learned Muslims from all parts of the world to join it, and (c) bridging the gaps between the contending sects of Muslims. Similar associations were to be formed in other Muslim countries too. The central organization, located in Turkey, supported by its branches, would eventually be so strong, it was hoped, that no European would dare interfere with it. The 'formulae' also pleaded, (a) the creation of honest political alliances between Muslim governments and wealthy Muslims, including intermarriage between the sultan's family and rich Muslims.[40] Although such formulae had little practical relevance, this reflected the urgency with which the Bengal Muslim press treated the question of pan-Islamic unity.

The *Nama-i-Muqaddas Hablul Matin* published a letter in 1912 which reminded Muslims that the Qur'an and the Prophet (sm.) had declared Muslims to be brothers. If one Muslim was subjected to tyranny others ought to come to his help. Describing the three hundred million Muslims of various different countries as hands of Islam, the letter urged all Muslims to at least ask their respective governments to check tyranny in their own countries. Muslims were again reminded that the integrity of the Islamic countries depended on their unity, and that sectarian differences between the Shi'ites and the Sunnis should not obscure the conflict between Islam and the infidel.[41] The paper published another letter from Haji Syed Mustafa of Kashan and Najaf, addressed to the Muslims of the world, stating that the tyranny perpetrated by the Christian powers upon the Muslim countries was the consequence of the selfishness, discord, and want of national feeling exhibited by Muslims. The Syed appealed to Muslims to unite: to abandon their differences and quarrels for the sake of God and the Prophet of Islam.[42]

Stressing the point further, the *Nama-i-Muqaddas Hablul Matin* asserted that the 'nationality' of Muslims was different from that of other people. Muslims, though living in different parts of the world were, as regards their religion, one people. Their belonging to different races and to different climates, following different rites and customs, should not affect their 'nationality'. Thus, Muslims living within the walls of China were closely connected with Muslims of Africa. Even if it was not possible for them to offer direct help to their brothers in other countries, their sympathy and support would always be forthcoming.[43] The *Mussalman* maintained that even if the worst happened to Turkey in the Balkan wars, Muslims would not fail to discharge their duty towards their fellow coreligionists in distress because 'the bond of religion is nowhere so strong as in Islam'. It observed that the war had already done something towards unifying the different communities in India, and what the Muslims in all parts of the world were doing at that time was an eloquent testimony to the solidarity of the followers of that creed and the sympathy which one Muslim felt for another in trouble.[44]

Around the middle of 1912, an association called the Anjuman-i-Ulama-i-Bangla was established. Maulana Muhammad Akram Khan became its secretary. Its objects were to create a band of *'ulema* able to preach Islam in modern times, to promote unity and create fellow-feeling by putting an end to narrow sectarian quarrels, to try to prevent Muslims from being converted to Christianity or any other religion, to reconvert those who had embraced Christianity, and to write books and pamphlets responding to those written by Christian missionaries misrepresenting Islam and the Prophet. One of the goals of the Anjuman was to create a great centre of *'ulema* and make them work in concert for the attainment of those objects. It was a unique organization and its necessity in Bengal was more pressing than in any other province of India. Some very earnest and well-qualified members of the Anjuman, such as Maulana Muhammad Akram Khan, Maulana Muhammad Maniruzzaman Islamabadi, Maulvi Muhammad Shahidullah, wrote books and pamphlets in refutation of the accusations made by Christian missionaries against Islam.[45]

The Anjuman-i-Ulama-i-Bangla, as part of its programme of 'safeguarding the interest' of Islam, initiated an organization to disseminate propaganda in 1913 called the Islam Mission. One of its principal goals was to counteract Christian missionary activities in Bengal. Despite the problems caused by the First World War, the Mission published a number of books and pamphlets, namely, *The Padre's Mistakes*, *Jesus of Nazareth*, *Worthlessness of Christianity*, *The Padre and His Three Disciples*, and *The Teachings of Islam*. The Mission gained further strength after Shah Abdullah, originally a Christian who had embraced Islam in the early 1900, joined it. The members of the Mission were devoted people and worked hard for it; the organization received regular donations from Muslims from all over the province.[46]

Political Activism among Bengal Muslims

Political activity naturally followed these sentiments; the colonial government's attempts to restrict pan-Islamic activity further crystallized it. One of the leading proponents of pan-Islamism in Bengal, Ismail Hossain Shiraji, was thus prosecuted by the government of Bengal for authoring 'seditious' works (especially, his poem *Anal Probaha* or 'the Flow of Fire', composed in 1899 and published in book form with other poems in 1900, twelve long poems all devoted to Islam and Islamic ideals). Warrants for the arrest of Ismail Hossain Shiraji and for his house to be searched were issued from Calcutta to the Magistrate of Pabna on 18 March 1910.[47] The poet was imprisoned for two years on charges of sedition and his book was banned by the British government. Freed from jail, Shiraji left for Turkey as a member of the Medical Mission headed by Dr M.A. Ansari on 2 December 1912, and came to be regarded as a hero by the Muslims of Bengal. He continued with his writings from Turkey and contributed a number of poems and articles which were published in various newspapers and periodicals of Bengal. These articles were later published in his book *Turashka Bhraman* ('Travels in Turkey'). Prior to his arrest for sedition, he wrote the epic poem *Mahashiksha Kavya*, based on a historical interpretation of the glories of Islam.[48]

However, besides Shiraji there was hardly any other prominent Bengali Muslim leader or intellectual who aggressively participated in anti-colonial and pan-Islamic activity in Bengal at this time, although newspaper reports indicate a growing support in the districts for the pan-Islamic cause. On the whole, Bengali Muslims continued to abstain from meaningfully participating in any agitation against the colonial government. The loyalist leader, Nawab Salimullah of Dhaka, continued to prevail until after 1916. By then Muslim opinion had crystallized in favour of separatist politics, irreparably breaking ranks with the Indian National Congress.

The possibility of reversal of the partition of Bengal, enacted in 1905, caused a great deal of misgiving among educated Bengali Muslims and galvanized them into action against the colonial government, but not in concert with the Hindus. It was in this context that on 9 April 1909 a mass meeting was held at the grounds of Ahsan Manzil, the home of Nawab Salimullah, to rally support in favour of partition.[49] In 1911 the Eastern Bengal and Assam Government observed that anxiety had been created amongst Bengali Muslims as a result of the decision to annul partition. In 1912 the government also noticed great apprehension amongst East Bengal Muslims about the possible repercussions on them as a result of the annulment of partition. Their leaders met and decided to make representations to the government of India regarding

the measures they believed were necessary to safeguard their interests.[50]

Soon after the annulment of partition in 1911, two important Muslim
conferences were held in Calcutta. The first was the Bengal Muslim
Conference held on 2 March 1912 in Dalhausie Institute at which about
1,000 Muslims were present. The object of this conference was to form
a strong representative association in Calcutta with branches in every
district of Bengal to 'safeguard Muslim interests' and to represent Muslim grievances to the government. In that conference the Nawab of
Dhaka appealed to all Muslims to unite and work together for the
benefit of the community. On 3 and 4 March 1912 the first Annual Session of the All-India Muslim League was held in the Town Hall, and
was largely attended. Several speeches were made dealing with current
political topics, but mostly focusing on the plight of the Muslims of the
subcontinent. The Nawab of Dhaka was bitterly critical of the Delhi an-
nouncements on the Partition of Bengal, in a sharp departure from his
well-known loyalist stance.[51]

Bengal Muslim's involvement in anti-colonial politics and, especially, in pan-Islamic activities greatly increased during, and immediately
after, the First World War. The British government found evidence that
scores of Bengali Muslim pilgrims to Mecca had joined the Turks in
their fight against the Allied Powers. In early 1915, the government
learned from a teacher in a Muslim school in Tippera district of Bengal,
who had returned from pilgrimage to Mecca, that a young man who
belonged to the same village as him had accompanied him to Mecca
and been recruited by the Turkish army with other young men of
different nationalities. The teacher stated that when he was at Mecca he
heard a Turkish officer deliver a very impressive and eloquent speech
urging Muslim pilgrims to join the Turkish army. The audience was so
impressed by the speech that over a thousand young men of different
nationalities immediately enlisted and were sent to Syria.[52]

In the meanwhile, the noted Ali Brothers, Maulanas Mohammad Ali
(1878–1931) and Shaukat Ali (1873–1938), had become the celebrated
leaders of the pan-Islamic movement in Bengal. Mohammad Ali, as the
editor of the English periodical, *Comrade*, was particularly active in
propagating anti-British views, thus setting a new trend in Bengal Muslim politics; Shaukat Ali had a similarly aggressive style. Consequently,
the wrath of the colonial government fell upon them, and both of
them were interned in 1915. Their arrests prompted loud protests in
Calcutta, and pro-Turkish sentiments were expressed and special

prayers offered in a number of mosques in Calcutta and elsewhere.[53] However, fearful of antagonizing the government, the premier Muslim mosque in Calcutta, Nakhoda Mosque, discontinued the special prayers and observances in favour of the sultan of Turkey. The imam of the mosque told the Muslims that as India was ruled by Christians, it was better to refrain from any outward expression of what they had in their hearts.[54]

By late 1915, the pan-Islamic intelligentsia in Calcutta, mostly Urdu-speaking Muslims, published a number of Urdu dailies and pamphlets (e.g. *Iqdam, Tarjuman, Risalat, Naqqash, Sadaqat, Al-Hilal, Jamhur, Millat, Rahbar, Al-Bilagh*, and *Hablul Matin*), which were pro-Turkish and anti-British in sentiment. These were designed to whip up communal and parochial sympathies of Muslims, especially of Calcutta, against the British and the loyalist Muslim leaders. Towards the middle of March 1916 the editor of *Hablul Matin* (Persian edition) was warned by the pess censor against publishing 'objectionable' poems. (The paper ceased to exist for a while, appeared again, and then again ceased publication.) At about the same time, *Al-Bilagh* published an article dealing with pan-Islamic ideals; its editor, Abul Kalam Azad (1888–1958), was warned by the government against publishing such articles in future.[55] In its issue of 25 July 1916, the *Sadaqat* of Calcutta published several answers to correspondence explaining that the paper was not permitted to publish any article or poem on the pan-Islamic subject.[56]

Towards the end of 1915, Abul Kalam Azad, one of the most persistent of the pan-Islamic propagators in Bengal, opened a school of Muslim theology in Calcutta, known as *Dar-ul-Irshad*. The Calcutta police obtained a copy of notes of a lecture delivered by Azad at the school in the first half of March 1916, expressing the view that the Qur'an forbade Muslims to remain in subjection; it was, therefore, incumbent upon the Muslims of India to strive to regain their lost control. There were two ways of working for freedom, according to Azad: one was for young men to form secret societies and prepare themselves to act with courage, and the other was to create a general desire for liberty amongst the masses, e.g. by delivering lectures on self-government and freedom.[57]

At this time, Muslim feelings in Bengal were profoundly stirred by events in Arabia leading to the rebellion of Sherif al-Husain (1853–1931) of Mecca. The news of the rebellion was received in Bengal with regret, and Britain was believed to be responsible for the Sharif's 'treachery'. There was some talk of starting an agitation to prevent any help being extended to the Sherif and his followers.[58] In Calcutta a small meeting was held at the house of the imam of Nakhoda Mosque, which passed a resolution of protest against the Sherif's activities. Similarly, a resolution was passed by the Bengal Provincial Muslim League against the Sherif and his Muslim sympathizers. The Central National Muhammadan Association, another Bengal Muslim 'political' organization, controlled mostly by government servants and pensioners, however, passed a resolution declaring neutrality on the subject. An advertised meeting of the Anjuman-i-Ulama-i-Bangla (which was pro-Turkish) took place in Calcutta and passed resolutions against the Sherif, reaffirming loyalty to the sultan of Turkey as the Caliph of Islam. The Muslims of Dhaka too were generally supportive of the sultan's position and believed that Britain had instigated the Arabs; they too denounced the Sherif as a traitor.[59]

The pan-Islamists became increasingly active in the rural districts during the First World War. Religious preachers often used their Friday sermons in the mosque to propagate the ideal of pan-Islamism. Leaflets were in circulation in many areas, and there were reports that many from the rural districts had travelled to Turkey to fight for the Turks. A Bengali leaflet, entitled *Jihad*, was found to be in circulation in Mymensingh district in East Bengal in November 1916, detailing the 'mistreatment' suffered by Indian Muslims under British rule and urging an overthrow of the colonial regime. It stated that Enver Pasha was on his way to India with a Turkish army, that Iran had joined him, and that Afghanistan was about to declare war on the British, and urged the Hindus and Muslims to unite to drive out the common enemy with Turkish help.[60]

The existence of a number of 'training camps' along the borders of North-West Frontier Province (NWFP), adjoining Afghanistan, which received and trained Muslim fighters at this time, is well-established. Reports indicate that towards the end of 1916 eight Muslims from Rangpur and Dhaka districts in eastern Bengal had joined these training camps.[61] Two Bengali Muslims who were attempting to convey money across the frontier to these fighters were captured by the colonial police. They were in possession of Rs 8,000, which reportedly had been largely collected from the districts of Dhaka and Mymensingh.[62] Three of the hundred rupee notes found in the possession of these two men had been traced through Muslim hide merchants in Calcutta to their agents in Rajshahi. The pro-Turk Muslims there organized under the leadership of one Maulvi Muhammad, the son of a man who had been deported at the time of the Wahabi trials in 1863–72. The maulvi had reportedly

50,000 followers in Bengal, and had been known to collect money for the fighters in the NWFP. When the government pursued him, he fled town. His safe was found to contain Rs 5,000 in cash obtained mostly from the sale of hide of cattle slaughtered during the festival of Korbani (an annual event commemorating the aborted sacrifice of Abraham's son). Much of the money sent from Bengal to the *mujahedin* (holy warriors) presumably came from this or similar sources. The government believed that the original contributors were not aware of the ultimate destination of the money.[63]

Government enquiries had continued in several districts to ascertain, (i) the system under which funds were collected by the the so-called Wahabis for transmission to the colony of *mujahedin* across the frontier districts, and (ii) how persons were recruited for the colony. It was found that in practically every district there were one or two influential Wahabi leaders who were looked upon by their followers as spiritual guides. These leaders had *sardars* (local chiefs) in many villages, especially where they (the Wahabis) had large numbers of disciples. The function of these sardars was to collect the hides of animals sacrificed at Korbani and other religious occasions. About three-quarters of the amount collected was spent in charity in the village, the remainder going to the spiritual guide who spent a portion ostensibly in maintaining a *madrassa* or some such establishment, and the rest on his own maintenance. A portion of the *madrassa* fund was believed to find its way to the *mujahedin* colony at Asmas. The most important districts in this chain appeared to be Rajshahi, Dhaka, Mymensing, Murshidabad, Birbhum, Dinajpur, Rangpur, and Nadia. Rajshahi and Dhaka, according to government information, were full of 'Wahabis'. In Dinajpur about a third of the Muslims were members of a particular branch of the Wahabi sect which actively helped the *mujahedin* colony across the border. Influential leaders in each district maintained *madrassas* out of funds they received. These *madrassas* appeared to have been the recruiting institutions.[64]

Meanwhile, internment of prominent pan-Islamic leaders caused a great deal of tension in Calcutta and elsewhere in Bengal. An agitation against the trial of these men under the Defence of India Act was well under way in 1918. Meetings, at which strong language was often used, were held in Calcutta to discuss this question, and also to demand the release of Maulanas Muhammad Ali and Shaukat Ali, and other detenus. Internment was the principal subject on which Muslim newspapers focused throughout the months of February and March that year. *Sadaqat* and *Jamhur* continued to publish strong articles against the internment of Muslim detenus.[65] Similarly, meetings were routinely organized to ventilate grievances against the colonial government's policy of internment. Thus, a meeting was held near Nakhoda Mosque, presided over by A.K. Fazlul Huq, on 3 April 1918. Hakim Abdur Rauf in his speech referred to the troubles in Turkey, Iran, Afghanistan, and other Muslim countries, and suggested that the object of the British government was to drive out Islam from India. Another speaker, Abul Hussain, explained incidents at Kanpur in UP, Bihar, and Jerusalem, and said the 'treachery' of the Sherif of Mecca had caused many to believe that the European war would end in a religious war, that a *jihad* would be the last resort, and that a true Muslim must be ready to sacrifice his life and property for the sake of religion.[66] In an interesting development, the Bengali-owned Muslim newspapers had joined the pan-Islamic cry by the middle of 1918.

Adding fuel to Muslim sentiments were publications by Christian missionaries and others. There was considerable agitation amongst the Muslims of Calcutta on account of an article (copied from the *Catholic Herald*) in the *Indian Daily News* allegedly linking the Prophet's tomb to a gutter. This incident interested the Muslim papers of Calcutta to the exclusion of every other topic. *Musalman* and *Jamhur* were most violent in their criticisms, forcing the government to issue orders requiring the submission of these papers and *Muhammadi* for censorship. The editors of *Millat* and *Jamhur* were externed from Bengal. *Mussalman* and *Muhammadi* suspended publication from 14 September 1918 for a time in order to avoid press censorship, and reappeared on 25 October 1918.[67]

There were signs that the Muslim leaders were becoming concerned about the terms of the peace settlement after the war, and endeavours were made to sort out differences between opposing views of Muslims on this question. British recognition of the claim of the Sherif of Mecca to the guardianship of the holy places of Mecca and Medina in February 1919, and the policy of the victorious Allies towards the Turks, especially the *khalifa*, were not reassuring to Bengal Muslims. The Muslim papers continued to discuss the future of the *khilafat* almost routinely. The *Muhammadi* in particular published strong protests against the dismemberment of Turkey, urging its readers to take a vow of passive resistance to fight against British policy towards the *khilafat*. There were further expressions of regret that no Muslim had been selected as a delegate at the peace conference.[68]

To allay the apprehensions of Muslims about the terms of the peace settlement, the colonial government took a number of measures. The governor of Bengal thus convened a meeting at Calcutta of 'leading Muslims' in May 1919 to explain the terms of the settlement. District officers were warned of the severity of the terms that were expected to be imposed upon Turkey, and had been asked personally to convey a similar warning to leading Muslims in their districts, invoking their assistance on the side of order, and to report to the government their assessments of the developing situation. It appears that government officers generally believed that there would be no trouble in the districts on the subject of Turkish peace terms provided that when announcing them it was made clear that Muslim institutions and holy places had been duly safeguarded.[69]

Even after the war, the Muslim press in Bengal continued to engage itself with the future of the *khilafat*. Although there was a general sense of satisfaction at the facilities offered by the colonial government to pilgrims going to Arabia, Muslim public opinion still remained dissatisfied over British handling of the Turkish *khilafat*. The *Muhammadi* had been actively campaigning against the dismemberment of the Turkish empire; it too deplored the existence of repressive laws that made it impossible for the press to ventilate their views on Turkey. The other Muslim papers, although somewhat cautious in the expression of their views, made no secret of their support for Turkey and consistently argued that the decision of the peace conference would seriously affect the position of Turkey. The Muslim papers in general, had a tendency to blame the British government entirely for the peace terms. In pan-Islamic conferences and meetings, and in the Muslim press (which discussed the Turkish question with increasing avidity), there were increasing signs of sympathy for the sultan of Turkey, and it was argued that the principle of self-determination ought to be equally applicable to the Muslim peoples. Similarly, the pro-Turk Muslim intelligentsia of Bengal felt that Arabia should not only remain under the spiritual control of the sultan, but also within his temporal jurisdiction. Muslim papers were assiduously pursuing the theme that Turkey deserved better treatment than she was rumoured to be getting. Britain was called upon to fulfil the wishes of her crores of Muslim subjects rather than pandering to other countries. They insisted that the Turkish sultan must remain the *khalifa*, and that unimpaired temporal power was indispensable to his spiritual dignity. Lloyd George's intention of securing a French mandate for Syria was described as a menace to Muslims, and Greece was alleged to be taking advantage of the delay in settlement by exploiting her own interests in Turkey. Great hopes were attached to various Indian missions that had gone to England. The Lucknow Conference which was to be held in September 1919 as a protest against any possible dismemberment of Turkey, and to be attended by delegates from Bengal, was widely advertised, and all Muslims were urged to attend the special Friday prayers for the welfare of Turkey to be held on 17 October 1919.[70] Similarly, the All-India Muslim League, which was emerging as a major Muslim political organization in Bengal, decided to hold a provincial conference at Krishnanagar (Bengal) primarily to organize support for a memorial regarding Turkey which the League intended to submit to the Viceroy. In early October 1919 the League sought to persuade the Muslim shopkeepers in Calcutta to down their shutters on 17 October 1919 in support of a general strike called in protest against the changes in the position of the *khalifa*. Maulana Hasrat Mohani, editor of *Urdu-e-Mualla* (Aligarh), came to Calcutta to supervise the arrangements on this occasion. Efforts were likewise made to induce Hindu shopkeepers to close their shops in token sympathy for the Muslim cause.[71]

Friday, 17 October 1919, was observed as the Khilafat Day in Calcutta and in a number of districts in Bengal. Urdu posters signed by Maulana Abdul Bari of Lucknow, Maulana Hasrat Mohani of Aligarh, and others were posted in Calcutta in support of the occasion. Similarly, a leaflet by Maulana Muhammad Akram Khan, editor of *Muhammadi* and a leading Bengali Muslim pan-Islamist, was widely circulated. The majority of shops owned by Muslims in Calcutta were closed on that day, as were a considerable number of those belonging to Bengali Hindu and Marwari businessmen. Special prayers were offered, and the imams of mosques took a leading role in explaining the problems that had led to this action. A crowded meeting was also held in the Town Hall, presided over by A.K. Fazlul Huq. It is estimated that between 10 to 15,000 people, mostly ordinary Muslims, were present in the meeting.

Meetings were also held in many districts, and in some places educated Hindus took part in the proceedings and made sympathetic speeches. Shops were closed in several towns. Efforts were made to reach out to ordinary Bengali Muslims and arouse their sympathy for the pan-Islamic cause. The opportunity was used also to promote Hindu–Muslim ties. The distribution by Muslims of fruits and flowers and paper handkerchiefs inscribed with eulogies of unity during the Diwali festival in 1919, and attendance of the Marwari *pinjrapole* ceremony (held at Sodepur on first October 1919) by a thousand Muslims including their leaders, such as A.K. Fazlul Huq, Mohammed Mujibur Rahman, Liaqat Hossain, Nazimuddin Ahmad, and A.K. Ghaznavi, indicated that the Muslim advocates of Hindu–Muslim unity were serious about seeking Hindu cooperation in their fight for the pan-Islamic cause.[72]

As indicated above, the Khilafat movement also offered an opportunity for different Muslim groups and sects to come together and promote a sense of togetherness. Their resentment against British policy towards Turkey promoted political unity amongst them and brought them closer to the Hindus, although this alliance with the latter proved to be short-lived. The Khilafat movement also won the support of Mahatma Gandhi, who sought to mobilize Muslims against the colonial government by combining the appeal of the *khilafat* with his Non-cooperation movement, the details of which are too well-known to be repeated.[73]

Bengali Muslim involvement in the Non-cooperation movement began in right earnest in the early 1920s; a conference organized by the Bengal Khilafat Committee in Calcutta Town Hall in February that year formally heralded the occasion. The key principles of non-cooperation were adopted at that meeting: it was decided to organize a *hartal* on 19 March 1920, and to send a telegram to the Viceroy, and the King–Emperor declaring that the Muslims of India would find it impossible to keep their secular loyalty intact unless their demands regarding the *khilafat* were accepted.[74]

With the Bengali Muslims actively involved in the Non-cooperation movement, it developed an organized and widespread agitation, especially in the lower districts of Bengal, against the British government. The movement continued to engender, in increasing measure among the masses, a widespread contempt for authority that manifested itself in the boycott and intimidation of loyal supporters of the government, molestation of government officials, confrontation with the police, and a growing refusal to pay taxes.[75] In 1921, the *khilafa*tists openly described Britain to be the arch enemy of Islam and predicted that a time would come when it would be incumbent upon all Muslims to draw the sword in defence of their religion.

Constraints of the Pan-Islamists and the Triumph of Separatism

Pan-Islamism in Bengal had to contend with manifold problems despite the show of unity discussed earlier. A number of 'leading Muslims' of Bengal, who did not approve of the aggressive programmes of the Muslim League and the other pan-Islamic groups, thus formed a new society in 1923 called the Indian Muslim Association to promote loyalty amongst Muslims towards the British. It was stated that the Association would 'abstain from adopting violent methods of agitation and resistance, active or passive, as a political weapon against government'.[76] Similarly, the question of rapprochement with the Indian National Congress soon came under close scrutiny. During the First World War the pan-Islamic press was quick to criticize the British, but its attitude towards Hindus was ambiguous. On the one hand, they remained sensitive to matters of Muslim concern, and on the other they were gratified by the sympathetic attitude of the Congress to the pan-Islamic cause.[77] Nonetheless, Mahatma Gandhi's Non-cooperation movement soon appeared to some Muslims as an inappropriate medium for the achievement of their long-term goals. The banning of cow-slaughter as a prerequisite for Hindu participation in the Khilafat–Non-cooperation movement, as demanded by many Hindus, was not supported even by many members of the All Bengal Jamiyat al-Ulama-i-Hind, who were generally supportive of the Indian National Congress. Backed by Mohammad Ali Jinnah (1876–1948) and Fazl-i-Hussain (1877–1936), various Muslim politicians soon began opposing the Non-cooperation movement. Similarly, although the movement imposed a ban on participation by Indians in the legislative council, various Muslim leaders of Bengal, including Nawab Syed Nawab Ali Chaudhury and Nawab Sir Syed Shamsul Huda, favoured joining it. A.K. Fazlul Huq supported the *khilafat* cause but opposed the Non-cooperation movement.[78] At another level, Bengali Muslim students had remained generally aloof from political demonstrations organized by the Congress, except in matters in which Muslim interests were involved or questions on Islam were raised.

The *khilafat* agitation generally fostered aggressive sectarian passion and inculcated a disregard for law and order, especially in matters that had a religious connotation. With the abolition of the *khilafat* this exasperated communal self-consciousness remained powerful: 'unable now to vent itself upon government, it turned upon the rival Hindu community'.[79] A growing sense of unease among many Muslims about their short-lived alliance with the Hindus gradually set in; that Muslim mosques (including Nakhoda Mosque in Calcutta and the Jama Masjid in Delhi) should have been thrown open to Hindu politicians contributed materially to this general reaction. Generally, loyalist Muslim leaders seem to have been at the forefront of this new shift in Muslim politics. For example, at a Muslim political and literary conference in Serajgunj, then in Pabna district, in April 1919 the President, Nawab Syed Nawab Ali Chaudhury, an arch loyalist, denounced fraternization between Hindus and Muslims in mosques.[80]

Mutual hatred of the ruling power had been the only cementing force for non-cooperation, but the considerations that led to discontent on the part of the Muslims eventually ceased to operate. The Khilafat movement, which had been the mainspring of Muslim agitation, lost its momentum when Turkey under the leadership of Mustafa Kemal Ataturk secured favourable terms under the Treaty of Lausanne signed in June 1923. The abolition of the *khilafat* by the Turks, the action of the Wahabis in seizing Mecca, and various other developments in the Muslim world undermined Bengali Muslim faith in the pan-Islamic ideal and diverted attention from pan-Islamic issues to internal politics.[81]

Thus, a growing sense of communal identity, coupled with despair in failing to achieve a meaningful understanding with the Hindus encouraged vast numbers of Muslims into ready acceptance of the concept of Muslim nationalism in India. Issues like Muslim employment and Muslim representation in the Calcutta municipality brought together Muslim leaders from Calcutta as well as the *mofussil*, united in their suspicion of the Congress, and their awareness of the need for Muslims to function as a distinct communal entity in the politics of Bengal and India.[82]

The Bengal Muslims had joined the Non-cooperation movement chiefly because of the *khilafat* question. This affected only Muslims, and as such no genuine sympathy for the *khilafat* cause could be expected from the Hindus. It was alleged in August 1921 that Hindu political workers scarcely took any active part in the Khilafat movement, and that the work of the Congress committees was quite different from that of the Khilafat committees insofar as the strategies to fight against the colonial regime. Even at the height of the Khilafat–Non-cooperation movement it was hardly possible to induce Muslims to take any interest in non-cooperation except in terms of the *khilafat*. When the Khilafat–Non-cooperation movement ended, Muslims left the Congress in large numbers. Pan-Islamic solidarity maintained itself as an undercurrent in the emerging notion of Muslim nationalism.[83]

Conclusion

Bengali Muslims' increased awareness of their Islamic identity, and as such part of a larger *ummah*, was the direct consequence of circumstances and political developments both in India and abroad. Their support for the sultan of Turkey, who was also the *khalifa*, was due to their sentimental attachment to the *khilafat*, and their belief that in the existence of the Turkish *khilafat* was bound up the honour and dignity of the entire Muslim world. This attitude was encouraged by a vast outpouring of works in print, religious propagation, meetings, and demonstrations, and finally by their attitudes toward Europeans and Hindus.

Muslim support for the *khilafat* caused a great deal of confusion in non-Muslim circles about their loyalty and patriotism, especially during the First World War when Turkey joined the war against Britain. Muslims insisted that the allegiance to the sultan was dictated solely by religious considerations, and that their political loyalty to India and to the colonial government was unaffected by this. The surrender of Turkey after the First World War and subsequent developments further exacerbated the confusion about Muslims. Even Muslim public opinion seemed uncertain and confused on various political issues. While the general body of Bengal Muslims refused to take part in the peace celebrations, observing instead Khilafat Day in Calcutta and other cities and district headquarters, many 'leading Muslims' questioned this strategy and sought to promote loyalty to the colonial government. Similarly, although their goals of preserving the *khilafat* had induced many Muslims to enter into an alliance with the Indian National Congress against the British, the failure of the *khilafat* cause, and the continued suspicion of the motives of the Congress increasingly drove the Muslims of Bengal into the acceptance of a territorial, pan-Indian, Muslim separatist nationalism. Pan-Islamism had affected their psyche deeply: although its immediate goal of safeguarding the interests of Turkey was not achieved, it did promote a kind of parochial nationalism in them, politically uniting them, at least for the time being, with the Muslims of northern India.

Notes and References

1. Several general studies have appeared on pan-Islamism, e.g., Jacob M. Landau, *The Politics of Pan-Islam: Ideology and Organization* (Oxford: Clarendon Press, 1990); Naimur Rahman Farooqi, 'Pan-Islamism in the

Nineteenth Century' in *Islamic Culture*, Hyderabad (October 1983). Kenneth McPherson has made some interesting observations on pan-Islamism in Calcutta in his work, *The Muslim Microcosm: Calcutta, 1918–1935* (Wiesbaden, 1974). *See* also Arminius Vambery, 'Pan-Islamism and the Sultan of Turkey', *The Imperial and Asiatic Quarterly Review and Oriental and Colonial Record*, London (January–April 1907) and Syed K. Jalaluddin al-Husaini 'Pan-Islamism: Khilafat, Non-Cooperation, Swaraj and Hindu–Muslim Unity' (lectures delivered in 1921), (trans. from the Persian by Maulvi Syed Ibni Imam), in *Roznama-i-Muqaddas Hablul Matin*, Calcutta, April 1921, p. 11.

2. *See*, for example, *Hablul Matin*, 9 Aug. 1897; *Report on the Indian Newspapers and Periodicals, Bengal* (RINPB), 14 Aug. 1897, 701; Valentine Chirol, 'Pan-Islamism', in the Earl of Ronaldshay (ed.), *Notes on a Journey Across Asia*, Proceedings of the Central Asian Society, London, 1906, 21–23; Roznama-i-Muqaddas Hablul Matin, 8 July 1901; and RINPB, 13 July 1901, 541.

3. *Report of the Rowlatt Committee*, 125.

4. *Roznama-i-Muqaddas* Hablul Matin, 25 Oct. 1897; RINPB, 30 Oct. 1897, 949. *Hablul Matin*, 15 Nov. 1897; RINPB, 20 Nov. 1897, 1015.

5. *Al-Punchr*, 26 Nov. 1897; RINPB, 4 Dec. 1897, 1061.

6. *Roznama-i-Muqaddas Hablul Matin*, 19 Aug. 1901; RINPB, 24 Aug. 1901, 659. *Roznama-i-Muqaddas Hablul Matin*, 26 Aug. 1901; RINPB, 31 Aug. 1901, 682.

7. An extract from page 132 of the book (containing 319 pages, printed at the Subhakari Pess, Jessore), as quoted by Meherullah, is as follows:
'Muhammad's character was worse than his religious teaching. It is doubtful whether there is a man who can equal him in the licentiousness and in doing of wicked acts. Not content with his wife and mistresses, he even took other men's wives and even his male and female servants did not escape his hands. Nay, he ravished even a girl of eight. He did not stick at age or relationship in gratifying the cravings of the flesh. He was a notorious robber . . . .'
[*Mihir o Sudhakar*, 30 June 1899; RINPB, 8 July 1899, 482.]

8. *Mihir o Sudhakar*, 29 Sept. 1899; RINPB, 7 Oct. 1899, 756.

9. *Roznama-i-Muqaddas Hablul Matin*, 24 June 1901; RINPB, 29 June 1901, 500.

10. *Roznama-i-Muqaddas Hablul Matin*, 19 Aug. 1901; RINPB, 24 Aug. 1901, 659. *Roznama-i-Muqaddas Hablul Matin*, 26 Aug. 1901; RINPB, 31 Aug. 1901, 682.

11. *Soltan*, 27 Sept. 1907; RINPB, 5 Oct. 1907, 1057.

12. *Soltan*, 5 March 1909; RINPB, 2 June 1909, 283.

13. *Soltan*, 28 May 1909; RINPB, 29 May 1909, 689.

14. *Mihir o Sudhakar*, 11 June 1909; RINPB, 19 June 1909, 752. *Mihir o Sudhakar*, 9 July 1909; RINPB, July 1909, 885–6.

15. *Mohammadi*, 13 Oct. 1911; RINPB, 21 Oct. 1911, 1281, 1283.
16. *Mohammadi*, 17 Nov. 1911; RINPB, 25 Nov. 1911, 1402.
17. *Mohammadi*, 24 Nov. 1911; RINPB, 2 Dec. 1911, 1430–1.
18. *Mohammadi*, 27 Oct. 1911; RINPB, 4 Nov. 1911, 1338.
19. *Mohammadi*, 7 Nov. 1911; RINPB, 25 Nov. 1911, 1404.
20. *Mohammadi*, 22 Dec. 1911; RINPB, 30 Dec. 1911, 1552.
21. *Nama-i-Muqaddas Hablul Matin*, 23 Oct. 1911; RINPB, 28 Oct. 1911; 1321.
22. *The Mussalman*, 3 Nov. 1911; *Report on the Indian-owned English Newspapers, Bengal* (RIENB), 11 Nov. 1911, 493.
23. *Nama-i-Muqaddas Hablul Matin*, 6 Nov. 1911; RINPB, 25 Nov. 1911, 1401. *The Nama-i-Muqaddas Hablul Matin*, 20 Nov. 1911; 2 Dec. 1911, 1431.
24. *Mohammadi*, 1 March 1912; RINPB, 9 March 1912, 274.
25. *Moslem Hitaishi*, 17 Jan. 1913; RINPB, 25 Jan. 1913, 69.
26. *The Mussalman*, 24 Jan. 1913; RIENB, 1 Feb. 1913, 71.
27. *Hablul Matin*, 18 March 1913; RINPB, 22 March 1913, 288.
28. W.C. Smith, *Modern Islam in India* (Lahore, 1943), 215.
29. *Safir*, 23 Aug. 1915: RINPB, 28 Aug. 1915, 1245.
30. *Hablul Matin*, 21 Sep. 1896; RINPB, 3 Oct. 1896, 971.
31. *Darussultanat and Urdu Guide*, 3 Dec. 1896; *RINPB*, 12 Dec. 1896, 1151.
32. *Mihir Sudhakar*, 27 Dec. 1889; RINPB, 4 Jan. 1890, 19.
33. *Mohammadi*, 10 May 1912; RINPB, 18 May 1912, 551.
34. *Hablul Matin*, 11 Oct. 1897, RINPB, 16 Oct. 1897, 934.
35. *Hablul Matin*, 14 May 1900; RINPB, 26 May 1900, 387. *Hablul Matin*, 25 June 1900; RINPB, 7 July 1900, 503.
36. *Roznama-i-Muqaddas Hablul Matin*, 27 Aug. 1900; RINPB, 8 Sept. 1900, 682.
37. *Roznama-i-Muqaddas Hablul Matin*, 10 Sept. 1900; RINPB, 22 Sept. 1900, 727. *Roznama-i-Muqaddas Hablul Matin*, 22 Oct. 1900; RINPB, 3 Nov. 1900, 788. *Roznama-i-Muqaddas Hablul Matin*, 5 Nov. 1900; RINPB, 17 Nov. 1900, 825.
38. From the Chf. Secy., Govt. of Bengal, to Secy, Govt of India, Home Dept, 17 Nov. 1911, 1.
39. From J. Stevenson, Chf. Secy., Govt. of Bengal, to Secy, Govt of India, Home Dept, 18 Dec. 1911, 1.
40. *Nama-i-Muqaddas Hablul Matin*, 9 Jan. 1911; RINPB, 21 Jan. 1911, 58.
41. *Nama-i-Muqaddas Hablul Matin*, 1 July 1912; RINPB, 13 July 1912, 770.
42. *Nama-i-Muqaddas Hablul Matin*, 29 July 1912; RINPB, 10 Aug. 1912, '905–6.
43. *Nama-i-Muqaddas Hablul Matin*, 12 Aug. 1912; RINPB, 24 Aug. 1912, 977.
44. *The Mussalman*, 22 Nov. 1912; RIENB, 30 Nov. 1912, 725.
45. *The Mussalman*, 23 Oct. 1914; RIENB, 31 Oct. 1914, 44.

46. *Mohammadi*, 30 Oct. 1914; RINPB, 7 Nov. 1914, 1201–2.

47. R. Nathan, Chf Secy, Govt of East Bengal and Assam, to Secy, Govt of India, Home Dept, 23 April 1910, 8.

48. Mizanur Rahman, 'Ismail Hussain Shirajee: A Poet of the Islamic Renaissance', in Syed Sajjad Husain (ed.), *Pakistan: An Anthology* (Dhaka: The Society for Pakistan Studies Series, 1964), 229–31.

49. From P.C. Lyon, Chf. Secy., Govt. of Eastern Bengal and Assam, to Secy, Govt of India, Home Dept, 11 May 1909, 6.

50. Le Mesurier, Chf. Secy., Govt. of Eastern Bengal and Assam, to Secy Govt of India, Home Dept, 22 January 1912, 7; C.J. Stevson Moore, Chf. Secy., Govt. of Bengal, to Secy., Govt. of India, Home Dept, 27 Jan. 1912, 4.

51. C.J. Stevenson Moore, Chf. Secy., Govt. of Bengal, to Secy., Govt. of India, Home Dept, 19 March 1912, 1.

52. *Weekly Report of the Director, Criminal Intelligence* (WRDCI), 2 March 1915, 5.

53. P.C. Bamford, *Histories of Non-co-operation and Khilafat Movements* (Delhi: Government of India, 1925), 121.

54. WRDCI, 1 June 1915, 4.

55. *Fortnightly Provincial Report* (FPR): J.H. Carr, Chf. Secy., Govt. of Bengal, to H. Wheeler, Secy., Govt. of India, Home Dept., 17 March 1916, 6.

56. WRDCI, 29 July 1916, 8.

57. WRDCI, 14 March 1916, 11.

58. J.H. Carr, Chf. Secy., Govt. of Bengal to H. Wheeler, Secy. to Govt. of India, Home Dept., 3 July 1916, 7.

59. WRDCI, 8 July 1916, 14; WRDCI, 15 July 1916, 20; WRDCI, 22 July 1916, 25.

60. WRDCI, 9 Dec. 1916, 2.

61. WRDCI, 6 Jan. 1917, 12.

62. WRDCI, 17 Apr. 1917, 3.

63. WRDCI, 27 May 1917, 10.

64. WRDCI, 22 Sept. 1917, 21.

65. J.H. Carr, Chf. Secy., Govt. of Bengal, to Sir James Duboulay, Secy., Govt. of India, Home Dept., 20 Feb. 1918, 8; W. Edgley (Bengal), to Sir James Duboulay, 4 March 1918, 11.

66. WRDCI, 16 Feb. 1918, 17.

67. *Confidential Report on the Political Situation in Bengal* (CRPSB), for the first half Aug. 1918, 12; second half of Aug. 1918, 11; first half of Sept. 1918, 11; second half of Oct. 1918, 7.

68. CRPSB, for the first and second half of Feb. 1919, 7; first half of March 1919, 2; second half of March 1919, 11; second half of April 1919, 12.

69. CRPSB, for the first half of May 1919, 9; second half of May 1919, 7.

70. CRPSB, for the first half of May 1919, 10; second half of May 1919, 8; first half of June 1919, 7; second half of June 1919, 11; first half of July 1919, 11; second half of July 1919, 10; first half of Aug. 1919, 9; second

half of Aug. 1919, 10; first half of Sept. 1919, 12; first half of Oct. 1919, 11.

71. CRPSB, for the second half of Aug. 1919, 9; first half of Oct. 1919, 10.
72. CRPSB, for the first half of Nov. 1919, 7–8.
73. *Administration Report, Bengal* (BAR), 1922–3, i–ii.
74. BAR, 1919–20, ii.
75. BAR, 1921–2, iv.
76. WRDCI, 3 Nov. 1917, 2.
77. McPherson, *Muslim Microcosm*, 31, 40–1.
78. Pradip Kumar Lahiri, *Bengali Muslim Thought, 1818–1947* (Calcutta: K.P. Bagchi, 1991), 93–4.
79. BAR, 1925–6, ii.
80. CRPSB, for the first half of April 1919, 10; second half of April 1919, 9.
81. BAR, 1923–4, xv.
82. McPherson, *Muslim Microcosm*, 141–2.
83. Albert Christian Niemeijer, *The Khilafat Movement in India*, 1919-24, (The Hague: Martinus Nijhoff, 1972), 38.

5

A Muslim Voice in Modern Bengali Literature: Mir Mosharraf Hosain

CLINTON B. SEELY

If a Muslim Bengali in the nineteenth century spoke Bengali (Bangla is the name for the language in English preferred nowadays by many of my Bengali colleagues) did anyone understand? The simple response is undoubtedly, yes. A complementary question, however, seems less definitively answered: If a Muslim Bengali wrote in Bengali in the nineteenth century, who read what he had written?[1] Inferable from these questions are two of the three issues I would like to address: those of language and audience. My third concern is with genre, specifically with the genre of the novel as it develops in Bengali, and with particular reference to the best known and voluminous work by Mir Mosharraf Hosain (1848–1912 CE)[2] *The Sea of Sorrows* (*Vishada sindhu*).

Background

The first part of the tripartite prose narrative *The Sea of Sorrows* appeared in 1885 and was entitled 'Maharam'. The second part, published in 1887, and the third, in 1890, bore the titles 'The Rescue' ('*Uddhara*') and 'The Slaying of Ezid' ('*Ezid-vadha*'), respectively.[3] *The Sea of Sorrows* relates, (i) the events leading up to the battle at Karbala and the actual slaying of Hasan and Hosain, grandsons of the prophet Mohammad; (ii) the rescue by Mohammad Hanifa of Zaenal Abedin plus the womenfolk, whom Ezid's forces had captured, and held prisoner in Damascus, following the decapitation of Hosain; and (iii) the eventual defeat of Ezid (not the slaying of Ezid notwithstanding the title of this part), who jumps into a well where he will live but burn eternally in fire sent from on high until the final day of judgment (*roz kiamat*). By the end of the third part, the metaphorical sea of sorrows has been traversed; on the other side, Zaenal Abedin assumes the throne of his forefathers and begins to rule over Damascus as well as Medina. 'Maharam', the subtitle of the first part, in addition to being the name of the first month of the Muslim lunar calendar year is the name given the annual commemoration (on the tenth day of Maharam) of the martyrdom of Hosain at Karbala, an event of utmost significance within Islam, more so for Shia Muslims, the minority within the greater Muslim community in Bengal, but also intrinsically a part of the heritage of the majority Sunni Bengali Muslim population.[4]

The Sea of Sorrows' subject matter is quintessentially Islamic and sincerely so. By that latter phrase, 'sincerely so', I mean to suggest that there is not the slightest hint of irony or disrespect to Islam in the work. At the same time, it should be noted that there is no animosity either: neither towards the Muslim community itself, nor towards those other Bengalis, the Hindus. The nineteenth century in Bengal witnessed several reformist Islamic movements, for example, the Wahabi and the Faraizi, which were directed inwardly at Muslims themselves and were meant somehow to purify a wayward practice of Islam.[5] *The Sea of Sorrows*, declares Anisuzzaman, shows none of the reformist or 'puritanic'—the English term is used in Bengali transliteration in the cited passage that follows—quality associated with those movements:

We cannot see any particular influence even on subsequent literature of the Faraizi or the Tarika-i-Muhammadiya movements. One or two writers, perhaps, like Pundit Riaz-al-Din Ahmad Mashhadi, paid their respects to the Wahabi movement, but this attitude did not become widespread. Had it become so, then somebody or other would have written a piece or two on the Titumir rebellion. Moreover, Mosharraf Hosain's *The Sea of Sorrows* or his *The Sacred Birth* (*Maulud sharif*) (on the life of the Prophet, Mohammad), or Hamid Ali's *The Slaying of Kasem* (*Kasemavadha kavya*), etc., are ample proof that the puritanic religious reform movements were unable to affect deeply the writers of this period.[6]

Not only was Mosharraf Hosain not a 'puritanic' Islamic reformist, he in fact, displayed genuine understanding of the Hindu point of view, at least for the first half of his life. In 1888, during the decade in which *The Sea of Sorrows* trilogy was being written and published, he brought out an essay and then a pamphlet entitled *Life of the Cow* (Go-*jivana*) in which he proposed, for the sake of communal harmony, that Muslims give up eating beef.[7] The reaction from more conservative Muslims, the

Riaz-al-Din Ahmad Mashhadi mentioned above for one, was rather harsh and predictably so. Wrote Mashhadi, without naming names: 'Under the influence of the Hindus, a couple of benighted Muslims, ignorant of scripture and lacking any sense of the spiritual, are these days expressing hostility toward *korbani* [the ritual sacrifice of an animal, usually a cow, according to Islamic scriptural dictates] of kine and the eating of beef'.[8]

A rejoinder to Hosain in the periodical press surmised that the author (Hosain) 'is not a Muslim'; at a meeting convened in the residence of a Muslim Sub-Deputy Magistrate, Hosain was proclaimed kafir and a fatwa was issued demanding that his wife be divorced from him.[9] Despite such vitriol from his own religionists, Hosain truly believed in Muslim–Hindu accord and boldly put his ideas on paper before the public.

Later in life, by the beginning of the twentieth century, Hosain had undergone a fundamental change of attitude and no longer could be so trusting of, or sympathetic toward, his fellow Bengalis who happened to be Hindu. This change of heart Anisuzzaman attributes in no small measure to the illiberality of the times which, in turn, stemmed from what has been called the Hindu renaissance (called so by some, though referred to as the Bengal renaissance by other scholars) and how the spirit of that Hindu renaissance got instantiated in the literature and society of those times. One aspect of that Hindu renaissance resulted not in a perception of some sort of transcommunal Muslim and Hindu (Bengali) congruity but in the cultivation of a memory—a revival or, indeed, a renaissance—of incongruity between the Muslim and Hindu communities fostering enmity. Although he names no one, Anisuzzaman in all probability has Bankim Chandra Chattopadhyay (1838–94) in mind here, particularly his novel *The Abbey of Bliss* (*Anandamatha*) (1882), with its very anti-Muslim warrior sanyasis, and probably his *The Character of Krishna* (*Krsnacaritra*), which came out serially starting in 1884 and appeared in its entirety in book form in 1892. Chattopadhyay's Krishna is the Krishna of the Bhagavad Gita, a warrior Hindu god not unlike the warrior Hindu sanyasis of *The Abbey of Bliss*.[10] Anisuzzaman may lament the change in Hosain's writings and rue the cause of that change, yet he can laud Hosain's earlier works for their lack of any hint of communalism. It is those earlier writings that are, in his opinion, truly worthy of being called 'literature', exemplified by the narrative in novel form, *The Sea of Sorrows*. He argued 'that this atmosphere of illiberality had much to do with the change in Mosharraf

Hosain's outlook'. Indeed, it was not just him; the fact that all writers of that time were accosted by this situation was indeed lamentable. However, to Mosharraf Hosain's credit, the entirety of his writings that can be called literature is free of the influences of this communalism.[11]

Genre

I am employing the phrase 'narrative in novel form' in the above paragraph in two ways. First, I mean to convey the sense of newness, novelty. The incident recounted in *The Sea of Sorrows* had been the subject of other texts, in languages other than Bengali but also in Bengali or, more specifically, a particular variety of Bengali called *dobhashi*, meaning quite literally 'of two languages': *do* ('two') and *bhashi* (adjectival suffix from *bhasha* ('language') meaning 'of such-and-such language' or 'speaker of such-and-such language'). Other names by which this form of Bengali is known are 'Mussalmani Bengali' and 'mixed-language mode', this latter locution being particularly apt since *dobhashi* comprises, in addition to Bengali, lexical items (individual words) borrowed from several languages including Hindi–Urdu, Turkish, Persian/Farsi, and Arabic, Arabic being the pre-eminent 'Muslim' language, the language of the most sacred Muslim texts.[12] *Dobhashi* Bengali was the language in which the best known precursor of *The Sea of Sorrows*, Shah Garibullah's *A Tale of Battle* (*Janganama*; 'tale' (*nama*, a Persian word), 'battle' (*janga*, also a Persian borrowing into *dobhashi* Bengali)) had been composed. Garibullah's dates are estimated to be 1670–1770.[13] Suffice it to say here that Mosharraf Hosain's *The Sea of Sorrows* was not the first text in Bengali to take as its subject matter the battle at Karbala and the deaths of the brothers Hasan and Hosain. The novelty of *The Sea of Sorrows*, however, lies in its mode of presentation: quite strikingly in the language itself, a very high-style, Sanskritized Bengali known as *sadhu* ('chaste, refined') Bengali; a mode of language not, with a lone exception, theretofore associated with Muslim texts or Muslim Bengali speakers. I shall have further observations on the matter of language later.

Garibullah's *A Tale of Battle* is in verse, not that novels, even the most modern of novels, cannot be composed in verse. One need only consider Vikram Seth and his wonderfully successful novel-as-a-set-of-connected-sonnets, *The Golden Gate* (1986), to realize that 'novel' and 'verse' are not mutually exclusive literary domains. Nevertheless, *The*

Sea of Sorrows and *A Tale of Battle* differ stylistically and in terms of culturally perceived genres. *A Tale of Battle* belongs to that class of literature in Bengali generally and rather casually known as *punthi*. Though *punthi* itself can mean quite literally both 'book' and 'manuscript, i.e. an ancient book predating the printing press', it comes to stand for certain pre-modern texts, inexpensive editions of many of which were published from Calcutta during the latter half of the nineteenth century. As pre-modern literature in Bengali is entirely in verse, *punthi* designates verse texts. Prose as a medium for literature came into being only within the nineteenth century. Furthermore, the texts known as part of the *punthi* genre are narratives, not lyric poetry, and are composed in *dobhashi* Bengali. In short, *A Tale of Battle* epitomizes *punthi* literature. Hosain undoubtedly knew Garibullah's text. In his autobiography he tells of reciting *punthi*s for his grandmother, for the village girls who would gather around when he began to chant melodically, and for the various female authority figures in his life, who used to summon him to their neighbourhoods to read a text aloud. One of the *punthi*s he mentions by name is Garibullah's entitled, after its hero, *Amir Hamza*. He adds proudly, 'I had probably read all of the *punthi*s that there were'.[14] *The Sea of Sorrows*, however, is no *punthi*. Although it may not conform perfectly to the then burgeoning genre known as the Bengali novel, it shares many traits with novels of that period, including those by Bankim Chandra Chattopadhyay, the nineteenth century Bengali novelist par excellence.

An author might identify the genre of his creation. Such was not the case with *The Sea of Sorrows* but was with Hosain's first work of fiction, *Ratnavati* (1869), which bears the subtitle 'entertaining novel' (*kautukavaha upanyasa*). I am translating the *tatsama* (that is, a word borrowed directly into Bengali from Sanskrit) Bengali word *upanyasa* as novel, meaning the literary genre by that name. T.W. Clark, in his article on 'Bengali Prose Fiction up to Bankimcandra', calls our attention to the two pieces of prose by Bhudev Mukherjee, published jointly under the title of *Aitihasika upanyasa*, which Clark translates appropriately as 'Historical Novels'. One of the two pieces is, in Clark's words, 'a short prose story, about twelve pages long'.[15] This is not exactly the stuff of which novels are made, or so one might now think. Clark quotes from the introduction to *Historical Novels* and notes that Mukherjee identifies the source of his first novel (the one of a mere dozen pages) as the initial story in *The Romance of History*, a book in English by the Reverend Hobart Caunter. What Clark translates as 'story' is *upakhyana* in Mukherjee's Bengali; what he renders 'novel' is *upanyasa* in the original.[16]

One might look upon the use of the term *upanyasa*, and also its generally accepted equivalence, both in English (novel) and in trans-literated Bengali (*nabhel*), as potentially anachronistic. Should we expect the Sanskrit word *upanyasa*, from pre-modern times, or the word novel, from contemporary English, to be compatible in meaning with whatever the term(s) *upanyasa*/novel meant in the nineteenth century in Bengal? I shall leave aside for the moment any discussion of the English lexeme and concentrate on the *tatsama* term. From the gloss for *upanyasa* in the standard Sanskrit–English dictionary by Sir Monier Monier-Williams, it is somewhat difficult to recognize anything even vaguely resembling what might be thought of as the novel in the nineteenth century, either in English literature or in Bengali: '*upanyasa*, n.—bringing forward, speaking of, mention; statement, suggestion, hint; quotation, reference'. *Upakhyana*, on the other hand, has much more of the feel of a literary genre: '*upakhyana*, n.—account, relation, repetition of an event; a subordinate tale or story, an episode'.[17]

Not all modern South Asian languages followed Bengal's lead in adopting *upanyasa*, nor did they opt for *upakhyana*, as the Indic, non-Western rubric for the novel genre. Marathi, to cite probably the most intriguing case, pressed into service the title, named after the narrative's heroine, of one of the best known Sanskrit prose *kavyas*, *Kadambari*, by Banabhatta, as a term by which Marathi novels can be identified.[18] The Sanskrit *Kadambari* is a lengthy, highly ornate narrative of the moon god and a talking parrot, and reincarnation and stories embedded in other stories. It is lush with language; it is embellished lavishly by figures of speech; it is intricately plotted; and it is richly, wildly fanciful. That such an ornamented narrative, albeit in prose, would be taken as a pre-modern counterpart of sorts to the new genre of the novel as it emerged in the nineteenth century in one part of South Asia is noteworthy. Bhudev Mukherjee, Bankim Chandra Chattopadhyay, and then Mir Mosharraf Hosain, Bengalis all, chose to designate their works *upanyasa*, not *kadambari*, not even *upakhyana*. The two novels in Mukherjee's *Historical Novels* were published together in 1862; Chattopadhyay's first novel, *The Chieftain's Daughter* (*Durgesa-nandini*), came out in 1865; Hosain's 'entertaining' novel *Ratnavati*, named after a female character, appeared in print in 1869. It is only in the 1860s that we have a number of works of literature calling themselves *upanyasa*; it is only then that the genre begins to achieve a critical mass in Bengali and assume a recognizable shape for that language; and, I suggest, it is only by an examination of the individual works called *upanyasa*, in other words, by induction, that we come to know what the genre *upanyasa* in the nineteenth century in Bengal actually is. Certainly the denotative meaning of *upanyasa* in Sanskrit is of no help in this regard as it does not define or describe a genre there. Hence, the term *upanyasa* as found in Bengali is not really an anachronism, for it does not stand for two different genres at two different times in history. As a genre, *upanyasa* is unique to Bengali literature beginning with the early modern period. At the same time, it must be acknowledged that this unique genre, emerging in the nineteenth century, owed much both to the narrative traditions extant in South Asia and to influences coming into South Asia from abroad, an inevitable result of British colonialism.

By translating *upanyasa* (or *kadambari* or *upakhyana*) into the English word novel, we immediately lose the luxury of allowing the genre to define itself, as I suggested we could do with *upanyasa* if left untranslated, reasoning inductively from the works of literature at hand that identify themselves as *upanyasa*. The English word 'novel' comes with its own predetermined, externally determined—that is, determined outside of the Bengali literary tradition—definition and description. That is not to say that the definition/description of the novel genre is uniform at any one moment or stable over time even in English. On the contrary, 'novel' can be a rather mercurial category. Some two decades ago, Oxford University Press brought out a volume entitled *The Theory of the Novel* (1974). At first blush, the title seemed both academically correct and innocuous enough to go unchallenged. Not so. George Steiner, who had confronted genre in his book entitled *The Death of Tragedy* (1961), which conversed academically with Friedrich Nietzsche's 'The Birth of Tragedy', excoriated the editor (and the press itself, if I remember rightly, though I cannot recall now where I saw that review), for presuming that there was but one theory, 'the Theory', and but one monolithic genre that could contain something so authoritative, so universal as to be referred to as 'the Novel'.[19] There are theories, and there are novels, not the one and only theory of the archetypal novel. Then in 1996, there appeared a massive monograph by Margaret Anne Doody entitled even more presumptuously, it might seem, *The True Story of the Novel*. Doody, however, does more to destabilize the notion of 'the Novel' than the title suggests with its definite articles. Much of her book is devoted to a study of 'the ancient novel', the modifier 'ancient' already expanding the genre's range into the pre-modern period and, one might anticipate, allowing for something like *Kadambari* or even more readily its modern incarnations, *kadambaris* and *upanyasas* of the nineteenth and twentieth centuries, to take their rightful place within her more inclusive novel genre. Her concluding remarks, at any rate, are encouraging: 'What my sort of interpretation of the genre itself, of the novel as Novel, does *not* allow is our making narrow definitions of the genre and shutting out half of the prose fiction of the world. My reading will also not allow national and temporal boundaries to be the perdurable affairs they are often imagined to be'.[20]

Despite an admonition like Steiner's of not presuming an immutable, pristine, idealized genre against which all actual novels can be measured, and despite statements such as Doody's cautioning against narrowly defining the genre, we still see a tendency to do just that. Even though Bankim Chandra Chattopadhyay almost single-handedly shaped the *upanyasa* genre in Bengali in the nineteenth century, Sudipta Kaviraj can say that Chattopadhyay's novels were not really novels: 'In terms of narrative form as well, Bankim relied quite openly and heavily on the resources of traditional Indian aesthetics. His narratives were called novels, but were actually structured more like traditional dramas or narratives'.[21]

Kaviraj is writing here in English, so he uses the word novel. However, since *upanyasa* and novel/*nabhel* are by definition, quite literally 'by definition', synonymous in Bengali, Kaviraj is saying Chattopadhyay's *upanyasas* were somehow not really *upanyasas*.

The right of Hosain's *Ratnavati* to be included in the genre called *upanyasa* was not questioned initially but has been challenged subsequently by modern literary scholars. It was reviewed in 1870 in the English-language periodical *Calcutta Review*, where the issue of genre did not arise:

Ratnavati. By Mir Musharaf Hosain, Calcutta: New Bengali Press. Samvat 1926 [1869]. This is a romantic tale designed to show that knowledge is of greater importance than wealth, but as it is founded on the marvellous and the supernatural, it is not likely to be of much use. The author's argument is to the effect that knowledge is more valuable than wealth, since the former enabled one Sumantu to turn some women into apes, while the latter was ineffectual to produce that wonderful result. But as no knowledge that we know of can turn women into apes, the superiority of knowledge over wealth may well be doubted. But we dare say the writer did not intend either to instruct or to argue, but merely to make his readers laugh. We take it that the author has concealed his real name under the *nom de plume* of a Musalman.[22]

More on the implications of this last sentence when we consider language and audience later. The suspicion concerning the name, however, was in a way understandable. Hosain's *Ratnavati* represents the first contribution by a Muslim writer to modern Bengali literature, modern at least in terms of language.[23] This initial publication of Hosain's is a rather short prose piece (not as short as the one novel in Mukherjee's *Historical Novels* but still coming to only 34 pages in his collected works) and divided into two sections, each labelled *pariccheda*, a term that came to mean in Bengali, and still means, chapter, as in chapters of a novel. *Ratnavati* differs substantially, and not in size alone, from any and all of Chattopadhyay's *upanyasa*s, but, despite that, it shares at least one feature: just as Kaviraj sees Chattopadhyay's narratives as other than part of the genre called *upanyasa*, so too modern critics have seen *Ratnavati* as not of the *upanyasa* class of literature. 'Despite the fact that it is advertised on the title page as an "entertaining novel" (*kautukavaha upanyasa*), the characteristics of a novel (*upanyasa*) are absent. It is a fairy-tale type of narrative', writes Anisuzzaman.[24] Qazi Abdul Mannan agrees, '*Ratnavati* cannot be called a novel (*upanyasa*). Within it a fairy-tale type of story is told'.[25]

Unlike *Ratnavati*, Hosain's *The Sea of Sorrows* does not announce itself as an *upanyasa*/novel or as any specific genre whatsoever, but some of the contemporary critical notices so identified it:

It is a novel-history [*upanyasa-itihasa*] about Maharam. The language is clear and clean, the events vivid; similarly, the characterizations of the heroes and heroines have been drawn exquisitely . . . . The activity portrayed is historical, but we read the work as though it were a novel [*upanyasa*]. The events themselves are novelistic [*upanyasa*-like], and the skill and sweetness of the writing has given them [the events] the appearance of a genuine novel [*upanyasa*] . . . . Those who wish to read an account of Maharam should read this book. Those who wish to read a pure and true novel [*upanyasa*], they too should read this book.[26]

That was then, when *upanyasa* was still in its formative phase in Bengali. In the twentieth century, critics continued in certain respects to examine *The Sea of Sorrows* through the lens of genre, the *upanyasa*/novel genre specifically, and found Hosain's narrative problematic. Take, for example, the comments by Mohammad Abdul Hai and Syed Ali Ahsan, who deem *The Sea of Sorrows* to be a 'hybrid creation' (*samkara srsti*):

The Sea of Sorrows is not a true historical novel [*aitihasika upanyasa*], not a biography, nor is it even a novel [*upanyasa*] of the tightly structured, formulaic

'*Organic plot*' sort. ['Organic plot' appears in English, in Roman script, within this Bengali passage.] It is a hybrid creation [*samkara srsti*], slathered liberally with romantic emotions from a hodgepodge of all manner of dramatic and narrative writings of the historical, novelistic [*upanyasa-dharmiya*], and purely creative sort. There are characteristics of the novel [*upanyasa*] in it; there is also a fundamental passion present. Moreover, an effort is made to unify the loosely structured plot [*plat* appears here in Bengali transliteration]. It has dialogue, and there is even a conscious effort to bring to closure all the various subplots. Still then, *The Sea of Sorrows*, by the standards of literary criticism, is not any one particular creation [i.e. not any one genre].[27]

Samkara, in the expression *samkara srsti,* is a *tatsama* word meaning literally 'made or making' (*kara*) 'with or together' (*sam*). With my translation of 'hybrid', one of the several acceptable glosses, I have held to what I consider Hai and Ahsan's intended meaning of this Bengali term. Though Hai and Ahsan might appear at first glance to be making a negative assessment of *The Sea of Sorrows*, that proves ultimately and absolutely not to be the case. However, we can see in their discussion of this work the problems confronting them by the concept of genre in general and the term *upanyasa* in particular. Immediately following the paragraph cited above, ending with '[it] is not any one particular creation', Hai and Ahsan state forthrightly that Mir Mosharraf Hosain had consciously wanted to write an *upanyasa*. Given the fact that the subject matter of his narrative concerns the historic events surrounding the battle at Karbala, is *The Sea of Sorrows*, then, a historical *upanyasa*? After reflecting on the historicity of events and characters as depicted in Hosain's narrative, Hai and Ahsan conclude that though the work displays beauty and excellence of a sort, it had been transformed into a, again this same expression, *samkara srsti* or hybrid creation and was not a typical historical *upanyasa*.

Mir Mosharraf Hosain makes unrequited love the reason behind Ezid's enmity toward Hasan and Hosain and thus the cause for the battle of Karbala. Consequently, Hai and Ahsan conclude, it is tempting to consider *The Sea of Sorrows* a romantic *upanyasa* of a type. However, here again, upon offering that generic classification, they continue with a paragraph that begins by rephrasing their qualms about the generic nature of the narrative: it is now called an *upanyasa* of 'mixed nature' (*misra jatiya*). Furthermore, the latter section of the 'Maharam' part does not, in their opinion, show much sign of being an *upanyasa*. In place of the *upanyasa*-like elements, Hai and Ahsan find little other than redundancy and a relatively lifeless attenuation of the story line. The second and third parts of *The Sea of Sorrows*, 'The Rescue' and

'The Slaying of Ezid', respectively, fare no better under Hai and Ahsan's critical gaze. The distinctive features of these two parts are prolixity (*vakabahulya*) and lack of control (*samyamahinata*), both unequivocally designated by Hai and Ahsan as faults (*dosa*). However, they follow this opprobrium with praise for *The Sea of Sorrows* as something new, novel. Mir Mosharraf Hosain, they tell us, managed to surpass the boundaries of *upanyasa* to create something new, something marvellous. The newness is identified, using the English words, as 'personal reflection'. Such personal reflection, they argue, elevates Hosain's narrative into 'prose poetry' (*gadyakavya*). After struggling again and again to find fits with genre rubrics but failing to do so, Hai and Ahsan come to the conclusion that *The Sea of Sorrows* is a historically grounded romantic *upanyasa* AND a prose epic (*gadya mahakavya*).[28]

I have spent considerable space here on Hai and Ahsan's discussion of *The Sea of Sorrows* in order to indicate how imbricated the concept of genre, and specifically the *upanyasa* genre, is with literary value judgment. Eventually Hai and Ahsan overcome their observation that *The Sea of Sorrows* would appear to fail as an *upanyasa*. They rescue the text in the end by identifying a combination of genres to which, in their opinion, *The Sea of Sorrows* partially belongs. Though not as interested in judging literary value, Kaviraj employed in essence the same strategy in relation to Bankim Chandra Chattopadhyay's prose fiction: Bankim's novels were, in a sense, failures as *upanyasa* but successful as 'traditional dramas or narratives'. Neither Kaviraj, understandably, nor Hai and Ahsan, somewhat less so, ever question the generic category of *upanyasa* and what it means in Bengali or, more precisely, what it meant in a historically situated Bengali literature of the last few decades of the nineteenth century.

By way of comparison, let me shift focus to Rabindranath Tagore's criticism of Michael Madhusudan Dutt's *The Slaying of Meghanada* (*Meghanadavadha kavya*) (1861), which provides an example of genre-based criticism, literary evaluation based upon how well a work corresponds to a preconceived genre. For any number of reasons, a comparison between *The Sea of Sorrows* and Dutt's *The Slaying of Meghanada* would be productive, yielding obvious similarities on many levels: characterization, language register, subject matter (heroic battles). Kazi Abdul Wadud had drawn our attention to what he called 'the profoundest of unions' (*nibiratama yoga*) between Dutt and Hosain.[29] Furthermore, each writer, though not without talented predecessors, initiated a new era or a new phase of an era in Bengali literature. The so-called modern period in Bengali literature can be dated from that point in the late 1850s when Dutt turned his back on English as his medium for literary creativity and embraced Bengali, his mother-tongue. Dutt's *The Slaying of Meghanada* is his magnum opus, his signature text. The Muslim voice in a common Bengali literature, as opposed to a separate *dobhashi* literature, is first heard with convincing authority when Mosharraf Hosain begins to publish. *The Sea of Sorrows* is that work that mature work, upon which this writer's reputation rests.

Both Dutt and Hosain, moreover, were innovators in the area of genre. They experimented, took chances, tried new literary forms. The nineteenth century, from one perspective, can be called the century of new genres in Bengali. It begins with the introduction of prose and with dramatic writings. It ends with Rabindranath Tagore's experimentations during the 1890s in the new genre of the short story. In between we find the *upanyasa*, the autobiography, the essay, and combinations and permutations of all these. Nothing like Dutt's *The Slaying of Meghanada* had been seen before, with its manipulation of the reader so that not the traditional Hindu epic heroes but the villain, Ravana, gains the reader's sympathies. Nothing like Hosain's *The Sea of Sorrows* had appeared in Bengali literature, with this Muslim tale of martyrdom now told through a language that had been the exclusive domain of Hindu (and Christian, e.g. Dutt) writers and in a novel-like manner.

Dutt's *The Slaying of Meghanada* had been subjected to genre criticism just a couple of years prior to when *The Sea of Sorrows* appeared in print. The critic who faulted Dutt for failing to meet genre standards was none other than Rabindranath Tagore, albeit a twenty-one years young Tagore, who delivered the *coup de grace* to Dutt's *The Slaying of Meghanada* in terms of genre: 'I found it had no breath of life. I found it was no *mahakavya* [epic] at all'.[30] In an ironic twist on this mode of criticism based on genre, we find Tagore faulting *The Slaying of Meghanada* for being more novel than epic: 'Who would call a piece of novelistic writing [*upanyasa lekha*], consisting of several narrative events artistically arranged and set to verse, a *mahakavya*?'[31]

The irony that runs through this criticism based on genre is manifold. First and foremost, all such criticism seems to assume a universally accepted understanding of genres. Recall George Steiner's challenge of this assumption and his dismay at the title of the Oxford University Press publication, *The Theory of the Novel*, and Steiner, I dare say, was not thinking about novels in Bengali from the nineteenth century when he questioned the homogeneity of both theory and the novel genre itself. Had he taken into consideration Mir Mosharraf Hosain's and Bankim Chandra Chattopadhyay's literary works, Steiner would have had greater reason to lambast a title that seemed to take for granted a single theory for a monolithic novel genre.

Furthermore, it is even more ironic that Hosain and Dutt were criticized for not conforming to genre expectations when at least part of what both writers, and Chattopadhyay can certainly be included here, were doing as artists, was breaking out of previous genre restrictions and producing something new. Dutt showed his countrymen that one need not be slavishly conformist to pre-modern or even modern genres. In *The Slaying of Meghanada*, he took much from the past, including the verse structure (fourteen-syllable lines known as *payar*) and the basic characters and themes (but adding, for instance, Pramila and Rama's excursion to the netherworld to meet his deceased father), and not only created new literature but demonstrated to the reading public what new literature, which was at the same time an outgrowth of the tradition, could be. Mir Mosharraf Hosain, in a comparable way, did the same thing. The tradition from which he drew was known as *punthi* literature, written in verse in a *dobhashi* idiom of, primarily, mixed Perso–Arabic and Bengali. The thematic content came straight from Islamic religio–history. In Bengal of the 1880s, *The Sea of Sorrows* joined similar texts by Chattopadhyay and others in the ever growing and self-shaping genre known generally as the Bengali *upanyasa*. The language was not *dobhashi* but *sadhu* Bengali, something no one spoke but all, or almost all, educated Bengalis of the latter half of the nineteenth century agreed was a fit medium for serious literature.

Language and Audience

I return now to the questions I posed at the outset: If a Muslim Bengali in the nineteenth century spoke Bengali, did anyone understand? And, if a Muslim Bengali wrote in Bengali in the nineteenth century, who read what he had written? The first question has to do with language. Without producing a disquisition on language, dialect, and speech register, let me just say that Bengali, from at least the mid-nineteenth century to the mid-twentieth century, is diglossic in that it has what is referred to in English as a literary form (*sadhu*, 'chaste' Bengali) as well as a colloquial form (*calit* Bengali). A distinctive feature of *sadhu* Bengali, as noted above, is its highly Sanskritized (i.e. *tatsama* Bengali) vocabulary. Colloquial Bengali, on the contrary, draws its parlance from various source languages: Sanskrit, Persian, Arabic, Hindi–Urdu, English, and Portuguese primarily. Moreover, the vocabulary so drawn is then often modified, phonologically and even morphologically, as it becomes part of the standard Bengali lexicon. Complementing this colloquial lexicon are what are known as 'deshi' or, even more colloquially, 'dishi' (local) words, those for which there is no discernible parent language. Dialects, of course, are evident throughout Bengali. and dialects can, in some cases, reflect not just regional differences but also religious differences. Mussalmani Bengali, as the very name implies, is a form of Bengali associated with the Muslim Bengali; community.

To return yet again to the first question posed: If a Muslim Bengali in the nineteenth century spoke Bengali, did anyone understand? One would want some clarification: What sort of Bengali (the language) is that Muslim speaking and who (what sort of Bengali, i.e. the person) is the audience? If the Muslim Bengali is speaking Mussalmani Bengali to another Muslim Bengali, the answer is yes, he or she would be understood. If it is to a Hindu Bengali, the answer is in general no, or we could say, the Mussalmani Bengali speaker is understood with difficulty by the Hindu listener. If the Muslim Bengali, with an education, is speaking the highly Sanskritized *sadhu* Bengali to an ordinary Muslim Bengali, the answer is no; the language would be too sophisticated, too Sanskritic for the listener to comprehend. If, however, it is to an educated Hindu Bengali, the answer is probably yes, even though *sadhu* Bengali in the main was reserved for writing and seldom employed, but was used occasionally, for formal speeches, for instance, as a spoken idiom.

Once more, without any pretence of being comprehensive, let me say a word or two concerning the type of language a Muslim Bengali might speak. Sufia Ahmed, on page one of her monograph *Muslim Community in Bengal: 1884–1912*, states: 'Within this area [the province of Bengal, as defined in the 1881 Census of Bengal, consisting of five Divisions, namely, Burdwan, Presidency (which included Calcutta), Rajshahi, Dacca, and Chittagong] the language spoken by all the Muslims, except for a few upper class residents of the major cities [who might speak Urdu], was Bengali'.[32]

Later in the book, she says of Muslim writings in Bengali:

Of these [religious works], the works in the first category, the works of [religious] instruction, were very commonly written in Mussalmani Bengali. This was important, for Mussalmani Bengali was the popular language of the mass of Bengali Muslims. These popular manuals of the tenets and principles of Islam provided for those unacquainted with Arabic and Persian a guide to their faith and a warning against un-Islamic practices in their religious and social life.[33]

Ahmed's point is that Bengali indeed serves as the language of almost all Muslim Bengalis but that the Bengali they speak is, on the whole, Mussalmani Bengali. W.W. Hunter, in *The Indian Mussalmans*, had impressionistically described this communal dialect back in 1871: 'So firmly did Islam take hold of Lower Bengal that it has developed a religious literature and a popular dialect of its own. The patois known as Musalman [*sic*] Bengali is as distinct from the Urdu of Upper India as the Urdu is different from the Persian of Herat'.[34]

Just as there is a difference between *sadhu* Bengali and *calit* Bengali, the former being a written medium and the latter a spoken form of the language, so too with Mussalmani Bengali there is a distinction to be made between the written and spoken idioms. The linguist Suniti Kumar Chatterji quantified for us what spoken Mussalmani Bengali might mean, in comparison to the written form otherwise known as *dobhashi* Bengali. In a (somehow typical, in Chatterji's estimation) Muslim Bengali household, possibly 15 per cent of the words in a normal conversation would be Perso–Arabic; in a *dobhashi* text by Garibullah, his *Amir Hamza*, for instance, more than double that, about 32 per cent of the lexicon, was found by Chatterji to be 'foreign'.[35] Given Hosain's statement in his autobiography, cited above, that he read aloud *punthi* texts for the women of the village, we can presume that even illiterate Muslim Bengali women (and men) would be able to comprehend *dobhashi* Bengali, at least understand enough to make the listening experience enjoyable. Such would most assuredly not be the case were the text to be in *sadhu* Bengali. Illiterate Bengalis of both religious communities would, on the whole, be unable to appreciate a *sadhu* Bengali text. Hosain's *The Sea of Sorrows* is in *sadhu* Bengali. For what audience, then, is it intended?

The Sea of Sorrows received notice in several journals, including an English-language periodical, *The Statesman and Friend of India*. A review published on 31 May 1885 included the apparently innocuous statement that 'the work [*The Sea of Sorrows*] will no doubt prove of much interest to the Mahomedan community'.[36] That it did, but in ways not anticipated, I should imagine, by the reviewer. Sufia Ahmed tells us that 'His [Hosain's] boldness in breaking away from the tradition of writing *Puthi* [also spelled *punthi*] literature in Mussalmani Bengali led to his being severely criticized and much humiliated by the Muslim society in Bengal'.[37] Then Ahmed adds in a footnote, 'In fact it was said about him and others among Muslims who followed this new trend that "their language was so 'chaste', that is to say, so Sanskritic, that it was indistinguishable from the writings of Hindu authors" '.[38] Recall, from the review of Hosain's *Ratnavati* cited earlier, that the reviewer considered 'Mir Mosharraf Hosain' to be a pseudonym for some Hindu author.

Contrary to the hostile reaction to his literature from certain of his coreligionists and the rather tepid response to *The Sea of Sorrows* in *The Statesman and Friend of India*, cited above, to wit—'the author has undertaken to write a history of the Mohurrum, being nothing more than the recital of the tragic event of the massacre of Hussein on the plains of Kerbala'[39]—some notices in the Hindu-edited Bengali language journals of the day expressed admiration for *The Sea of Sorrows* generally, and for Hosain's facility with the language, the *sadhu* form of the Bengali language. 'Very few of the Muslims texts have been translated and published in this sort of highly refined Bengali', wrote one reviewer. 'The thoughtful reader can readily understand that all texts of that nature extend the Bengali language in a new direction and, moreover, are garnering the respect of Muslims for the [their/our mutual] mother tongue, Bengali. We convey our thanks to Brother Mosharraf'.[40] Added another:

If there cannot be unity between the Hindus and Muslims of Calcutta, there cannot be genuine progress in this land—many sage individuals have come to understand this fact. And a shared language is the basis for national integrity.[41] There are some who hope that our Bengali language will one day be the tongue of all India. Yet, when we see there is no unity of language shared by the two main communities of Bengal, then how can we be so bold as to entertain this type of unattainable desire in our hearts? It can be shown that in terms of the numbers of inhabitants of Bengal, the figures for Hindus and Muslims are about equal. Now take those 30 million Muslims—Bengal is their motherland and Bengali their mother tongue. Muslims, however, do not accept this. Though they cannot point to any other country as their motherland, still then they think of Perso–Arabic as their mother language. Lower-class Muslims, of course, converse in abominably coarse Bengali, but educated Bengali Muslims are utterly opposed to speaking in refined Bengali or to studying that language. They consider it a very serious offense to forego their bastardized Urdu and carry on a conversation with a Bengali gentleman in genteel Bengali. This is most unfortunate for both Hindus and Muslims. Recently, though, educated Muslims have become engaged in cultivating the Bengali language. Mir Mosharraf Hosain is the principal figure among them. His command of Bengali is truly impressive. . . . For a Muslim Bengali, this is a matter deserving of no small pride and praise. . . . For those who love tasteful, elegant Bengali, *The Sea of Sorrows* is a most readable book for them. Let us hope that Bengali Hindus, by reading this work, shall learn to call Muslims brothers, and that Bengali Muslims, after reading it, shall learn Bengali, pure Bengali.[42]

The Muslim Bengali reading audience, or at least some of them, were peeved that Hosain had given up what they saw as their (Muslim) literary language, *dobhashi* Bengali, and taken up *sadhu* (in their eyes, Hindu) Bengali. Clearly, the Hindu Bengali reading audience's reaction was just the reverse. Hindu readers were, it appears, surprised but at the same time quite favourably impressed. These two Bengali audiences, the Muslim and the Hindu, differed markedly in numerical strength. Qazi Abdul Mannan's assertion that in nineteenth-century Bengal 'educated middle-class' meant Hindu and Hindu only might be an exaggeration, but only slightly.[43] The readership for a work in *sadhu* Bengali would have been anticipated to be overwhelmingly Hindu.

Mosharraf Hosain, by means of the preamble to 'Maharam', the first part of *The Sea of Sorrows*, gives his reader some idea of his expectations with regard to audience. In that briefest of forewords, he states succinctly, in one compound sentence, the gist of the story. In the following sentence he suggests that many (in nineteenth century Bengal) may be ignorant of the motivating factors behind the horrific battle at Karbala. Such a characterization would apply to a Hindu readership primarily but not exclusively. There is no reason to presume that all Muslims know everything there is to know about their religion, just as there is no reason to presume that all Christians know Christianity thoroughly, or that all Hindus know every facet of that constellation of religious lore and practice now called Hinduism.

Next, Hosain claims to have composed *The Sea of Sorrows* based upon Persian and Arabic texts, a claim that Mannan points out may be true but might also be made, true or not, to lend authority to his own text.[44] Were it true that he was presenting in Bengali material from Persian and Arabic originals, then there would be reason to surmise that part of the intended audience might be Hosain's fellow Muslims. We know from his autobiography that he was sorely disappointed in the erudition of even those who taught, and thus purported to know, Arabic, though it should be noted that his comments pertain to the rural area, which was, of course, most of Bengal:

In the village, learning Arabic and Persian was not the general rule, and in fact there really was no particular need to do that. One studied Arabic to acquire merit, for the purpose of reading the Holy Koran. And what an odd reading it would be. The practice was to recite the Holy Koran as soon as one mastered the alphabet. That recitation remained recitation only. No one in our local area understood the meaning of the Arabic Holy Koran. Still today [1908–10] the Mollahs [the term Mollah designates one who knows Arabic and Persian and the Islamic scriptures] who earn money by reading the Holy Koran do not comprehend what they recite. Their education consisted of simply reading the words. For a Muslim Bengali, acquiring knowledge is indeed most difficult.[45]

Since Garibullah's *A Tale of Battle* in *dobhashi* Bengali may not only have been the source of inspiration for Hosain himself but could also be read/heard by his coreligionists and understood, it seems unlikely that Hosain would have seen his composition as the only or even the primary vehicle for informing Muslim Bengalis about their religious heritage. If he were adding something not from a *dobhashi* Bengali telling of the event but from an older literary tradition, then, of course, he could see himself as instructing his fellow Muslim Bengalis. As a potential translator of those ancient Arabic and Persian books in verse, he is demure. Were he even to attempt a flawless rendering of those texts, such an effort would be futile, he says, comparable to, employing a classic South Asian literary conceit here, a dwarf reaching for the moon. Instead of producing the perfect translation, his stated intention is to make readily accessible to his dear readers, 'those lovers of the Bengali language', the essentials of Maharam, something every Muslim would undoubtedly more or less know. The epithet 'lovers of the Bengali language' most aptly applies at this time to the Hindu educated middle-class. Hosain goes on to apologize for using of necessity a few 'communal' (*jatiya*) words and begs forgiveness if this offends anyone in learned circles. By *jatiya* Hosain means Perso–Arabic; there are certain Perso–Arabic terms for which no suitable Bengali word, *tatsama* or no, exists. That Hosain should feel reticent about including language of this sort in his text is, as Mannan points out, completely justified, since Hindu Bengalis had been critical of any such contamination of *sadhu* Bengali, calling texts with a mix of lexical items, some from Arabic or Persian or, more likely, Urdu, despicable.[46] If the reviews cited by Qazi Abdul Mannan, editor of Mir Mosharraf Hosain's collected works, are any indication, the Hindu readers forgave Hosain for the appearance of the non-*tatsama* lexemes in his narrative. The preemptive apology, however, demonstrates quite well that Hosain expected Hindu Bengalis to be among the readership of *The Sea of Sorrows*.

From the body of the text itself, one can infer that Hosain foresaw fellow Muslims also to be among his audience. Put another way, there was something in the text for the educated Bengali Muslim not only to appreciate, by way of powerful modern (for the times) prose, but also to learn about his Islamic past. For example, the second chapter begins with Ezid dispatching a messenger to the home of Abdul Jabbar, whose wife he (Ezid) covets. The person so sent is referred to a '*kased*', with quotation marks in the text highlighting that word. The second paragraph begins by addressing the reader directly:[47]

Reader! Though a *kased* is a messenger, do not think of him as your Bengal-style postal courier [*daka harakara*]. He is a bearer of royal missives, yet dignified, discreet. The venerable Muslim authors referred to such a one as *kased*. The attributes of a *kased* include those associated with civility. If not wise and truthful, reserved, well-spoken, and of pleasant appearance, one is not deputed to the post of *kased*. Still, there is a slight difference between *duta* [a *tatsama* term meaning messenger, envoy] and *kased*; a *kased* does not command quite the respect that a *duta* does.[48]

Kased is a term not only new to his Hindu readership, the presumed majority of his audience, but also quite likely unfamiliar or only vaguely familiar to his potential Muslim readers. Garibullah, in *A Tale of Battle*, refers to this person sent off from Damascus to Abdul Jabbar's as the *kased*, with no further elaboration.[49] Hosain fleshes out the character of Abdul Jabbar and of his wife and also shows his reader a facet of their somewhat contentious domestic relationship, all through dialogue, before the *kased* arrives at the couple's home. With due civility that includes a requisite paean to Allah and praise for the ruler of Damascus, the *kased* delivers the letter into Jabbar's hands. This second chapter ends with Abdul Jabbar excitedly making preparations to depart for Damascus. The *kased* appears briefly again in the next chapter to announce to Ezid that Abdul Jabbar has arrived at the palace and has been properly, deferentially greeted. This *kased* is by no means fully developed as a character in Hosain's narrative, but far more developed than in Garibullah's *punthi*. Still, the reader, both Muslim and Hindu, comes to learn through *The Sea of Sorrows* of a functionary within the Arabian courts of Islam's infancy, a character type, Hosain tells his reader, found in other (pre-modern, Arabic and Persian) texts composed by Muslims. Then, when later on, after one *kased* has been felled by an arrow through the chest and we encounter Moslem (also known as Mosel) in the eighth chapter, a character introduced previously and now serving in the capacity of royal *kased*, on his way to Medina to announce the failing health of Mabiya, Ezid's father, and to summon the brothers Hasan and Hosain to Damascus, we have a sense of both the person, Moslem, and the post—not simply a menial messenger but an emissary of some stature.

There are those parts of *The Sea of Sorrows* meant exclusively for the Hindus in his audience, and Hosain does not hesitate to identify them as such. For instance:

At this point it is necessary to say something to the Hindu readers. If I do not explain in brief our marriage customs, it will take some effort on their part to understand the wedding ceremony presented here. Until the nuptials have taken place, no male from the groom's side is allowed to see the prospective bride.

If the bridegroom is of age, then, irrespective of the country wherein the marriage occurs, the groom, guided by the officiating cleric, must pronounce a few words in Arabic. A person chosen by the bride's guardians to represent her must respond to those words with like words. The words upon which a marriage is based are these: '[marriage] proposal' and 'acceptance' (*izab kabul*).[50] Proof that the pride has agreed to the marriage requires two witnesses. Other than this, there are no religious rituals, no recitation of texts, no activities of any kind connected with our weddings. However, there are those individuals, swayed by local customs and themselves a bit undisciplined when it comes to religion, who, considering the rest of us ignorant, put on a ritual of sorts. That, however, is not sanctioned by the scriptures. Even if such rituals are not performed, the ties that bind are no less secure. Neither side need fear that some misfortune might result from failure to heed [unsanctioned] rules and regulations.[51]

Other assistance to the Hindu reader, superfluous for the Muslim, is provided by parenthetical glosses of Perso–Arabic terms within the text itself at various places, e.g. '*janaja* (*mrta sharirer sadgatira upasana*)' (Arabic: 'prayers for the spiritual salvation—"good passage"—of the deceased person'); '*talak nama* (*stri parityager patra*)' (Arabic: (*talak*), Persian (*nama*); 'a document declaring the man divorces his wife'); and '*vivahapayagam* (*prastava*)' (*tatsama* Bengali (*vivaha*), Persian (*payagam*), with only the Persian word glossed in Hosain's text; 'marriage-proposal').[52]

What immediately follows the passage above, the one explaining Muslim marriages, is a paragraph denouncing the institution of dowry as it had developed within the Muslim communities of South Asia. Unlike his explanation of weddings, I read Hosain's rumination on dowry as something intended more for his fellow Muslims than the Hindu readership. He does not defend or explain the practice but instead criticizes it. It is not, however, a criticism of the puritanical sort, associated with the reform movements of the nineteenth century. His is a criticism from a pragmatic point of view. The institution of dowry is making paupers of people for no good reason, and what is more, (benevolent) British rule is conniving:

The manner in which the practice of *den mohar* amounting to tens of thousands of rupees has caught on these days in the Muslim communities in India, the way in which by convention the entire wealth of the husband goes straight into the coffers of the bride, thereby reducing the husband to a street beggar, is utterly horrifying. British law, moreover, recognizing this as in accord with religious beliefs and conforming to scripture, at the moment of the pledge itself holds the husband liable for the pledged money as if it were an actual debt and then, selling off his ancestral wealth, his home and lands, and ultimately incarcerating his very person in prison with other prisoner types, goes about using that wealth as it wishes. And it is not as though we ourselves are free from blame. Wishing the best for our own daughters, we gradually, day by day, are driving up the amount of *moharana* [the same as *den mohar*]. You readers would be amazed to learn how modest was the *moharana* within the family of Lord Mohammad, they who are the rulers of both this world and the next. Lord Mohammad's daughter, Bibi Fatemah, mother of Hasan and Hosain, received as *den mohar*, if figured in today's currency, no more than four rupees and four annas.[53]

Mosharraf Hosain explained Muslim marriage practices for the benefit of his Hindu readers; he criticized the *moharana* or Muslim dowry system with the Muslim audience in mind. Much of the time, I think it is safe to say, he wrote for a combined educated Muslim–Hindu reading public, as when he adds culturally specific information about the position of the *kased* in an Arabian court, to cite just one example.

Concerning that combined Muslim–Hindu educated Bengali reading public of the latter half of the nineteenth century, Bankim Chandra Chattopadhyay, in the opening editorial of his literary journal *Bangadarshana* ['Mirror of Bengal'], complained bitterly:

Those who are engaged in publishing books and periodicals in the Bengali language are indeed an unfortunate lot; for no matter how hard they may try, the local educated Community will turn away from reading their writings. These English-loving elites have decided that nothing worth their reading could possibly be written in Bengali. By their reckoning, all authors who work in Bengali either are stupid and devoid of writing skills, or are translators of English works. This is their belief: 'Whatever is put into print in Bengali is either unreadable trash or a mere shadow of some English original. And since the latter is available in English, why should we insult ourselves by reading it in Bengali. We are readily caught out, anyway, for having dark skin and in various ways go around trying to absolve ourselves of that crime; why admit our guilt openly by reading Bengali?[54]

Chattopadhyay's concerns were, no doubt, real. (His satirization of the anglophilic Bengali gentleman cuts deep here, as it often did.) English had been for some time not just the language of government but a medium dear to many an educated Bengali's heart, yet Bengali literature had an audience, too. Chattopadhyay was read: well read. *The Slaying of Meghanada* went into its sixth edition during Michael Madhusudan Dutt's lifetime. The foreword to the expanded eighth edition of *The Sea of Sorrows*, dated 10 Caitra 1315 BS (1909), is reprinted in the collected works. Hosain ends it with the following: 'My primary aim is to please the readers'.[55] Clearly he succeeded. Critics aside, the number of editions alone bespeaks his success.

Notes and References

1. The masculine pronoun 'he' is justified here; there were no Bengali Muslim women writers, novelists or otherwise, until Begam Rokeya Sakhawat Hosain (1880–1932), whose published works began to appear in the first decade of the twentieth century. Mir Mosharraf Hosain and Begam Rokeya Sakhawat Hosain are not related.

2. CE stands for 'common era' and represents the current academic convention for indicating dates formerly marked by AD. The AD designation is seen as too Christian and thus potentially offensive to non-Christian cultures. All dates in this article are CE dates.

3. Anisuzzaman, *Muslim manasa o Bamla sahitya: 1757–1918* (Dhaka: Lekhaka Samgha Prakasani [Dhaka University], 1964), 234. Qazi Abdul Mannan gives 1891 as the date of publication for the final part; Mannan, *Adhunika Bamla sahitye Muslim sadhana*, 2nd edn. (Dhaka: Student Ways, 1969), 144.

4. A Shia, or as that person is also known in English, Shi'ite, considers Ali (husband of Fatemah, Prophet Mohammad's daughter, and father of Hasan and Hosain) the lawful successor to the Prophet. A Sunni recognizes the first four Khaliphas, Abu Bakar, Umar, Usman, and Ali, as the legitimate successors to the Prophet.

5. *See* Rafiuddin Ahmed, *The Bengal Muslims, 1871–1906: A Quest for Identity* (Delhi: Oxford University Press, 1981, 1988) on the role such movements played in the shaping of the Muslim Bengali identity and community.

6. Anisuzzaman, *Muslim manasa o Bamla sahitya*, 448.

7. Ibid., 228–9.

8. Cited in ibid., 319.

9. Ibid., 230.

10. Sudipta Kaviraj notes this connection between Chattopadhyay's Krishna and the fictional warriors of his political-cum-historical novels; Kaviraj, *The Unhappy Consciousness: Bankimchandra Chattopadhyay and the Formation of Nationalist Discourse in India* (Delhi: Oxford University Press, 1995), 102.

11. Anisuzzaman, *Muslim manasa o Bamla sahitya*, 252.

12. The expression 'mixed-language mode' (*mishra bhashariti*) is proposed by Anisuzzaman (*Muslim manasa o Bamla sahitya*, 117) who justifies it on the grounds that *dobhashi* is not, in fact, made up of only two languages but instead of at least five: Bengali, Hindi–Urdu, Turkish, Persian/Farsi, and Arabic.

13. Mohammad Abdul Jalil, *Shah Garibullah o janganama* (Dhaka: Bangla Academy, 1991), 17.

14. From the autobiography of Mir Mosharraf Hosain, *Amar jivani*, quoted in Qazi Abdul Mannan (ed.), *Masharraph racana sambhara* (Dhaka: Bangla Academy, 1980), 2, xxii.

15. T.W. Clark (ed.), *The Novel in India: Its Birth and Development* (Berkeley & Los Angeles: University of California Press, 1970), 49.

16. Ibid., 51.

17. Monier Monier-Williams, *A Sanskrit–English Dictionary* (London: Oxford University Press, 1899 (rpt. 1970)).

18. Gwendolyn L. Layne, *Kadambari: A Classical Sanskrit Story of Magical Transformations* (New York: Garland Publishers, 1991), Introduction.

19. John Halperin (ed.), *The Theory of the Novel: New Essays* (New York: Oxford University Press, 1974). Almost coincidentally, MIT Press had published in 1971 a translation of a work by Gyorgy Lukacs entitled in English *The Theory of the Novel: A Historico–Philosophical Essay on the Forms of Great Epic Literature*.

20. Margaret Anne Doody, *The True Story of the Novel* (New Brunswick, New Jersey: Rutgers University Press, 1996), 484–5. Conspicuous by its absence from Doody's study is literature from South Asia, apart from a brief mention of Salman Rushdie's *The Satanic Verses*; Calcutta and the goddess Kali make an appearance via a citation from Yukio Mishima's *The Temple of Dawn*; and E.M. Forster's *A Passage to India* completes the South Asia references.

21. Kaviraj, *The Unhappy Consciousness*, 160.

22. *Calcutta Review*, 50 (1870), 235. I thank Sudipta Chatterjee for calling this review to my attention and for emailing me a copy of it. This review is mentioned and partially cited in Anisuzzaman, *Muslim manasa o Bamla sahitya*, 222, endnote 2; there the number of the issue is given as 99 with no date or volume indicated.

23. Qazi Abdul Mannan credits Hosain's *Ratnavati* with initiating the era of literary prose by modern Muslim writers: Mannan, *Adhunika Bamla sahitye Muslim sadhana*, 138. Anisuzzaman also acknowledges *Ratnavati* for its prose, a mark of modernity, but refuses to grant it full status as an example of modern literature, claiming that it still reflects premodern literary tastes, a claim that Mannan would not dispute. Contributions to 'modern' Bengali literature by Muslim writers are to be found only from 1870 onward, contends Anisuzzaman: *Muslim manasa o Bamla sahitya*, viii, 447.

24. Anisuzzaman, *Muslim manasa o Bamla sahitya*, 222.
25. Mannan (ed.), *Masharraph racana sambhara* (Dhaka: Bangla Academy, 1970), 1, 4.
26. The first citation is from the periodical *Bharati*, Phalguna, 1293 (1887), the next two from the periodical *Sulabha samacara*, 19 Vaishakha, 1293 (1886), in Mannan (ed.), *Masharraph racana sambhara*, 2, xv, xii–xiii.
27. Mohammad Abdul Hai and Syed Ali Ahsan, *Bamla sahityer itivrtta (adhunika yuga)*, 2nd edn Dhaka: Student Ways, 1964), 79.
28. Hai and Ahsan, *Bamla sahityer itivrtta*, 79–83.
29. Wadud's article, simply entitled '*Vishada sindhu*' ('*The Sea of Sorrows*'), was published in 1934 and subsequently became part of his book *Shashvata Banga* (Calcutta, 1951); cited in Mannan (ed.), *Masharraph racana sambhara*, 2, xvii–xix. Mannan points to Wadud's article as the model for nearly all criticism of *The Sea of Sorrows* since then. Among the connections joining Dutt's *The Slaying of Meghanada* and Hosain's *The Sea of Sorrows*, Wadud noted parallels between the characterizations of Ravana and Ezid, and between that of Sita, who suffers through no fault of her own, and Zainab, a married woman after whom Ezid lusted, who, faultless like Sita, is fundamentally the cause of the conflict.
30. Rabindranath Tagore, '*Meghanadavadha kavya*' ('The Slaying of Meghanad'), in *Rabindra-racanavali, acalita samgraha* (Calcutta: Visva-harati, 1962), 2, 81 (misprinted as 79); first published in *Bharati*, Aug. 1882. Tagore would subsequently explain away his attack on Dutt's text as just so much youthful exuberance: ibid., 718.
31. Ibid., 78.
32. Sufia Ahmed, *Muslim Community in Bengal: 1884–1912* (Dhaka: Oxford University Press, 1974), 1.
33. Ibid., 325.
34. W.W. Hunter, *The Indian Mussalmans* (London, 1871), 152; cited in Ahmed, *Muslim Community in Bengal: 1884–1912*, 307 fn.
35. Chatterji's findings are paraphrased in Anisuzzaman, *Muslim manasa o Bamla sahitya*, 117. Chatterji writes: 'The percentage of Persian words in a typical "Musalmani [*sic*] Bengali" work, the "Bara Dastan Amir Hamza" *the Great Tale of Amir Hamzah*, is about 31.74 [per cent], as seen from computing the words in 5 pages of a folio edition from the popular Battala printing houses of Calcutta . . . . In a Bengali Moslem home, it [Persian words in Bengali] would rise to higher than 7.1%, it may be even 15%, but it could never be as high as 30%, even in the most preponderatingly Mohammedan parts of Bengal': Chatterji, *Origin and Development of the Bengali Language* (Calcutta: Calcutta University Press, 1926), (London: George Allen & Unwin, 1970), 1, 211.
36. Cited in Ahmed, *Muslim Community in Bengal: 1884–1912*, 354.
37. Ibid., 309; in support of this point, Ahmed cites M.A. Hakim, '*Banga sahitye Musalamana*', *Islam darshana*, 11th issue, 1921, 534.

38. Ahmed, *Muslim Community in Bengal: 1884–1912*, 309; the quoted material is from Q.M. Husain, 'Bengali Literature', in S.M. Ikram and P. Spear (eds.), *The Cultural Heritage of Pakistan* (Karachi, 1955), 141.

39. Oddly, whereas this reviewer seems to diminish the worth of the narrative by calling it nothing but a history, Hosain's near contemporary, Kaikobad (1857–1952), faulted *The Sea of Sorrows* for misrepresenting the historical facts, in reaction to which he (Kaikobad) composed the poem *Maharam sharif* (1932); Anisuzzaman, *Muslim manasa o Bamla sahitya*, 265.

40. Cited from the periodical *Gramavartta prakashika*, 11 Jyaishtha 1292 (1885), in Mannan (ed.), *Masharraph racana sambhara*, 2, xi.

41. This sentence, almost word for word, and the sentiment pertaining to language throughout this review had been seen previously, in a notice of Hosain's third work: *Gorai brij athaba gauri setu* ['The Englishman's Bridge, or the Span across the River Gauri'] (1873), a verse piece on a bridge of all things. That notice by Bankim Chandra Chattopadhya appeared in his *Bangadarshana*, Pausa, 1280 (1873); cited in Mannan (ed.), *Masharraph racana sambhara*, 1, 7–8.

42. Cited from the periodical *Caruvartta*, 23 Jyaishtha 1292 (1885), in ibid., xiii–xv.

43. Ibid., ix.

44. Mannan (ed.), *Masharraph racana sambhara*, 2, xxii.

45. Mir Mosharraf Hosain, *Amar jivani*, ed. Devipada Bhattacharya (Calcutta: General Printers & Publishers, 1977), 78.

46. The eminent Sanskrit pundit, Haraprasad Shastri, referred to Ram Ram Basu's *Raja Pratapaditya caritra* ('The Life of Rajah Pratapaditya'), one of the very earliest pieces of Bengali prose, as 'ugly and not worth reading', just because Perso–Arabic words are to be found in that text; ibid., ix–x.

47. There is an 1889 edition of just the first part of the trilogy, the title page of which is both in Bengali and English. The English title reads *Bishad-Sindhu!!!: The History of the Moharam*. Note the abundance of exclamation points. Note too the placement of an exclamation point after the direct address to the reader (*pathaka!:* Reader!). In the collected works of Mir Mosharraf Hosain, there is no punctuation after the word *pathaka*, and yet it is the reader who is addressed.

48. Mannan (ed.), *Masharraph racana sambhara*, 2, 9.

49. Jalil, *Shah Garibullah o janganama*, 141; the spelling is *kached* in Garibullah's text.

50. The Arabic words are given in Bengali transliteration in parentheses; the words I translate as 'proposal' and 'acceptance' are in the original *tatsama* Bengali lexemes, *prastava* and *svikara*.

51. Mannan (ed.), *Masharraph racana sambhara*, 2, 18–19.

52. Ibid., 5, 20, 24.

53. Ibid., 19; *den mohar* and *moharana* gloss as 'the money that the husband

pledges at a Muslim wedding to give to the bride'; also known as *kabin*; Mohammad Enamul Haq and Shivaprasanna Lahiri (eds.), *Bamladesher byabaharika Bamla abhidhana*, 2 vols. (Dhaka: Bangla Academy, 1974, 1984).

54. *Bangadarshana*, vol. 1, no. 1, Vaishakha 1279 (1872): 1–2.
55. Mannan (ed.), *Masharraph racana sambhara*, 2, 5.

6

The Changing World of Bengali Muslim Women: The 'Dreams' and Efforts of Rokeya Sakhawat Hossein

SONIA N. AMIN

Background

Rokeya Sakhawat Hossein (1880–1932), pioneer feminist writer of Bengal, was born into a conservative Muslim zamindar family of Payrabund in the northern Bengal district of Rangpur. A contemporary of literary stalwarts like the Nobel-laureate Bengali poet, Rabindranath Tagore, the 'revolutionary' Bengali Muslim poet, Kazi Nazrul Islam, and the novelist, Sarat Chandra Chatterjee, she lived through an age that saw the cultural awakening in Bengal enter a new phase, marked by intense political activism, and the beginnings of an anti-colonial struggle against British rule in India. The last decades of the nineteenth, and the first quarter of the twentieth century were particularly significant for Bengal's Muslims because of changes in their socio–economic, educational, as well as political structures, especially in the districts of lower Bengal, which fundamentally altered the character of that community. The growth of a middle class, with its roots in the countryside, albeit a belated phenomenon, was instrumental in that community's experience with 'modernization' and increased participation in the nationalist struggle. This 'awakening' played a critical role in revitalizing the community and in redefining its political identity. Although these changes have received the attention of scholars in recent years,[1] the women's question, which was part of it, has not.[2]

The struggle of the emergent Bengali élite, both Muslim and Hindu, had to be waged on many fronts. Outside, in the economic and political domain, it was primarily directed against the British: the transformation of the colonial society into a form of modern state had resulted largely from an encounter with the West. This had provided the impetus to what came to be called the women's reform movement, which had compelled the male reformers and nationalists of the time to actively consider the question of middle class women's participation in public life.[3] Simply put, the aspiring élite had to validate their claim to modernity (inherited in part from post-Enlightenment Europe's rational–utilitarian Liberalism), and at the same time establish the validity of tradition. Women had to be both the emblem of the nation's/community's modernity and a fortress against the denigrating onslaught of that very change. Apart from this, struggles had to be waged on other fronts too, for while the reformers/nationalists fought to counter colonial dominance, they also sought to preserve their dominance in the home while reshaping it. This gave many twists and turns to the progression of the women's reform movement making it difficult for it to follow a linear route. Resolutions were sought at every turn. Tradition had to be invented, circumvented, or accommodated.

Reformists went about this in various ways. They constructed a 'golden age' that synthetically absorbed much of present concerns and grafted them onto a period of Vedic antiquity in the case of Hindus, and the time of the Prophet or the pious caliphs, in the case of Muslims. More importantly, they reinterpreted scriptures in the light of the liberal precepts of the day to suit their rationalizing agenda. How far this strategy of negotiation was successful is widely debated. Some argue that in widening the bases of reform by making it more acceptable to a larger segment, the reformists ultimately chose to make 'sacrifices' to accommodate the demands of middle class women. It is against this complex background that we must evaluate Rokeya and her career.

Pioneer Female Educationist

Rokeya has been a symbol of the educational aspirations of Bengali Muslim women since the early twentieth century, and consequently, has received much attention from scholars. There are several well researched monographs in Bengali on her life and work. However, attempts to historicize her in the context of the ambivalence experienced by the writers of the Bengal renaissance have not been undertaken. At a time when the Brahmo reform movement had taken off in Bengal and Hindu women were preparing for the first ever university degrees,[4] girls from an upper or middle-class Muslim family were not allowed to step out of the inner quarters: the *andar mahal*. Although Rokeya's father Zahiruddin Saber's fortunes were on the decline,[5] his two sons were able to find their way out from the decadent atmosphere of the ancestral home to the metropolis of Calcutta where they received an English education. Perhaps the brothers brought back the winds of change to Payrabund: consequently, the three sisters, Karimunnessa, Rokeya, and Humaira received a reasonably good education at home despite the prevailing negative attitude toward female education in upper class Muslim society.

Rokeya herself learnt Bengali and English from Karimunnessa (herself a poet), and her brother, in addition to Urdu, which was considered the 'appropriate' language of the Muslim aristocracy in Bengal.[6] The world of Payrabund—with its semi-feudal expanse, seclusion of women (a condition termed by Rokeya as '*aborodh*' or 'captivity' to distinguish it from the acceptable norms of female modesty—known as purdah), the decadent life-style of the zamindar, and glimmerings of change viewed from afar—was a microcosm of the Muslim aristocratic world in India at the time.

Rokeya's brothers arranged a marriage for her at 16 to Syed Sakhawat Hossein, a widower 22 years her senior. Despite the age difference, Sakhawat had three important qualifications—an English education, a government job and an honourable character—which made it easy for Rokeya to pursue her own interests. She left for Bhagalpur in the neighbouring province of Bihar to set up home. For the next 14 years she managed a small and neat household, a picture of Victorian orderliness. She tended her husband (who helped her with her English), practiced thrift, and gave birth to two babies who died in infancy. Most importantly, however, a room was set aside for her, and here, with her husband's encouragement, she started to write and publish.

Rokeya's husband died in 1909. It was during the period 1902–19 that Rokeya wrote her most significant pieces. She formulated her feminist theory exposing patriarchy and the oppression of women in pieces, such as 'Alankara' or 'The Badge of Slavery' (1903), later retitled 'Streejatir Abonoti' ('The Degradation of Women'), 'Ardhangi' ('The Other Half') (1904), 'Griha' ('Home') (1904), 'Sultana's Dream' (in English) (1905), 'Bhrata Bhagni' ('Brother and Sister') (1905), and and 'Kupmonduker Himalaya Darshan' ('A Frog in a Well Sees the Himalaya') (1904). Rokeya did write 'radical' pieces in later life, but the kernel of her feminist thought had been formed in these early years. Undoubtedly the Bhagalpur years were a very creative phase for her.

After her husband's death, family tension, especially with her step-daughter, compelled Rokeya to leave Bhagalpur. Widowed and childless, she set out for Calcutta, where almost alone and unaided she founded the Sakhawat Memorial Girls' School in 1911. She now entered a different phase in her career: that of educationist and social reformer. Though she continued to write, she now became more involved in promoting the education of Muslim girls. Her every effort was spent in popularizing the school in Calcutta, getting guardians to send their daughters to it, soliciting local and government support, effectively managing the institution as its principal. Alongside this, she worked to develop the Anjuman-i-khawateen-i-Islam, a small social service association for Muslim women, set up by her in 1916. From the unbounded space of her writing desk, Rokeya now had to move among the Urdu-speaking, conservative Muslim community of Calcutta, who dominated Muslim society of the city at that time and whose support was essential for keeping the school alive.

It must have been very difficult for a young widow to run a school in Calcutta in the early decades of this century, when female education was somewhat of an anathema to the accepted norms of upper and middle class Bengali Muslim culture.[7] This perhaps also partly explains the transformation in her own life. In the one rare conjugal photograph of Rokeya and Sakhawat, the young wife is seen standing, her head unveiled, with her hand on her husband's shoulder. In the few photographs of her in later years (she was very reluctant to have her photograph taken at this stage of her life), when she became better known, she appears with her head covered, and increasingly took to a 'conservative' lifestyle. Thus, she began observing the rules of strict purdah for women by (a) wearing the *burqah* (long cloak-like garb covering body and face), and (b) conducting the business of her school from behind a curtain when receiving a male visitor.

Scholars who have written on Rokeya have sometimes been intrigued by the various images that she presented: the apparent contrariness between one piece of writing and another, or between one passage and another. As her career as an educationist progressed (ca 1911–1932), she began addressing meetings and wrote for the Muslim edited journals that were then becoming increasingly popular. One of the principal focuses of her presentations was to highlight the 'ideal education' imparted at her school *in keeping with the tenets of Islam.*

The syllabus of the school was very 'proper' in inculcating socially desirable values: domesticity, piety, and obedience. These were also in keeping with the Victorian-inspired Brahmo values of ideal woman-hood[8] as well as the norms of ideal female conduct in Muslim society. Here, Rokeya trod very cautiously, reiterating time and again that the school aimed at producing the new woman fit for the new (middle-class) Muslim home, society, and polity. She used conventional arguments to legitimize her unconventional programmes.

Caution, conservatism, and deference to convention on Rokeya's part are understandable. Founding a school for Muslim girls almost single-handedly in the wake of intense reaction against her 'feminist' pieces published a few years earlier was surely a provocative act. Ostensibly contradictory to this 'mission' was her acknowledged weaknesses for conservative religious values, both in published writings as well as in private correspondence, which makes the task of evaluating her very complex. One must, however, view this apparent contradiction in the context of the Bengali Muslim social traditions of the time of which she was a part. By no means was she trying to imitate the values of Western feminism, which were practically unknown to her. Her goal was to challenge the dominant patriarchal structure of the society, not break away from the society itself: female education was for her one of the principal means of achieving that goal.

The Feminist Discourse

Nowhere does the complexity in evaluating Rokeya surface more clearly than in a textual analysis of her works. We turn to this now with an examination of some of her most significant pieces with an eye to certain internal inconsistencies. (This may be venturing into 'foreign' territory for those not thoroughly familiar with Rokeya's texts. However, the scholarship on Rokeya in Bengali has advanced far enough to warrant a textual reading at a more critical level like that proposed here.) Subversion, then subsequent accommodation and textual modification, were undertaken by Rokeya herself from very early on.[9]

Contemporary writers never strayed far from the assumption that religion as the repository of tradition was a basic ingredient of the social structure. One of Rokeya's earliest pieces, '(*Alankara*)' ('Ornaments' or 'Badge of Slavery'?) published in *Mahila* in 1904 (later retitled 'Streejatir Abonoti' or 'The Degradation of Women') was one of the boldest articulations of her feminist theory in essay form. It was not passed off as a fantasy as in *Sultana's Dream* or the novel *Padmarag*. Here she deals with the issue of religion in a patriarchal society in a straightforward manner. Like Vidyasagar before her, she navigated between the subtle ridicule of religious practices (carefully termed 'social' phenomena) and a painstaking interpretation of religious/Islamic tenets in the light of Rationalism. With regard to Islam, the religion she was born into, she upheld the rights granted to women in the Shari'a, the Prophet's solicitude for women, and his code of conduct for them (as well as towards them). Like others of her time she wrote about the pristine, golden age of Islam which resembled in so many respects the rationalistic one the reformers were helping to construct. At the same time, however, she did not shrink from using her innate sarcasm with regard to certain practices associated with Islam, which again she was careful to characterize as social constructions. For instance, in 'Alankara' she commences with a clear statement about the historical genesis of women's subjugation, much in the vein of Engels. However, the paragraph that caused the real stir was the one on revealed religious texts which is worth quoting at length:

As the world advanced men saw it did not suffice any longer to call themselves mere prophets. So the wise Jesus declared himself Son of God, a part of the Creator, and gave the Bible. It was written there that women are subservient to men . . . and ignorant woman accepted the dictum with bowed head. Sisters, those revealed texts are naught but books written by men. How different the contents of these books would have been had they been written by women instead! The religious books are neither revealed nor sent by God. Had God sent us a female prophet she would surely have travelled beyond Asia. Why have the messengers of God never crossed the bounds of Asia? Did not God's kingdom extend over the Americas?[10]

Rokeya in anticipation of the disapprobation that might follow, was quick to modify her use of the term religion by stating that it was not her intention to hurt anyone's religious sentiments: 'In this case by religion I mean its social manifestations', she now writes. Then, however, she reverts to her radicalism again:

Why, one may ask, do I drag in religion while dwelling on social issues? I do so because religion has intensified the chains of our bondage. Men have used it to perpetuate their sway over women. That is why I am compelled to drag in religion.[11]

However stunning the message penned by this remarkable lady from the Muslim *andar mahal* who never went to school, she carefully avoids mentioning the religion she was born into, Islam. It must however be pointed out that Christianity, according to Islamic tenets, is its (Islam's) revered precursor, and Christians are considered 'the People of the Book', i.e. people to whom divine books have been revealed. The famous passage above generated a strong reaction in contemporary journals: Rokeya was quick to sense the Muslim community's pulse. She agreed to have the controversial passage omitted in the subsequent anthology which contained the essay.[12] We may ask: What prompted Rokeya to have this passage excised? Was there a change of position or conviction on her part? or was it a strategic toning down? Judging by the negative reaction aired in the popular journals, one is tempted to think the latter may have been the cause of this change of mind. However, Rokeya herself never set down any reasons for the changes in her position.

The year 1904 was a very creative one for Rokeya. After 'Alankara', she published 'Ardhangi' (The Other Half) in *Nabanur*. Here she spelt out once again her thoughts on woman's place in society, as it was and what it should be, in the most specific terms. Male and female, she wrote, were like two wheels of the same cart, which cannot move if one or the other is broken. She declares in unequivocal terms that man and woman are equal. What engages us here, however, are the various disclaimers she makes in the essay, and her analysis of Islamic inheritance law. We encounter such a disclaimer (which is an act of accommodation interwoven into an act of subversion) in the very second paragraph: 'Here I feel it necessary to say a few words for our conservative sisters. I have not taken up the pen to disparage the custom of purdah. If anyone on perusing my "Stree Jatir Abonoti", concludes that it is against the purdah, then he/she has missed my point and misread the essay'.[13] Rokeya then lays down the foundation of one of her master strokes of 'strategic circumvention': the purdah versus *abarodh* formulation. She builds up a case for female emancipation (particularly mobility and education) by showing her acceptance of female modesty, propriety, and moderation, exemplified by the notion of purdah, and a rejection of *abarodh* (captivity), which was the socially-accepted definition of purdah. In *abarodh* a woman is shut off from public space, or any healthy participation in society, a state that Islam never condoned, argued Rokeya.

This subtle and clever distinction between purdah and *abarodh* recurs in many of Rokeya's writings. It was to become a popular leitmotif and served to allay much of the conservative fear regarding female emancipation. In this essay, Rokeya also pays homage to the 'golden age' of Islam by suggesting that Islam, in its true form, offered women freedom and equality: 'When the female species were being oppressed in Arabia, Prophet Muhammad (pbuh) arrived as their saviour . . . He set an example by his love for his daughter Fatema who filled his life with joy. Alas! he is here no more to save us from our plight'. [14] She then turns to the critical question of man–woman relations, a central concern she often circumvented but never strayed from. She focuses on the question of women's status in Islamic Inheritance Law: 'Let us now turn to Muslim society. According to Muslims we women are half of men; that is, two women are comparable to one man. Or two brothers and one sister make "two and a half"! According to Mohammedan law a daughter inherits half of what a son inherits. But this law is confined to the book . . . The daughter in reality gets nothings'.[15] Then Rokeya goes on to ask that, should the Prophet take accounts and inspect what had been given to daughters, what would Muslims have to say? Thus, Rokeya starts out by a clear elucidation that man and woman are equal in all respects; then allows herself a little humour and produces an interesting statistic: 'Two brothers and a sister equal "two and a half"'. She even adds an exclamation mark after this last comment. As this 2 : 1 ratio is a basic tenet of Islamic law insofar as women's inheritance is concerned, one is left musing how Rokeya reconciled this with her theory of total equality of the sexes.

In the anthology *Motichur* (1905), Rokeya inserted one of her 'domestic pieces', 'Sugrihini' ('The Good Housewife'), which she starts thus:

Hithertofore I had attempted in *Streejatir Abonoti* to depict a truthful picture of the condition of women. But as the truth is always bitter, many did not like my essay. I then proceeded in *Ardhangi* to demonstrate how men and women are like two wheels of a cart, two vital organs of the same body . . . The whole is dependent on both for its proper functioning. If the language of equality is too difficult for women, let us abandon high ambition and lofty thought and move to a more pleasant topic. Today if I ask you: what is your goal in life, you will probably answer—to be a good housewife. Well, let us turn to this.[16]

Rokeya then spells out her formulae for domestic success: account keeping, cooking, cleanliness, interior decoration, infant care, nursing, gardening, etc. The only topic missing is sexual relations. However, Rokeya cleverly puts the good wife/mother argument to her own use. The argument is skilfully deployed to convince the reader that a sound education is a prerequisite for the above. In the central argument she inserts like a palimpsest an advocacy for female education to the extent of a knowledge of chemistry and horticulture, proving once again where her heart (and mind) lay! Such domestic pieces on typical advice to the good housewife formed one of the principal means through which she sought to reach out to women. In the several public addresses which she was invited to deliver on various occasions, she upheld all the standard values manifest in the domestic ideology of the time. However, at the same time she was also writing, in impeccable English, the amazing *Sultana's Dream* challenging the patriarchal structure. That fantasy tells of 'Ladyland', where gender roles are reversed: men stay home and women wisely administer the state and run society. This little book on the inversion of the public and private was written, however, in a language read by few women of the time and published from remote Madras in south-east India. However, its significance lay in the fact that while she was handing down tips to the dutiful wife, she was conjuring her vision of an inverted, subversive reality: a world dominated by women.

The Contradictions

A sharp contradiction in her social thoughts is reflected in two of her essays, namely, the 'Burqah' (1904) and 'Abarodhbasini' (1929). In the earlier work she justifies the use of the cloak-like garment and offers arguments in favour of its use. The 'Burqah' is a truly conservative piece of work in which the *burqah* is held up as the ultimate symbol of female modesty. Rokeya even states that '*abarodh* is an ethical improvement on the natural state', and, 'we believe *abarodh* and improvement in women's status are not contradictory'. [17] It seems apparent that when Rokeya wrote this essay, she had not worked out her later strategic formulation of the purdah–*abarodh* question, where *abarodh* is a phenomenon to be condemned while purdah is defined as female modesty. This becomes apparent in Rokeya's later collection of 47 episodic essays: 'Abarodhabasini' ('The Secluded Ones') published serially in the Bengali Muslim journal, *Mąsik Mohammadi*.[18]

The episodes of 'Abaradhabasini' depict the absurdity and horror of seclusion. Though the pieces (several drawn from real life experience) traverse many aspects of *abarodh*, a few ridicule the use of the very *burqah* celebrated in earlier writing (e.g. episodes 13, 14, and 43). One episode records the death of her aunt-in-law, who, while travelling, stumbles over her *burqah* and falls on to the railway tracks from the platform. Her maid refuses to let any male stranger rescue her. The aunt dies unprotesting, run over by a train, unable to disentangle her *burqah*. These two pieces, 'Burqah' and 'Abarodhbasini', read together would indeed confuse the reader as to Rokeya's position on female seclusion. Indeed, there is a certain contradiction in her thoughts in this regard throughout her writings which is partly reflected in her own lifestyle: for example, in her later years she increasingly took to some form of veiling in deference to the traditional Muslim social custom of female segregation while at the same time remained openly critical of *abarodh*. 'Abarodhasini' is a later work, which she (with a touch of irony?) dedicates to Rahatunnessa, her mother, who was an ardent supporter of *abarodh*.

In 1931, the year before she died, Rokeya published another article in English in *The Mussulman*, namely, 'Educational Ideals for the Modern Indian Girl'. Here she sets down her thoughts on the ongoing project of constructing the ideal Indian girl, who was to be the beneficiary of an English education tempered with the noblest elements of the Indian heritage: 'We should by all means broaden the outlook of our girls and teach them to modernize themselves. Yet they should be made to realize that the domestic duties entrusted to them cover a task on which the welfare of the country depends . . . . In short, our girls should not only obtain university degrees, but must be ideal daughters, wives and mothers—or may I say obedient daughters, loving sisters, dutiful wives and instructive wives'.[19]

It is easy to lose sight of the other Rokeya, the Rokeya of 'Stree Jatir Abonoti', 'Ardhangi', *Sultana's Dream*, or the *Padmarag* (1924), if one confines oneself to her educational and domestic pieces. One must however constantly read 'Sugrihini', or the piece on educational ideals against *Sultana's Dream* or 'Sireejatir Abonoti'. Existing gender roles are rejected outright in *Sultana's Dream*, and in *Padmarag* the female protagonist renounces the institution of the family and the domestic code by refusing to go back to the man she loves.[20]

In Rokeya's work one finds both the limits of liberal ideology and its transcendence. Her philosophy of education was being spelt out in the heyday of liberalism in Bengal at the same time as Ismail Hossain Shirazi, S. Wajed Ali, Lutfur Rahman, not to mention Tagore and other male writers were expounding their views on social reform. Rokeya reiterated much of what they said. They were all in it together: the rationalization of scriptures, evocation of the 'golden age' and the creation of the new woman embedded in a selective modernity. However, where Rokeya differed from the others was in her ability to see education not as an end in itself or as an aid to woman's familial role only, but also as a means to economic independence, for here was the last forbidden frontier: education as a means to wage-work. The sexual and the economic were the two areas in which the liberal Muslim, like his Hindu/Brahmo counterpart, was not willing to change. Over these he sought to retain his traditional grip. Rokeya was aware of this. Though she agreed on the first count, she did not on the second. She referred many times to the economic aspect of female education. That is why, while writing domestic pieces, she encoded into her arguments an advocacy of woman's economic role.

Perhaps, we could close this part of the discussion by visualizing Rokeya at her writing table on the eve of her death on 9 December 1932, as reported by her cousin Mariam Rashid, who was living with her at the time. Mariam reports that Rokeya was seen poring over papers at her desk till the early hours of the morning of the 9th. These could have been school documents, or her last work *Narir Adhikar* ('Rights of Women'), published posthumously in 1957. Mushfeqa Mahmud, a disciple of Rokeya who collected and published an invaluable anthology of Rokeya's letters, writes about *Narir Adhikar*: 'Rokeya worked late at her desk the night on which she died. This unfinished essay was found under a paperweight on the table where she spent her last working hours'.[21] In *Narir Adhikar*, Rokeya was returning to the subject that was her lifelong passion: the oppression of women. In the fragment she completed, she addresses a specific problem in Muslim society: the plight of women who are victims of easy divorce, particularly in rural areas (a phenomenon that continues to this day). The husband divorces the wife at the slightest pretext, packs her off, and prepares for his next marriage. Rokeya is ruthless in her portrayal of male lust. While she was enjoining girls to be dutiful wives, she was sitting at her desk late at night exposing the hypocrisy and cruelty of the husband.

Conclusion

This brief analysis based on selected writings of Rokeya should illustrate the problems encountered by Bengali Muslim women and Rokeya's dreams and efforts to bring about a change in societal attitudes to women, or at the least to create an awareness in society about the problems suffered by women. Rokeya's shifting positions on women's issues create a problem for us in evaluating her role, especially her writings. What are we to make of the varying positions and strands in her work? How do we evaluate those areas where she seems to take leave of the logic and single-mindedness that characterized so much of her work? First of all, we must not measure her against any absolute standard of the 1990s, but 'read' her rather against her own historical context, and against the internal logic of her work. It is evident to scholars of the Bengal renaissance that the reformist agenda had often to negotiate with tradition. Rokeya, whom we must place within the Bengali intellectual tradition of her time, merely continued in the path of Vidyasagar and Rabindranath and did not visualize a dramatic change in the roles and functions of women. Throughout the era of reformism, each measure of change had to be entertained on the basis of a sanction, whether real or constructed, in tradition or scripture. Every person who advocated change in any sphere realized that he/she would have to navigate with caution, accommodating tradition here and rejecting it there.[22] In Rokeya's case the situation was more complex in that she came from the more conservative Muslim society, and was a woman who had taken up the mantle of social reformer. For her the challenge must have been more personal, more arduous. Her strategies for survival would have to be more diverse and well-planned. Finally, there is always the possibility that a social critic or writer might evolve over time and occupy various intellectual positions. Rokeya was a religious person, as some of her writings and lifestyle assert, living in an age concerned with retrieving the culture from the onslaught of the West while at the same time refashioning it along the lines of a selective Western modernity. The apparent contradictions and ambivalence in her writings may not satisfy someone seeking constant clarity and consistency, but about 100 years later her works survive and her school still stands. She is rediscovered and reread with much admiration today. She has become a symbol of women's progress in Bengali Muslim society.

Notes And References

1. *See*, for example, Sufia Ahmed, *Muslim Community in Bengal 1884–1912*, 2nd edn (Dhaka: University Press Ltd, 1996; 1st edn 1976); and Anisuzzaman, *Muslim Manas O Bangla Sahitya* (Dhaka: Muktadhara, 1974).
2. *See* Sonia Nishat Amin, *The World of Muslim Women in Colonial Bengal 1876–1939* (Leiden: E.J. Brill, 1996) for an account of the change in the material and ideological world of Bengali Muslim women in the late nineteenth and early twentieth centuries.
3. *See*, for details, Partha Chatterjee, 'The Nationalist Resolution of the

Women's Question', in Kumkum Sangari and Sudesh Vaid (eds.), *Recasting Women: Essays in Colonial History* (New Delhi: Kali for Women, 1990).

4. However, one should not overemphasize this point: although a few Bengali Hindu women were ready at that time for a university degree, the number was insignificant. Overall, there was little qualitative difference between women's education in the Hindu and Muslim societies of Bengal. Sudha Mazumdar, an upper caste Hindu woman who lived during the time (b. 1899), explains in her memoirs: 'The vocation of every girl was to be a wife and mother, and the ideal held up to her for her future life was *seva*, service to others . . . , Since much would be required of the girl when she attained womanhood, a system of education began to prepare her for her future life from her earliest days. As nearly all things in India hinge on religion, this training was also centred in religious thoughts and practices'. (*See* Sudha Mazumdar, *Memoirs of an Indian Woman*, edited with an Introduction by Geraldine Forbes (Armonk, New York: M.E. Sharpe, Inc. [An East Gate Book], 1989), 16–17). As such, a formal public education was not considered essential for women, either Hindu or Muslim, with few exceptions. (*Editor's note.*)

5. *See* Muhammad Shamsul Alam, *Rokeya Sakhawat Hossein: Jivan O Sahitya* (Dhaka: Bangla Academy, 1989), 87.

6. For a discussion on Urdu–Bengali dichotomy, *see* Sufia Ahmed, op. cit., esp. ch. 1.

7. *See* Shamsun Nahar Mahmud, *Rokeya Jivani* (rpt Dhaka: Riyadh Mahmud, 1987; 1st edn Calcutta, 1937), 53–4.

8. For an account of Victorian–Brahmo roots of the new domestic ideology in Bengal, *see* Sonia Nishat Amin (1996), op. cit., ch. vii.

9. For Rokeya as a subversive writer, *see* Syed Manzoorul Islam, 'Subaltern Worldview: A Reading of *Sultana's Dream*', in Firdous Azim and Niaz Zaman (eds), *Infinite Variety: Women in Literature and Society* (Dhaka: University Press Ltd., 1994).

10. Rokeya Sakhawat Hossein, cited in Muhammad Shamsul Alam, op.cit., 314.

11. Ibid.

12. *Motichur,* vol. 1, published in 1905. *See Rokeya Rachanavali,* ed. Abdul Qader (Dhaka: Bangla Academy, 1973).

13. Rokeya Sakhawat Hossein, *Ardhangi* (1904), in *Rokeya Rachanavali*, op. cit., 35.

14. Ibid., 42.

15. *Rokeya Rachanavali*, op. cit., 41.

16. Ibid., 45.

17. Ibid., 51.

18. The collection has been translated into English by Roushan Jahan, entitled, *Inside Seclusion: The Abarodhabasini of Rokeya Sakhwat Hossein* (Dhaka: Women for Women, 1981).

19. Cited in Muhammad Shamsul AIam, op. cit., 340–1.
20. For a discussion of *Padmarag*, *see* Sonia N. Amin, 'The New Woman in Literature in the Novels of Nojibur Rahman and Rokeya Sakhawat Hossein', in Firdous Azim and Niaz Zaman, op. cit.
21. Cited in *Rokeya Rachanavali*, op. cit., 315.
22. *See* Kumkum Sangari and Sudesh Vaid, op. cit., Introduction.

7

Radicalism in Bengali Muslim Thought: Kazi Abdul Wadud and the 'Religion of Creativity'

SHAHADAT H. KHAN

Background

A radical rational humanist movement, the 'freedom of intellect movement' (*buddhir mukti andolan*), began in Dhaka in the 1920s. Its intellectual motto was: *Jnan jekhane simabaddha, buddhi sekhane arashta, mukti sekhane asambhab*, or 'Where knowledge is restricted, there the intellect is inert, there freedom is impossible'. This freedom of intellect movement was the most unique and striking expression of rational humanism among twentieth century Bengali Muslims before independence from British colonial rule in 1947.

The movement's central intellectual organization was the Dhaka Muslim Sahitya Samaj (MSS), or the Muslim Literary Society of Dhaka, and its views were published in its Bengali journal, *Shikha*. The MSS and *Shikha* were founded by Western-educated Bengali Muslims. Unlike many other Hindu, Muslim and Brahmo associations, and journals in Dhaka, a parochial and religious exclusiveness was foreign to the MSS and *Shikha*. This is evident in MSS's definition of membership, its composition, resolutions, rules of procedure, intellectual activities, and the contents of its journal.[1] In none of the areas was any discrimination permitted by reason of religion, gender, or professional status. The essential contribution of the MSS was not its advocacy of any particular viewpoint but to provide a framework within which a range of divergent views could not only be expressed, but mutually assessed in orderly discussion and debate. The topics of essays in the

MSS ranged across Bengali Muslim literature, society, religio–cultural life, and nationalism. However, the ways of thinking about these topics were deliberately structured to be diverse and critical.

The founder of this movement was Kazi Abdul Wadud (1894–1970), a Bengali-speaking and Bengali-writing Muslim intellectual, born and raised in an average rural family in Eastern Bengal, currently Bangladesh. Despite economic hardships, his father had managed to give Wadud an English education. Indeed, he received the highest academic degrees from Presidency College and Calcutta University in 1917 and 1919. Wadud never visited the West, as Sir Sayyid Ahmad Khan and Sir Mohammad Iqbal did, and never had an opportunity for any significant dialogue with European intellectuals or with high ranking Europeans in Bengal. This notwithstanding, some of the finest strands of modern rational humanism of the West were discussed in his writings. This came initially, perhaps, from Waduds's English education, but, more importantly, from his creative individual effort to study Bengali humanist intellectuals, mostly Hindus, already in dialogue with the West. If historians argue that Rammohun and Rabindranath, two stalwarts of the Bengal renaissance, were inspired by 'British Orientalism', then rational humanist Muslims like Wadud may be considered to be the first generation of Bengali Muslims inspired by British Orientalism through Tagore and Rammohun.

This essay does not propose to analyse Kazi Wadud's intellectual orientation to, and influences from, non-Islamic sources, such as the ideal of 'unfettered rationalism' of Raja Rammohun Roy and the 'universal humanism' of Rabindranath Tagore.[2] Its goals are to elaborate on Wadud's views on the 'religion of creativity' (*srishti dharma*) for an understanding of his views on religion, nationalism, and communalism in British India. I intend to focus specifically on three components of Wadud's *srishti dharma*. First, I will analyse Wadud's thoughts to indicate the extent to which his mind was liberated from the communal self-consciousness of being a Muslim, which was necessary for him to develop so novel a conception as *srishti dharma*, 'the religion of creativity'. I will then examine Wadud's secular or humanistic standpoint in relation to British rule in particular and the West in general. Indeed, Wadud expected that British rule would play a positive role in freeing Indians from a fixation with religious communalism. Thirdly, I will explore the most important component of *srishti dharma*, namely accommodation of Muslims with the Hindus, not on the basis of their respective religious apologetics, but through accommodation of

Muslims with Hindus via rational humanism and human creative endeavours. Wadud's standpoint was that Muslim accommodation with Hindus should be unconditional and unrestricted.

Kazi Abdul Wadud and Shrishti Dharma

Kazi Abdul Wadud was not an activist in the nationalist politics of India. He had no formal or informal, social or political links with political clubs or organizations of the All India Muslim League, the Indian National Congress, or the Jamiyatul Ulama-i-Hind, etc. Wadud's diary, *Nana Katha* (published in Kazi Abdul Wadud's Collected Works in Bengali), and his written correspondence indicate that he had no social or intellectual intercourse with the nationalist Muslim or communal Muslim political figures, yet he was not an uninvolved intellectual who kept to himself his views on political developments in India. Wadud wrote a long article on the Khilafat movement, reacted in print to the Civil Disobedience movement, commented on British rule in India, and responded to the political question of 'mixed electorate'. Then, in 1935, he developed a clear, detailed thesis on the causes of, and solutions to, Muslim–Hindu division in India.

What emerged out of Wadud's response was in fact a new thesis: a secular humanistic nationalism for India. Wadud called this thesis *srishti dharma* or 'religion of creativity'. Its objective was not to rush a nationalist movement for an end to Indian political bondage but to initiate a movement to achieve social freedom for Indians, first from an obsession with religion so that 'Hindus and Muslims can lead an integrated life' (*Hindu-mussalmaner sanmilita jiban*).[3] He also told the educated Bengali Muslims that their life-style ought to be changed to a 'life of knowledge and love' (*jnan o premer jiban*). On another occasion, Wadud lectured his Muslim audience on 'humans' loving union with their surroundings' (*paripasvikatar sange manusher prembandhan*).[4]

Wadud wrote a lengthy article in 1921 on the Khilafat and the Non-cooperation movements entitled, '*Non-cooperation ba Asahajogita*'. The essay was written before he conceived the *buddhir mukti* motto, yet it does not conform to the views of nationalist Muslims on the Non-cooperation movement. For example, the Urdu-speaking nationalist Muslim leaders, such as Abul Kalam Azad, Hussain Ahmad Madani, Mahmud Hasan, etc. sought to 'give the Non-cooperation movement a religious sanction'.[5] In other words, the 'nationalist' ulema claimed Quranic sanction for non-cooperation against British rule.

Wadud stressed several issues of the Non-cooperation movement. He wrote that 'we believe we have to understand Non-cooperation by our intellect, which is the greatest resort of humans'. He restricted his definition of the movement to its political meaning; 'Non-cooperation', he wrote, 'is only a political issue. In larger human life there cannot exist anything called, non-cooperation'.[6] Political non-cooperation against British rule in India, according to Wadud, should not set a precedent for non-cooperation with a democratic political system in India.

Wadud expressed his objections to British rule by using several strong Bengali phrases: *danab shakti* or monstrous power, *dharmahin*, or irreligious; and said that the British attitude to India was filled with *atma-nirbharita* or arrogance. These objections were largely repetitions of Gandhi's and nationalist Muslims' accusations against British rule. For example, following Gandhi, Wadud wrote that the British were determined to rule India by the sword, and in this age of science, learning, freedom and equality, British rule marked a differentiation of value between Indians and the British. However, unlike Gandhi, and the nationalist Muslims, he saw this 'monstrous rule' as an outgrowth of the highest development of European democracy and material civilization. It is interesting that Wadud showed a deep respect for the development of democracy and material culture in Europe. He wonderfully described three ideals of European democracy: 'Equality, Fraternity, Liberty (*Samya, Maitri. Svadhinata*)'.[7] The European *raj shakti*, or 'highest executive power' of European states, according to Wadud, is not concerned with the well-being and happiness of vested interest groups, but of all citizens who live within a *raj shakti*. The rise of the democratic type of *raj shakti*, according to Wadud, began a new phase in human history in Europe. Its direction is 'not so much concerned with development of a spiritual life of humans'. The modern *raj shakti* of Europe, while creating a new order of state and society, has also created avenues for the unrestricted development and fulfilment of the ambitions, hopes, and aspirations of humans. Wadud also expressed respect for other influences of democratic (*ganatantra*) development in Europe. For example, he cited the rising 'power of masses' (*ganashakti*) and also observed that humans were given incredible opportunities to shed 'all kinds of superstitions' (*sarba prakar samskar bimukti*). This freedom of thought of the masses in Europe, according to Wadud, 'is always essential for humankind's highest achievement of civilization'.[8] According to him, the form of government in Europe, the way it functions through a parliament or gathering of people, should be taken by all as a universal standard of state mechanism, because it is the highest form of government that can guarantee 'well regulated freedom'.

Wadud contrasted this European development of democracy and materialism with Asian civilizations. He argued that Asian civilizations had also stressed materialism, but only at the cost of yet greater emphasis on spirituality. On the contrary, '*raj shakti* in Europe found out the secret truth of human life—a new truth, the splendours of the desire for enjoyment'.[9] Wadud described the amazing splendours and elegance of the material civilization achieved by Europe. He wrote that in this perceptible world a variety of earthly pleasures (*bhog*) has made human life charming. The earthly pleasures have given human life a new vigour (*nabasphurti*) and new strength (*nabashakti*). Now people no longer have to wait like dull-witted persons for pleasures in the next world (*parakal*). The ancient sages of Asia had stated that for heavenly pleasure people should promote spiritual life in their society, but modern people have brought pleasures into this earthly world by the power of intellect (*buddhi*). 'We should not hesitate to eulogize the beauty of human intellect that has been inspired in the heart of the Europeans'.[10]

Wadud was disappointed with British rule in India. He argued that 'Equality, Fraternity, Liberty' were also ambitions of the Indian nation (*bharatiya jati*), yet the British would not grant these to India. British rule was inflated by an arrogance (*atma-nirbharita*) arising from their highest achievements in material and democratic development: 'British rulers want in India the highest fulfilment of their selfish purpose, no matter by what honest or dishonest means they achieved them'.[11] He did not, however, claim that the British rulers in India were the only examples of this arrogance. Neither did he exclusively blame India for being the first victim of European arrogance. Wadud argued that the highest form of European arrogance was expressed in Nietzsche's ideal of the superman. Germany had begun the First World War as a consequence of Nietzsche's superman ideal. After Germany's defeat, the victors of Europe themselves adopted this ideal and rendered ineffectual the 'American scholar president' Woodrow Wilson's ideals of the League of Nations and the self-determination of nations.

Notwithstanding these criticisms, Wadud thought that non-cooperation against British 'political rule' should be non-violent and peaceful: 'It is only non-violent non-cooperation which is our goal'.[12] For self-restraint in the face of British rule, he offered several suggestions. He forbade any form of physical violence. He appealed for a guarantee of the personal safety of British officials and their staffs. More importantly, Wadud understood non-violent non-cooperation only as: *srishti dharmi asahajogita*, or 'non-cooperation based on the principles of the religion of creativity'. Its one positive aspect is that non-cooperation vis-a-vis the British is also the 'cementing bond amongst ourselves [Indians]'. He reminded that our miserable loss of freedom was not only effected by our rulers, but was also our own creation.

Wadud also proposed reforms for problems for which he blamed Indians. His reform proposals were so extensive that at times he forgot that his target was British rule in India. For example, when the Central Khilafat Committee asked students to leave all British educational institutions, Wadud did not accept this proposal outright. His answer was ambivalent, vaguely stating that unless students were properly indoctrinated in the broader purpose of non-violent non-cooperation, they should stay in schools and colleges. Teaching 'universal humanity' (*vishva-manabata*) as part of education was one of his principal concerns. To achieve this, Wadud proposed a reform of 'national education'. The proposal suggested new curricula in school and college education, one central purpose of which was to resolve Hindu–Muslim division. The secondary purpose was to popularize vocational and adult education. These proposals tended to deflect attention from any direct or indirect indoctrination of students against the British colonial power in India.

Wadud also articulated some of the views of nationalist Muslims. The destruction of Khilafat means to Muslims the loss of their worldly power. Political freedom of Muslims is indispensable for Islam and for Muslims.[15] Wadud did not elaborate where and how British rule had destroyed Muslim traditions and Islam in India. Similarly, he did not share the view of nationalist Muslims that it is simply un-Islamic for Muslims to live under a Christian ruler.

However, Wadud did suggest that Muslims should not forgo the religious identity of Islam. It is, however, important to note that it was only during the Khilafat/Non-cooperation movement that Wadud spoke favourably about Muslim and Hindu identities, but Wadud's religion was the religion of creativity. Wadud argued that true religious feeling is involvement of Indians in wider social and material life and abandonment of repressive meaningless religious ceremonial. In other words, the highest order of all religions is that humans have entered into an inseparable organic unity, because humans are united under Allah or *Bhagaban*.

During the Khilafat movement, Wadud also resolved, in his own thinking, one of deep-rooted contradictions of composite nationalism: 'Are we Muslim or Indian first?' To this question, a typical response of nationalist Muslims was: 'India is the physical and Islam the spiritual force for the Indian Muslims'.[16] Wadud's argument was: 'If the Khilafat, for the restoration of which we are fighting today, were to attack India tomorrow, then it would be our obligation to fight back . . . . Because nobody has the right, not even our Khalifa, to impose bondage on countless Muslim–Hindu–Christian–Buddhists in India'.[17] In other words, Wadud's own resolve, in the ongoing tension between religion and nationalism, was to embrace an 'unconflicting patriotism', of the *bharatbasi*, or Indian. He wrote: 'The national patriots sometimes would help Muslims against non-Muslims; but also [sometime] help non-Muslims against Muslims'.[18]

Whatever Muslim communal self-consciousness Wadud had expressed during the Khilafat movement began to change steadily in the aftermath of the Khilafat campaign. From 1924, the ideals of freedom (*mukti*), intellect (*buddhi*), and creativity (*srishti*) had been evolving in Wadud's thought. A rational humanistic tendency in his understanding of Islam was also evident in the essays and comments that he presented in MSS. Furthermore, one could see, post-1924, his reduced emphasis on 'Hazrat Mohammad' in comparison to the view of composite nationalist Muslims who saw 'Prophet Mohammad' as an Islamic justification for Muslims' cooperation with Hindus in India.[19]

Despite Wadud's initial support for the Khilafat and the non-violent Non-cooperation movement, his diary in 1924 was privately cheerful over the destruction of Khilafat: 'The destruction of Khilafat was most necessary'. He had also denied that Indian Muslims had political and financial responsibility for preservation of Khilafat, 'We will protect all Muslim countries—this is largely not true . . . . Why should we protect them? Who are you to protect them? Above all, how long should the Khilafat arrangement continue, like a plant protected in a pot?'[20] Wadud thought that Muslim countries until now had survived on physical force and not on the strength of modern science and knowledge. Under the name of the 'so-called Khilafat', Muslims ruled their countries with imposition of religious dogmas. The destruction of Khilafat would give them relief: 'They would not allow religious rules to dominate the human intellect'. As for those who argued that the destruction of the Khilafat had hurt the image of Muslims, Wadud commented, 'I agree with them, but I am not sorry for it. It is now very essential that a part of 'mussalman feeling' (*mussalman bhab*) should be destroyed. Up to now, religion had brought torture. Now it would be cut back and would be situated in its proper place in [human] life'.[21]

Privately, Wadud was also critical of the two most noteworthy nationalist Muslim leaders, Maulana Abul Kalam Azad and Maulana Mohammad Ali. He criticized Azad for aiming to found 'an international Muslim association' (*bishvabyapi mussalman-samuha*) for 'the protection of the interests of Muslims in the world'. 'The fault of this organization is not', according to Wadud, 'because it is a huge organization. The problem of this organization is that its basis for unity is religion and religion of the tradition'. Wadud compared Azad's international Muslim association with Romain Rolland's International League of Intellectuals, and concluded on the latter: 'In today's world, one society is coming into acquaintance with other societies. Such an introduction and familiarity should lead to a mighty civilization. Pan-Islamism is opposed to universal humanity. As a result, the Muslim world is not able to adjust to its own time'.[22]

The starting point of Wadud's criticism of Mohammad Ali was the latter's proposal demanding an exclusive territory for Muslims. Wadud pointed out this demand in a speech that Mohammad Ali delivered in the aftermath of the Khilafat movement. Wadud quipped about this proposal that for Islam it is essential to have such territories, *'Jejirat-ul-Arab'*, over which there would be no control by non-believers. To this communal comment, Wadud replied, 'Well! It has a cultural value ... But what is its relation with a true religious life? ... It is not impossible, but it is difficult to get a true sign of religion in life-style closed in by rules of shariat ...'.[23]

Not only privately, but publicly, Wadud urged Bengali Muslims to think about *manab dharma*, or 'religion of humanity'. He repeated his appeal for a change of attitude towards Prophet Mohammad in 1926 on the occasion of Mohammad's birth and death anniversary when he paid a tribute to Mohammad's humanity. Wadud's three-page article, 'Fateha-i-Doyajdaham', did not make laudatory comments about Mohammad's socio–political reforms, but only politely referred to his glorious humanity. Wadud spoke of Prophet Mohammad as *mahaguru* (great guru): 'If we look into our mahaguru's life, we become silent because of our praise and respect'.[24]

Wadud also reviewed several biographies of Prophet Mohammad. In 1926, he reviewed one entitled *Manab Mukut* (1922) or 'The Crown of

Humanity', by an 'Islamic liberal', Yakub Ali Choudhury (1888–1940). He praised Choudhury for not making the biography a 'neo-orthodox' restatement on the greatness of Islam, that 'Mohammad was the last and greatest Prophet and his coming had been mentioned in holy books of Jews and Christians'. He equally appreciated the author's treatment of the Prophet as a 'human being'. He, however, criticized the author for his statement that 'Hazrat Mohammad's ideal of humanity is the greatest of this world'.[25] Wadud termed this attitude of Muslims 'partisanship' (*pakshapatita*).

This partisan attitude was criticized from several directions. First, Wadud argued that Muslims are so infatuated by the dazzling glory of Mohammad's power that they had no time to look anywhere other than at Mohammad. Secondly, Wadud cautioned the author that while his love of fellow Muslims and love of Islam may be wonderful, yet a person who believes in the 'religion of creativity' would look at these differently. He quoted the American humanist philosopher, Ralph Waldo Emerson (1803–82): 'No facts are to me sacred, none are profane; simply experiment, an endless seeker with no past at my back' (English quotations are from Wadud).[26]

In the following year, Wadud's article, 'Sahitya Samasya' (1927), stated a fundamental standpoint of modern intellectual criticism: 'A genius (*pratibhaban*) is not infallible' (the English word is Wadud's). He pointed out that 'it is not true that monotheism was completely unknown in the brutal and idolatrous society of Arabia'.[27] He emphasized that Mohammad also faced severe opposition from the Arabs: 'Throughout his life, Mohammad had physically suffered torture and torments by some ordinary Arabs. After his death, even the majority people of his own tribe, Quraish, did not understand his basic teaching'.[28]

When the 'neo-orthodox' weekly Bengali journal, *Sultan* (16 November 1927), edited by Maniruzzaman Islamabadi, condemned Dhaka radicals, Wadud fought back. Two weeks after the Calcutta neo-orthodox had attacked the rational humanists of Dhaka, he wrote a lengthy reply (30 November 1927) to the editor of *Sultan*, with a request that his reply be published in the journal. This was not done. Nevertheless, Wadud reiterated in the letter his earlier point that Prophet Mohammad is a human and as a human has limitations. He specifically pointed out, in this context, a biography of Prophet Mohammad, *Mostafa Carit,* written by a neo-orthodox Muslim Bengali intellectual, Maulana Akram Khan. Wadud pointed out that the 'biography was all about criticizing the

Christians', but 'nowhere did the book portray the human character of Mohammad, for example, how Mohammad's human thought grew day by day, how he loved his family life, and for that matter how from time to time also committed mistakes . . .'.[29] Wadud also cited a fundamental Islamic tenet of neo-orthodox Muslim thought which held *inter alia* that 'the person who would be the last messenger of the truth must be truthful and possess all the virtues. Prophet Mohammad was the last messenger of truth and therefore he must be truthful and virtuous'.[30]

Wadud posed two fundamental questions against blind allegiance to the so-called Islamic ideals. First, 'What does it mean to say that the Quran is the message of Allah (*Quran Allahar bani kon arthe*)?' Secondly, 'The way Muslim society was asked to obey the phrase "last messenger of truth", does it not distort humans relation with God and constitute idolatry?' He cautioned the neo-orthodox intellectuals not to 'repeat answers that have already been given. We are not satisfied with those answers. Because those answers do not recognize complete and unfettered freedom of human thought'.[31]

The two questions were not answered by the editor of the *Sultan*. On the contrary, the journal asked Wadud, 'If he [Wadud] respects the Quran in any sense as the Word of Allah', and 'If he [Wadud] respects Hazrat Mohammad as a prophet and last messenger of Allah'. Wadud cautiously avoided any direct answer. However his reply (3 or 4 December 1927) to the neo-othodox intellectuals was categorical: 'You are supposed to know already what is the framework of our debate and how you should debate with "free-thinkers" [English phrase is Wadud's] of Dhaka . . . . If you had the strength to answer these modern questions, then, by this time, Muslim society would have changed completely'.[32]

At this point in the debate, the editor of the *Sultan* withdrew and did not bring further accusation against the 'free-thinkers' of Dhaka, but Akram and his journal, the *Mohammadi*, did not spare them. Wadud continued to defend his radical theological views in replies to Akram.

Wadud and Muslim Communalism

In tracing the origins of Muslim communalism, Wadud looked to early Islamic history and found intolerance of one group of Muslims for another Muslim group. The emergence of a Muslim 'rationalist group' in early Islam is well known. During the Abbasid rule, the leader of the rationalist group was Imam Abu Hanifa. Under Imam Hanifa, Wadud stated, rationalism had continued for some time in the Muslim world, 'until the extreme scriptualists under Imam Ghazali persecuted the rationalist group'. The rationalist group could not tolerate the differing opinions of the extreme scriptualists. This culminated in the 'inhuman torture and killing by the rationalists of the scriptualist leader, Imam Hambal'. After Imam Hambal died, the 'extreme scriptualists' in the thirteenth century were organized under Imam Ibn Taymiya, who had started a movement for a 'return to puritan Islam'. Wadud wrote that the intolerance of Taymiya had gone to the extreme, and 'except the Quran and reliable Hadith, all other sources of knowledge—Khalifa, Sufis, philosophies—are declared unreliable'. However, the Sufis, who were dominant in Muslim society at that time, 'tormented Taymiya'.[34]

In the eighteenth century, a disciple of Ibn Taymiya, Mohammad ibn Abd al-Wahhab, had successfully re-established puritan Islam in Arabia. In the nineteenth century, Wahabism became a powerful trend among Indian Muslims. Wadud accounted for the communalism of the Wahabi movement in two ways: a return to primitive Islam (*adim Islame pratyabartan*) and use of Islam as a political force. On both counts, Wadud argued, the Wahabis aggravated Muslims' intolerance toward non-Muslims. By a fatwa declaring India a 'Darul Harb', the Wahabis justified the political use of Islam, i.e. to declare a jihad against British rule. Also, through an Islamization movement for a return to puritan Islam, Wahabis had destroyed Hindu–Muslim unity in rural Bengal. He wrote: 'Before the Wahabi influence came to Bengal, rural Muslims were not intolerant of worship of idols. Some respected Muslim families in those days used to worship Hindu deities, for example, Kali and Durga'. After the Wahabis came, the relationship was destroyed. 'The honest minded Hindus', according to Wadud, 'were now sad. They complained that while Muslim peasants used to take part in our pujas, and did not even mind to eat with us . . . . now they are not willing to know their Hindu neighbours'.[35]

Wadud objected to what the Wahabis thought to be a perpetual religious duty to return to 'primitive' Islam. He reacted to this rigid ideal arguing that it 'is needless to say that this kind of thought is always inimical to expansion of human thought and is suspicious of all new experiments of humans . . . . The Indian Muslims could not get free of this, because of their consciousness of Muslim weaknesses in India.' It was because of their weakness and 'inferiority complex' (English phrase is Wadud's), according to him, that 'two objects become a special subject of respect of Muslims of India—the Quran and the messages of Mohammad or to put it bluntly subservience to both'.[36]

Wadud analysed an aspect of communalism, obsession with Islam, in the thoughts of several late nineteenth and early twentieth century Muslim modernist intellectuals, notably, Sir Sayyid Ahmad Khan, Sayyid Amir Ali, and Sir Mohammad Iqbal. Sayyid Ahmad had an innate liberality that was free from Wahabi intolerance, but his emphasis on Islam was fairly explicit and intense: 'Islam is an "unrivalled eternal light" (Wadud quoted Sayyid Ahmad's Urdu phrase, *ek lajoab nur*), i.e. 'Islam is universally bright and universally perfect'. He also argued that Sir Sayyid's thinking on Muslim separatism in education and politics was not merely on account of the latter's backwardness, it was his (Sayyid Ahmad's) ingrained belief that Islam is the best civilizing force in the world. He said frequently, 'Were not the Muslim civilization and culture unforgettable things in the annals of human history? Why then should not Mussalmans of India, the lawful inheritors of those proud traditions, exert themselves to have at least as honoured and useful an existence as any other nation or community?'[37]

Wadud interpreted Amir Ali's obsession with Islam in another direction. Amir Ali was not totally in the dark about the Bengal renaissance that was influencing his 'non-Muslim fellow citizens' in Bengal where he was born, but his acquaintance with it was 'outrageously imperfect and meagre', The Central National Mahomedan Association that he established undertook even more 'absurd' politics than the association established by Sir Surendranath Banerjee. The Mahomedan Association had succeeded to establishing *anjumans* ('associations') in different areas of Bengal 'but the long and short of all their orations and thundering seems to have been that Mussalmans are different from the Hindus . . . Sir Sayyid, although a separatist, was creative, but Amir Ali had almost nothing except separatism'.[38]

Wadud acknowledged that Iqbal wrote genuinely patriotic poems. Iqbal had even expressed in an All India Muslim League conference (1930) that he would have accepted Indian nationhood had it been established on a lead given by Akbar and Kabir. Wadud, however, criticized this rhetorical nationalism. Why, in the absence of Akbar and Kabir, could he not think of any other solutions except 'strengthening each religious community of India in its particular ideology and way of life?' In response Wadud wrote, 'The old inarticulate suspicion of Indian Mussalmans of their uncharitable environs has under its [Iqbal's work] influence, flared up to undisguised belligerency'.[39]

The aspect of non-communalism (humane, humanistic) that Wadud was expecting from Muslim intellectuals was 'unfettered reason'. As Rammohun's 'unfettered reason' had broken out of particular religious bonds, Wadud expected the same from so-called creative Muslim modernists. They should be free from obsessions and infatuations. The model of adjustment to modern non-communal life for Wadud was Rammohun, and the necessary condition for reaching agreement with other religions was ridding oneself of obsession or infatuation with one's own religion. However, this model of 'unfettered reason', Wadud was unable to find in many intellectuals, apart from those of the Bengal renaissance and some of its twentieth century followers, especially his young rational humanists among the Muslims of Dhaka.

During the Civil Disobedience movement, Wadud gave his verdict in favour of 'mixed electorates'. Among Muslim politicians, mixed electorate was supported only by a few nationalist Muslim leaders. Wadud did not call them 'nationalists' but 'friends of the mixed electorate'. He summarized two reasons for their support of a mixed electorate: First, they say that they are children of this country, and therefore, want to fight for the welfare of this country. Second, Islam is a universal brotherhood, and therefore its interests would be narrowed and falsified if its followers did not look out for other people's interest. Wadud praised their support for mixed electorates, yet differed with them: their motivation for support of the mixed electorate was religious and this he could not appreciate. He wrote: 'I am a realist [English word is Wadud's] . . . . Whatever is the reason, Hindus and Muslims are divided in this country . . . . For this, I do not want to say anything, good or bad, about their past because to say something forcefully good or bad about the past is [another] sign of force'.[40] When he did blame anyone for communal tensions, he tended to blame his fellow Muslims; at any rate their leaders. Wadud criticized the so-called respected 'Muslim political leaders [who] are bowed down to the feet of the powerful in the hope of minor gain'. About Muslim religious leaders, Wadud's comments were more devastating: 'Even today, Muslim religious leaders are a group of destitutes who are habitually illogical, immoral, even ignorant of religion. And their world of literature is still being dominated by a group of tasteless half-educated people'.[41]

Wadud constructed a new role for Muslim representatives in an elected 'national parliament'. For this new role, Wadud suggested Muslims adopt 'creative power' (*srishti kshamata*). This he did by pointing Muslims to the creative power of the Jews in the multinational societies of Europe. He wrote that the Jewish community is a minority group in Europe, and because of this they had suffered violence and insult for long years in Europe, yet the Jews had reached the highest position in European material and intellectual life. 'For one special reason, the Jews have achieved this highest position: for self-protection a minority's sense of creative power must be higher'.[42]

Wadud wanted to rouse the creative power (*srishti kshamata*) of the minority Muslims of India in order to follow this intellectual and material development of the Jewish population in Europe. Wadud suggested several ways of doing this. First, Muslim leaders must fully realize that they are demographically a 'minority community' (*chota dal*) in India. Therefore, Muslim leaders must keep away from the communal path, for otherwise it would be inevitable for the 'Muslim masses' to fight with other Indian communities. For example, Muslim leadership should not battle with a majority community on issues of 'music before mosque', 'cow slaughtering', and 'separate electorate'. This would undoubtedly mean Muslims making concessions to Hindus, yet such concessions, according to Wadud, would be valuable for Muslims: 'I am telling Muslims to "accept this defeat" because it is only by accepting this defeat that the mental depression and discomfort of the Muslim in the present time would go. His whole intellect would be creative and simultaneously he would help India in many ways to be creative. Secondly, Indian Muslims must 'get rid of infatuation' that Muslims are the majority in some provinces and in time of danger they will be rescued by some 'invincible religious brothers from outside India'.[43]

Finally, Wadud wanted Muslims to be strong and powerful only through creative ability in unison with Hindus. He argued that in politics a country would give up an established principle to rule a minority community. Let the majority community continue to dominate. By giving up a separatist talk, the minority party would devote itself only to various creative actions to enable the majority community to direct various projects for human welfare.

In public speeches and writings, Wadud sought to liberate the Muslims of Bengal from a Muslim communal self-consciousness. In 1926, Wadud was invited to lecture at a Hindu ashram in Rajshahi. He declared: 'It is not right to categorize humans into two groups, Hindu and Muslim'.[44] These two religious categories 'may be true according to Shastras, but not in the life that the Creator (*bidhata*) has given to them'. He also stated that if a religious distinction is made to supersede

the everyday way of life of Hindus and Muslims, and if their relationship is not categorized as 'close relative' based on 'normal human
self-identity then all efforts at achieving Muslim–Hindu unity would be
in vain'. In 1927, Wadud told a young Muslim audience in Faridpur:

Strengthened by an inspiration of love, stand up strongly in the bosom of the
modern age, and say—'My inheritance lies in the deeds of humans. If I deprive
myself of this claim of inheritance, I shall not only be a destitute, but the flow
of human history will be thwarted in me' . . . . You also say, young Bengali
Muslims, 'I am a human first, simply by my human birthright. I am a relative
of the humans, regardless of their birth in any specific country, age, jati and
religion'. After that, . . . 'I am a child of Bengal, Bangalee [Bengali], [and I
have] lifted my head under an open sky'. And say lastly, 'I am a Muslim'.[45]

Wadud's essay 'Bangali Mussalmaner Sahitya Samasya' (1927), also
claimed that Muslims are human first. His view of universal human
identity thus takes as the primary standard of value of anything its
ability to enhance the potential of human life. Implied by this grand
view was Wadud's judgement that Islam and the much vaunted Muslim
cultural ethos were of secondary importance, and often served to positively block the greater good, the universal potential of human life.

During the Civil Disobedience movement, Wadud also searched
for an understanding of nationalism in Bengali literature and wrote an
article, entitled, 'Bangla Sahitya Jatiyatar Adarsha' (1931) or 'Ideals of
Nationalism in Bengali Literature'. It analysed nationalist thought of
some eminent scholars of Bengali literature, namely, Bhudev Mukho-
padhyay, Swami Vivekananda, Keshab Chandra Sen, Sarat Chandra
Chattopadhyay, and Bankim Chandra. Wadud was a harsh critic of
Bhudev's rationalist Hindu identity. He acknowledged some concern
for *jatiya jiban*, or a 'national life', beginning in Bhudev's essays,
Samajik Prabandha (Social Essays) and *Paribarik Prabandha* (Domestic Essays), that sought a solution for Hindu–Muslim tension. Yet
Bhudev, feeling threatened by the Young Bengal attack upon Hinduism,
wanted to prove that 'Hinduism is the greatest religion in all ages of
history'.[46] Wadud did not object to Bhudev's 'self-esteem', but to the
purpose: that this self-esteem is not derived from habitual self-esteem
stemming from the ability to move freely and to gain strength in this
world. Rather, this self-esteem is generated for the purpose of a debate:
an ongoing effort to defeat a powerful opponent and safeguard a
religion. Therefore, for an energized national life in India and Bengal,
Wadud argued, perhaps nobody should be indebted to Bhudev.[47]

Wadud criticized Vivekananda on two counts. First, he objected to

Vivekananda's concept of 'benevolent hermitage', which, though it may have originated from a sense of patriotism, would downgrade human dignity, he believed. Secondly, he found Vivekananda's prescription for resolving Hindu–Muslim tension, as expressed in the statement, 'The character of Indian nationalism would be, Islam is the body and Veda is the brain' as weak and unworkable. He argued that it is probable that 'Islam is in the Vedanta and Vedanta is in Islam', yet that synthesis is only 'an accommodation of several old and conflicting religious ideals', and not a 'clearly defined resolution of human "welfare and misfortune" in today's practical world'.[48] Equally, Wadud found Bankim Chandra Chattarjee's ideal of Hindu revivalism 'narrow and harsh'. Bankim was unable to form a single ideal of nationalism suitable for all Indians because Bankim's talent, he argued, was not a talent 'rooted in the religion of creativity'.

Wadud was critical of Hindu revivalist nationalism because such nationalism did not fit with his conception of secular humanistic nationalism. That is why he never advised Muslims to refrain from reading Bankim's writings. On the contrary, to reconcile Bankim with Bengali Muslims and to stop the latter from branding Bankim as a communal Hindu, Wadud wrote apologetics of Bankim's writings designed to counter Muslims' demand for separation from Hindus because of Bankim's alleged anti-Muslim stance. Wadud interpreted Bankim's humanism from 1919 to 1931 in several essays which were not exclusively written on Bankim.[49] It was however the 'high noon' of Muslim separatism from Hindus in Bengal after the civil disobedience movement that inspired Wadud to write his major interpretations of Bankim's writing. He wrote five essays in this vein from 1931 until 1939.

The five essays defended Bankim's Hindu revivalism in several ways. First, Wadud reminded those 'rootless Muslims' of Bengal who feel pain today by Bankim's remarks that once upon a time Hindus also felt helplessness and shame because of Muslim conquests. By way of example, he wrote: 'By Sultan Mahmud's onslaughts, India's wealth was looted . . . . The Hindus, like dust, were blown away . . . . This uprooting of Hindus is the cause of anti-Muslim antipathy'.[50] Today, if the defeated *bharatbashi* (Indian) has begun a reaction under Bankim's leadership, it is not abnormal. However, he agreed that it is an offence for a 'genius' like Bankim to show an inordinate and exclusive concern for the brotherhood of Hindus. He, however, asked whether it really indicated that Bankim was not a humanist? His answer was:

'Bankim tried hard to glorify Hinduism, but the significant glorification that he actually achieved was glorification of truth and humanity alone; hence his claim to be reckoned as a man of genius . . .'.[51] He argued that even Bankim's love for Hindus is another example of strong attachment to kith and kin. He also asserted that in order to focus on the 'universals' a writer can be concerned with the 'particular' or concrete. In other words, Wadud recognized that an emphasis on the 'particular' (religion, language, time, and space) could also be a kind of creativity if it focused on the universality of 'love, truth and humanity'.

Wadud reinterpreted Bankim's controversial novel, *Anandamath*, arguing that a strong feeling of Hindu revivalism was not conspicuous in the novel. A Hindu resurgence was portrayed to the extent that Hindu rebels wanted to wreck a Muslim state. He however added: 'The Muslim state was already suffering in a decrepit condition' before the Hindu rebels wanted to wreck it. Wadud also pointed out that, despite the Hindu rebellion against Muslim rule, Bankim did not in the novel re-establish a 'Hindu Kingdom' in India. For that, Wadud wrote, Bankim pointed his finger to the distant future: 'The great possibility of the reinstallation of the Hindu power with the help of the English, who are skilled teachers in secular things'.[52]

Wadud also asked the question: 'What exactly is the "Hindu" or "Hindu way" that Bankim Chandra describes in the *Anandamath*?'[53] He directly quotes from *Anandamath*, suggesting that Bankim's definition of 'Hinduism' was not based on orthodox interpretation but on knowledge. Wadud argued that this definition places Bankim in opposition to many authorities on Hinduism. For example, he pointed out that Bankim's remark, 'ignorant cult', had been rejected by Ramakrisna Paramahansa as 'a betrayal of ignorance of matters of religion'.[54] Wadud also expressed doubts about Bankim's eagerness to understand 'religion [as] the submission of all human faculties toward the Isvar'.[55]

Wadud refuted the charge that Bankim distorted Muslim historical figures as 'mean characters'. He defined a mean character in literature as one 'who is wanting in vigour, misshapen and—when the character is not nourished by the emotion of its creator—fails to excite emotion of the reader'. In this sense, Bankim did not distort the Muslim character, Zebunnissa. Wadud wrote: 'In the eyes of connoisseurs, Zebunnissa towers head and shoulders above the big personalities and the battles and intrigues of Rajsingha. The author first presents her to his readers as a monstrosity who toys with love, but he goes on revealing with delicate care and curiosity the loving woman hidden in that monstrosity'. If communal Muslim intelligentsia disregard this human image, Bankim should not be blamed. Bankim presented the Hindu woman character, Shaibalini in Chandrashekhar as a 'sinful woman' and Hindu male character, Bhabananda in *Anandamath* as 'a vicious scoundrel'. From the perspective of literary execution, these three 'sinners' far outbalance in magnificence the 'goodies' Bankim draws in his novels. Wadud, therefore, concludes that Bankim was a humanist notwithstanding his concern for establishment of the Hindu kingdom and the Hindu way.[56]

Nationalism and Hindu–Muslim Conflict

During the early 1930s, Mahatma Gandhi was pursuing a policy to bring about Hindu–Muslim unity; the political slogans of 'satyagraha' and 'swaraj' proposed new forms of actions to challenge the legitimacy of British rule. These, it seemed to Gandhi, would bring about Hindu–Muslim unity through a shared political consciousness of Indian nationalism. The Salt satygraha defied British rule by producing salt illegally by boiling sea water. The campaign also included other types of satyagraha, '. . . . boycott of foreign cloth. . . , non-payment of certain taxes, contravention of forest laws, and disobedience to the Ordinances with which government attempted to control the movement'.[57] These tactics, however, failed to bring about Hindu–Muslim unity. The majority of Muslims kept aloof from the satyagraha and by the end of 1930, 'out of a total of 29,000 in prison, only 1,500 were Muslims'.[58]

Wadud became a critic of Gandhi's political nationalism by the 1930s. This shift from support of Gandhi's non-violence in 1920 to a critique of civil disobedience in 1930 was due to several factors. Tagore's influence on Wadud was one. Tagore had not supported Gandhi's Non-cooperation movement in 1920. After Turkey was declared a republic in 1923, Tagore characterized Gandhi's 'communal entente' as a 'fragile solution'. In a private correspondence, Tagore wrote that, apart from curing the disease of religious orthodoxy, he saw no alternative to solving the Hindu–Muslim problem, and Wadud endorsed this attitude.[59] Like Tagore, he was unwilling to accept Gandhi's 'fragile solution'.

Wadud's discomfort with the civil disobedience, and communal participation in it, was further evident in his correspondence with Abdul Kadir during the Civil Disobedience movement. When Gandhi launched the movement in 1930, Kadir saw an apparent parallel in the anti-British appeals by the Wahabi and Swadeshi movements. Wadud immediately cautioned Kadir. The Swadeshi leaders, he said, at least thought about the economic emancipation of Indians generally. On the contrary, the Wahabi movement was a purely Muslim religious movement, or at best an 'attempt of the defeated [Muslims] to stir themselves up'.[60] Kadir wrote in one editorial of the Bengali journal, *Jayati*: 'Without doubt we [Muslims] should stand side by side with Hindus. If we ignore this movement, there will be no welfare for Muslims [in the present] and there will be endless problems in the future'. In reply, Wadud told Kadir: 'We have said "Hindu" and "Muslim" too many times. Let us forget those symbols . . . . Freed from a symbol of "Muslim", we are born under an open sky . . . . It is better that we should delete terms like "Islam" and "Muslim" from our dictionary'.[61]

Wadud opposed Gandhi's programme at several levels. He complained that Gandhi's towering leadership had not produced any 'creativity' in India. Gandhi's leadership did not even sustain whatever 'creative power' had already existed in India before him. Apart from engendering jealousy and bitterness, Gandhi's non-violence is now meaningless for his disciples. Gandhi's movement for freedom and the rights of the untouchables has been interpreted by many Hindus and Muslims as manipulation by the Hindu establishment. Gandhi by and large had failed to understand and correct the underlying problem of communalism: 'Mahatma's leadership has raised very much the country's "political consciousnes", but not its "conscience". In human society, a person is dangerous whose consciousness has risen, but not his conscience'.[62]

Wadud's conscience in nationalism was not founded on anti-British political or social outcries: 'I respect Europe more than I respect ancient India and ancient Islam'. He, however, cautioned that this respect does not mean that: 'We have to surrender our *srishti shakti* [creativeness]. . . . We will adopt European things and ways, not because they are European, but because these are necessary for us'. Wadud also described another purpose of *srishti shakti*: 'To make the power of the state more effective'. At the same time, Wadud also wrote, 'We have to try to free ourselves from all intellectual destituteness'.[63] The two meanings of *srishti shakti* are not antagonistic, but complementary. For example, Wadud wrote that peoples' minds should be built first and then the *raj shakti* would take initiative. In other words, for any new endeavours, individuals would first take the initiative and then the *raj shakti* would function in relation to individual initiatives. For this, Wadud by the 1930s supported continuing British rule in India because he expected that British rule would help minimize the religious barriers and end communal identity.

Furthermore, Wadud objected to Gandhi's Civil Disobedience movement on another account. He thought it to be 'a dangerously extreme measure' (English phrase is Wadud's) because 'it has shaken respect for law, which is a very basic norm of a civilized society'. He rebutted those who say 'extreme measures should be taken in an extreme situation'. His reply was that extreme measures may or may not lead to a positive impact: 'After flood water subsides, the ground could be either fertile or there could remain a big concentration of contaminated water in the soil'. This supportive attitude towards British rule does not indicate, however, that Wadud was opposed to the eventual political freedom of India: 'We do not oppose a separate nation state for India. The real question is which course we should follow'.[64]

Wadud narrowed down solutions to Hindu–Muslim conflict in modern times to the viewpoints of two Bengali spokesmen: Ramakrishna Paramahansa and Rabindranath Tagore. Regarding Ramakrishna's dictum, 'As many views, so many paths', Wadud argued that 'the phrase has a tendency toward new creativity, but there is more in it of worship of ancient *shastras* and society'.[65] Tagore's unifying viewpoint has two aspects. On the one hand, it can be categorized as, 'As many views, so many paths', which respects human diversity. On the other, 'he also believed in *srishti dharma* that sees humans not as divided into groups by country or class, but members of an interrelated society in which the humans' only truth is the highest development in social life'. Wadud frankly admitted that his ideal, *srishti dharma*, or 'religion of creativity', was inspired by Tagore's Hibbert Lectures, 'The Religion of Man', at Manchester College in Oxford (May 1930). In those lectures, Tagore did not use the Bengali phrase, *srishti dharma*, or its English equivalent 'religion of creativity'. The nearest expression to *srishti dharma* that Tagore used in the Hibbert Lectures was 'The Creative Spirit'. One difference in approach was that Tagore defined creative spirit in the Hibbert Lectures in metaphors but did not directly criticize Hinduism or Islam. On the contrary, Wadud, though he drew inspiration from Tagore's creative spirit and appears to have coined the term *srishti dharma* in response to that idea, used *srishti dharma* as an ideal on the basis of which he criticized historical religious systems, especially his own Islamic system.[66]

Wadud saw *srishti dharma* as the only real solution for Hindu–Muslim conflict. He declared: 'Unless a movement of *srishti dharma* begins in our thought, the sorrows of Muslim–Hindu conflict, as we understand them, will not be driven from our country. This is our solution'. He creatively defined *srishti dharma* as:

the boundless curiosity of humans toward knowledge and enterprise . . . . Age after age, it was by *srishti dharma*'s inspiration that humans had dreamt of new possibilities of human life and sacrificed their lives for celebrating all new efforts. This does not indicate that *srishti dharma* changed humans suddenly and completely into something marvellous. Humans would only change slowly in their new profundity of understanding . . . . *srishti dharma*, also, does not reject humans' relation with surrounding living beings with whom they have entered into intimacy. Rather, by fully recognizing this intimacy, *srishti dharma* creates new potentiality of human life and this process has been continuing steadily. This ability of the humans to bloom into new life along with their surroundings is not only a wonder, but it is inevitable—as oxygen is fundamental for the burning and reconstitution of the cells of a human body.[67]

Wadud's *srishti dharma* was intended to challenge blind faith in religious, including Islamic, ideologies. 'It is possible to escape from this difficulty if we do not think of religion as a matter of rules but as a matter of discovery. Then religious books and great men—like the thinkers of the word and works—would be the objects of trust/respect by mankind; but not the objects of worship and ritual'. *Srishti dharma*, therefore, is not antagonistic to Hindu–Muslim unity on the basis of religion; but it must be religion as new creation (*srishti*); not as restating (*punar-gathita*) religious rules. Religions could be used for a unity, but only by an application of "unforced knowledge and intellect" to religious rules. Wadud applied this understanding of religion to Islam in a debate on 'Hindu–Muslim conflict' with a Bengali Islamic liberal apologist. Wadud wrote to the apologist that to Muslims the Quran is the message of Allah and Prophet Mohammad is merely the carrier of that message. This thought may have two implications. One is essentially that of 'Quran puja', or blindly and literally following the Quran, which is bound to be excessive, like blind puja to the *pir*s. The other implication could be in terms of uncoerced knowledge or reasoning. For example, the Quran as the message of Allah, means knowledge. Knowledge indicates the varieties of knowledge. 'Therefore it is desirable for humans to search for knowledge of various sorts, from the Quran or, if necessary, to reject the Quran'.[68]

Wadud's *srishti dharma* demanded a redefinition of Indian culture'. He criticized Indian culture as the fragile and emotional thinking of those cultural nationalists who recognize only the 'Indianness' of their culture. The cultural nationalists pay no respect to the innate creativity of humans as humans. They also cannot clearly answer: 'What is really meant by Indian culture?—Buddhist, Vedic, Puranic, Mughal, or British? If it means a synthesis of all these, in which ways and what areas would there be a synthesis? And why should there be a synthesis?' Therefore, in Wadud's redefined sense of culture it is neither essential nor possible that *bharatiya samskriti* or Indian culture (what to speak of Hindu or Muslim culture) would be the only meaning of *samskriti*, or culture, in India. Conversely, Wadud stated, 'It is inevitable and essential today not only to be acquainted with the world but also be one who is blended into this world'. This meaning of 'universality' of culture, Wadud expressed in various Bengali phrases, for example: *vishva-manab* (universal human), *vishva-kristi* (universal culture), *antarjatikbad* (internationalism), or *paribestaner sange nibir jog* (one's intimacy with the surroundings).

Finally, to implement the ideals of *srishti dharma*, Wadud was looking for a new political and intellectual leadership in India. Wadud wrote that the qualities of the new leadership would be to 'respect traditions', but not as their worshipper (pujari). Their expectations would not be the unity of 'ancient Hindus and Muslims', because that would be an untruth and an impossibility. Instead, the expectation should be to build a 'new nation' of humans in India. The new leadership should never recognize a nation divided by religion, because that would result in an anathema, the 'division by *jati*'. It is not division by *jati*, or communal and cultural division, that should be the goal of new leadership. Rather, the new leadership should work tirelessly to infuse *srishti dharma* into political and intellectual life.

Conclusion

Kazi Wadud's *srishti dharma* was a new thesis for the Bengali Muslim intelligentsia, of adopting a secular humanist approach to Islam, communalism, and nationalism in India. *Srishti dharma* was new because it contradicted both the separatist Muslim nationalists' and the Indian nationalist Muslims' views of British rule and Muslims' relationship with the Hindus. The fundamental objective of the Muslim nationalist and separatist movements was to eject British rule from India, because British rule was considered basically incompatible with Islam. The pro-British attitude of such rational humanist Muslims as Wadud was quite different. Wadud wanted the British to stay in India because he did not hold them responsible for Hindu–Muslim conflict. Moreover, he understood nationalism not primarily in terms of gaining immediate political freedom, but in terms of social freedom, or freedom of thought of people away from the shackles of religio–communal bigotry. They saw continuing British rule and Western influence as supporting such social freedom and 'freedom of intellect'.

Unlike the composite nationalists, Kazi Wadud did not argue for a fragile 'cooperation' with Hindus. *Srishti dharma* demanded a more fundamental and permanent relationship based on Muslim 'accommodation with Hindus'. This would be accomplished through *srishti dharma*, not through an apologia featuring what in current circumstances would be good for the Islamic religion. Instead, *srishti dharma* urged Muslim accommodation and solidarity with Hindus which would come about through lessened emphasis on religious rules and a rejection of Muslims 'obsession' or 'infatuation' with Islam.

A year before the independence of India in August 1947, Wadud was frustrated as he watched communal agitation gathering momentum for the division of India and Pakistan. Publicly he did not make a last bid to reassert his outspoken advocacy of *srishti dharma* in favour of Muslim accommodation with Hindus. He felt that in the charged environment of communalism it was fruitless to appeal to Muslims for oneness with Hindus: 'By heart and soul Muslim separatists are now coming to a climax. They have never united with Hindus and they will not be united in the future'.[70] Wadud condemned the separatist Muslim leaders, who were proposing an 'Islamic foundation' of the new Muslim state. He condemned some of the Muslim separatist leaders as 'Nazis and Bolsheviks'. He even demanded of the Muslim leadership who insisted on a communal state of Pakistan that they 'must go to the North-west of India and form an independent religious kingdom'; one to which Bengal would not be a party. Wadud flatly declared that 'Bengali Muslims' geographical and cultural union with Punjabi Muslims is impossible'.[71]

Notes and References

1. For details, *see* Shahadat H. Khan, 'The Freedom of Intellect Movement' ('Buddhir Mukti Andolon') in 'Bengali Muslim Thought, 1926–1938', Ph.D. dissertation, University of Toronto, 1997, 128–92 .
2. Ibid., 52–127

3. Kazi Abdul Wadud, 'Samskritir Katha', in *Kazi Abdul Wadud Racanabali*, vol. 1, ed. Abdul Huq (henceforth *Racanabali*, 1) (Dhaka: Bangla Academy, I988), 578.
4. Wadud, 'Abhibhashan', in *Bulbul* (periodical), vol. 4, no. 7, 1937, 578.
5. Rizwan Malik, 'Mawlana Hussain Ahmad Madani and Jami'yat-Ulama-i-Hind, 1920–1957: Status of Islam and Muslims in India', Ph.D. dissertaton, University of Toronto, 1995, 76.
6. Wadud, 'Non-cooperation ba Asahajogita', in *Racanabali 1*, 568.
7. Ibid., 561.
8. Ibid., 560.
9. Ibid., 559.
10. Ibid., 560.
11. Ibid., 571.
12. Ibid., 583.
13. Ibid., 577.
14. Ibid., 578.
15. Ibid., 606–14.
16. Aziz Ahmad, *Islamic Modernism in India and Pakistan*, 1857–1964 (London: Oxford University Press, 1967), 192.
17. Wadud, 'Non-Cooperation ba Asahajogita', in *Racanabali 1*, 613.
18. Ibid., 614.
19. *See*, for example, Rizwan Malik, op. cit., 85–6; Mushir-ul Haq, *Muslim Politics in Modern India* (Meerut: Meenakshi Prakashan, 1970), 118; and Yohanan Friedmann, 'The Attitude of the Jami'yat-i-Ulama-i Hind towards Indian Nationalism', in *Journal of Asian and African Studies*, vol. VII (1977), 164.
20. Wadud, 'Nana Katha', in *Kazi Abdul Wadud Racanabali*, vol. 2, edited by Abdul Huq (henceforth *Racanabali* 2) (Dhaka: Bangla Academy, 1989), 298–9.
21. Wadud, 'Nana Katha', in *Racanabali 2*, 299.
22. Ibid., 302.
23. Ibid., 301.
24. Wadud, 'Fateha-i-Doyajdaham', in Kazi Abdul Wadud, *Naba Parjay*, vol. 2 (Dhaka: Syed Imamul Hosain, 1929), 43.
25. Wadud, 'Manab Mukut', in *Naba Parjay 1*, 33.
26. Ibid., 34.
27. Wadud, 'Sahitya Samasya', *Naba Parjay 1*, 16.
28. Ibid., 16–17.
29. Wadud, 'Bad Pratibad', in Wadud, ed., *Shashvata Banga* (Calcutta: Kazi Khurshid Bakht, 1951), 404.
30. Ibid.
31. Ibid., 405.
32. Wadud's letter to the editor of *Masik Mohammadi*. *See* Wadud, 'Amader Katha', in *Jayati*, vol. 1, no. 5 (1930), 158–60.

33. Wadud, 'Hindu-Mussalmaner Birodh', in *Racanabali 1*, 323.
34. Ibid., 322. Some scholars reject this argument. Fazlur Rahman, for example, writes: 'Ibn Taymiya has an important and interesting passage which clearly shows that contrary to the opinions generally held, he was not only not inimical to Sufism as such but considered it as necessary a part of religion as law'. Fazlur Rahman, *Islam* (Chicago: University of Chicago Press, 1979), 112.
35. Wadud, 'Hindu–Mussalmaner Birodh', in *Racanabali 1*, 323. For a comprehensive study of the impact of Wahabi movement in rural Bengal, see Rafiuddin Ahmed, 'Fundamentalist Reform and Rural Response', in *The Bengal Muslims 1871–1906: A Quest for Identity* (Delhi: Oxford University Press, 1981), 39–71.
36. Wadud, 'Hindu–Mussalmaner Birodh', in *Racanabali 1*, 322, 329.
37. Wadud, 'Our Nineteenth Century Renaissance', in Wadud, *Creative Bengal* (Calcutta: Thacker & Co., 1949), 75.
38. Ibid., 77.
39. Ibid., 78.
40. Wadud, 'Nirbacan Prasanga'; Wadud to Abdul Kadir. See *Jayati*, vol. 1, nos. 11–12 (1931), 281–2.
41. Ibid., 284.
42. Ibid., 282.
43. Ibid., 282, 283.
44. Wadud, 'Milaner Katha', in *Naba Parjay* 1, 12.
45. Wadud, 'Abhibhashan', in *Naba Parjay* 2, 35.
46. Wadud, 'Banla Sahitye Jatiyatar Adarsha', in Wadud (ed.), *Samaj o Sahitya* (Calcutta: Moslem Publishing House, 1934), 51.
47. Ibid., 53.
48. Ibid., 58.
49. Wadud, 'Mussalman Sahityik', in *Prabasi*, May–June, 1919; rpt. in *Racanabali 1*, 527–34.
50. Wadud, 'Bankim Chandra', in *Ajker Katha* (Calcutta: General Printers, 1941). In a separate article, Wadud wrote of Sultan Mahmud's attacks on Hindu temples in India. See Wadud, 'Ekti Aitihasik Coritra', in *Ajker Katha*, 116–19.
51. Wadud, 'Bankim Chandra', in Wadud, *Creative Bengal*, 92.
52. Ibid., 92.
53. Ibid.
54. Ibid., 93.
55. Wadud, 'Bankim Pratibha', in Wadud, *Samaj o Sahitya*, 164.
56. Wadud, 'Bankim Chandra', in Wadud, *Creative Bengal*, 94–5.
57. Judith M. Brown, *Modern India: The Origins of an Asian Democracy* (Delhi: Oxford University Press, 1988), 267.
58. Ibid., 270.

59. Wadud, 'Ekkhani Patra', in *Jayati*, vol. 1, no. 4 (1930), 141; *see Racanabali 1*, 149–53.
60. Ibid., 77.
61. Ibid.
62. Ibid., 141.
63. Wadud, 'Jnan o Prem', in Wadud, *Samaj o Sahitya*, op. cit., 83.
64. Wadud, 'Ekkhani Patra', in *Jayati*, vol. 1, no. 4 (1930), 78.
65. Wadud, 'Hindu–Mussalmaner Birodh', in *Racanabali 1*, 345.
66. *See* Rabindranath Tagore, *The Religion of Man* (New Delhi: Harper-Collins, 1993 (rpt.); Rabindranath Tagore, *Manusher Dharma* (Calcutta: Visvabharati, 1972 (rpt.).
67. Wadud, 'Hindu–Mussalmaner Birodh', in *Racanabali 1*, 345.
68. Wadud, 'Hindu–Muslim', Wadud to Mohammad Wajed Ali, *Bulbul*, vol. IV, no. 1, 7 Feb. 1937, 59.
69. Wadud, 'Hindu–Mussalmaner Birodh', in *Racanabali 1*, 349.
70. 'Griha Yuddher Prakkale' (1946), in *Racanabali 1*, 349.
71. Ibid., 494.

8

The Bengali Muslims and the State: Secularism or Humanity for Bangladesh?*

JOSEPH T. O'CONNELL

Background: Dilemmas of Secularism in Bangladesh

The core of this essay goes back to a paper on the dilemmas of secularism in Bangladesh, written early in 1975 (O'Connell, 1976), the final year of rule by Sheikh Mujibur Rahman, when secularism was still one of the four pillars of the 1972 Constitution of Bangladesh. There are two principal justifications for returning to that paper, condensed, revised, and reframed after reflections on pertinent developments during the more than two decades of Bangladesh history that have elapsed since then. One is the persisting salience of the underlying dilemmas that advocacy of secularism was an attempt, albeit short-lived and probably counter-productive, to resolve. The other is the return to power, after over twenty years in opposition, of an Awami League government in Bangladesh. While the current Awami League regime may share many of the ideals and goals of the late Mujibur Rahman's government, the historical contexts are markedly different, and suitable means to effect redefined goals will have changed as well. A reconsideration of the erstwhile much touted and much berated secularism, and of the related dilemmas entailed in restraining Muslim communalism while motivating public commitment to national goals, may still to be worthwhile. Later in the essay, it is suggested, though not argued at length, that a more promising ideal or principle than secularism for Bangladesh would have been (or might yet be) humanity or humanism. Accentuating humanity (or humanism), which may be defined both generically and in particularized variants (e.g. Muslim, Hindu, Christian, Buddhist, rational, secular conceptions of humanity or humanism), might stimulate commitment to constructive national goals, while avoiding the backlash triggered by secularism. Also, the ideal of humanity, when articulated through the idiom and values of a particular religious tradition, might serve as a principle of critique from within that religious community and discredit those who might try to interpret the religion in anti-human ways.

Sympathetic though I was to some of the basic concerns and aspirations behind the advocacy of secularism in the early 1970s, I doubted that it would have the widespread appeal needed to motivate Bangladeshis to support much required development objectives. I was also anxious lest emphasizing secularism might inhibit alternative sources of motivation, especially those stemming from the more humane and tolerant strains of indigenous Bengali Muslim self-consciousness, and instead occasion a backlash of an intolerant communal kind. It was not my intention then, nor is it now, to declare that advocacy of secularism was simply a mistake; wrong for Bangladesh. Rather, I saw the founders of Bangladesh as caught on the horns of a genuine dilemma. To advocate secularism (and enforce policies implied by that term) might well alienate the greater part of the Bangladesh population who are at least nominally religious (the vast majority of these being Muslims), but not to advocate secularism, or some tolerant humane ideal akin to it (and not to enforce the implied policies), might well open up public affairs to a resurgence of intolerant communally focused politics.

Undoubtedly there were then and remain now in Bangladesh many individuals, including some of the most creative in literary, intellectual and professional fields, who are profoundly dedicated to the progressive humanistic ideals clustered around the rather abstract term, secularism. For them, secularism is not merely a political or constitutional category, but a symbol of their highest aspirations; a verbal expression of their faith, if you will, in secular humanism (in its varying shades). They have had their share of martyrs to that faith, including those murdered on the eve of Bangladesh independence. They no doubt sensed that their own lives and well-being would be at risk should the kind of Bangladesh envisioned by the original four pillars (nationalism, socialism, democracy, secularism) not come to pass. Accordingly, in the first year or two of independent Bangladesh, in a political climate especially conducive to their vision of a secular, democratic, and socialist nation of Bengalis, many strove enthusiastically to define and project that vision.

However, those who enthusiastically shared secularism as an ideal were not all that numerous, nor were their political grass-roots all that deep, notwithstanding the official endorsement by the Awami League, the constitutional provisions, and the personal support of Sheikh Mujibur Rahman. However, by the end of his tenure as president of Bangladesh (and of his life), Mujib himself was speaking in a more Muslim idiom and acting in ways much more ingratiating to Muslim sentiments, but by that time Mujib's' secularism and alleged subservience to India (with which country secularism was especially associated) had become vulnerable points of attack by his opponents.

When Ziaur Rahman took power, as is well known, he moved quickly to remove secularism from the Constitution of Bangladesh as a pillar of the state and replaced it with an affirmation that Bangladesh is based on absolute faith in the almighty Allah and Islam. Bangladesh was formally declared to be a Muslim state with Islam as the official religion. However, the civil rights of non-Muslims were not curtailed nor was sharia installed in place of modern civil and criminal law. Successor governments up to and including the present Awami League regime (headed by Sheikh Husina Wajid, Mujib's daughter) have retained these changes.[2]

One of the key constitutional implications of Mujib-era secularism had been to outlaw any use of religio–communal issues for political purposes. The Muslim League and the Jamaat-i-Islami were thereby excluded from formal electoral politics (though they continued to function in para-political and clandestine ways) until Ziaur Rahman did away with secularism. However, in its zeal to forestall the fundamentalist-intimidation of the Jamaat-i-Islami and the communalist politics of the Muslim League, the first Awami League government and its supporters effectively banned a wide range of political and semi-political public activities by Muslim groups which need not have constituted fundamentalist/communalist intolerance. Moreover, the way that secularism was projected by some advocates (and caricatured by its opponents) seemed to imply the stigmatization, and exclusion from the arduous tasks of-nation-building and social development, of Muslim ideals and values *en bloc*.[3]

Ironically, one of the factors that may have defused further communalization of politics was the rapidity with which secularism ceased to be a pillar of the state once the Awami League ceased to be the responsible governing party. Whatever has gone wrong, or failed to go as right as might have been hoped, in Bangladesh public life for the past two decades cannot be laid at the doorstep of Mujib, the Awami League, and secularism, but of the series of martial law administrators and the parties they constructed or coopted on the way to quasi-civilian and civilian rule. By the same token, the re-emergence of the Awami League after twenty years of exclusion from goverment suggests the continuing rootedness of some of its core values, though not necessarily of its previous outspoken advocacy of secularism.

The fundamental dilemma involving Islam and secularism in Bangladesh remains how to tap into the positive motivational force of Islam without opening the floodgates to a rising tide of Muslim fundamentalism and communalism; and conversely, how to discourage or contain such fundamentalism and communalism without offending Muslim sensibilities generally. Interestingly, the successor regimes (military, quasi-civilian, and civilian) hostile to the Awami League may to a certain extent have succeeded in resolving (or blunting) this dilemma where the Awami League failed. They removed the offensive term secularism from the constituton and declared Islam to be the state religion, but they did not impose sharia or restrict the civil rights of non-Muslims. They allowed explicitly Muslim parties to participate in electoral politics (and courted their support, when needed) but did not define their own parties in an explicitly religio–communal mould. They ingratiated Bangladesh with supportive oil-rich Muslim countries by fostering public and private Islamic activities, but managed not to alienate Western (governmental and NGO) support or provoke India by blatant harassment of non-Muslims. While there has been much official and unofficial encouragement of Muslim religious and socio–cultural life in Bangladesh, there has been no attempt to reduce the status of Bengali language and literature. The national poet is indeed a Muslim, but the most non-communalist of Muslims, Qazi Nazrul Islam; and the national anthem continues to be 'Amar Sonar Bangla', composed by Rabindranath Tagore, a humanist among Hindus.

Indeed, even the current Awami League regime, led by Sheikh Husina Wajid, thus far has maintained much the same balance of Islamic and non-communal (secular, if you wish) policies as imposed by the preceding post-Mujib regimes. At one point, it even made common cause, for electoral purposes, with the Jamaat-i-Islami. How much this continuity is due to conviction (Sheikh Husina Wajid is personally reputed to observe various Muslim customs), constitutional restraints (lack of the two-thirds majority in the legislative assembly necessary to amend the constitution) or political judgment (that the current balance of Muslim and non-communal [secular] factors is prudent for Bangladeshi electoral politics) I do not know, but I suspect that all three factors are operative.

Secularism of the Awami League Regime of Mujibur Rahman

A. Basic dilemmas behind Bangladeshi secularism

The People's Republic of Bangladesh, by its fourth year since liberation (16 December 1971), faced a formidable array of problems.[4] One of the most basic was the need to forge an effective sense of national identity and national purpose. To some extent, a sense of identity and purpose did exist, but it seemed doubtful that in its then current form and degree of intensity it would prove sufficient to maintain cohesion and stimulate developmental change. As a historian of religion by training, I viewed this problem as a religious one, using religion in a broad functional sense, e.g. as in Paul Tillich's oft quoted expression, 'what concerns one ultimately', or as 'one's way of valuing most intensively and comprehensively'.[5] Alternatively, one could speak of an existential problem or of a problem of value commitment. Commitment to the defence or consolidation of one's nation and to supporting or resisting socio–economic change, if done wholeheartedly, is bound to involve one's 'ultimate concerns'; what a person 'values most intensively and comprehensively'. If one happens to be a faithful Muslim (as most citizens of Bangladesh claim to be) or Hindu, Christian, or Buddhist, then one's traditional religious faith must impinge in some way upon one's public societal commitments. In a similar way, the ultimate concerns and most intensive and extensive values of an agnostic or atheistic individual must influence that person's public societal commitments. If serious conflicts develop between one's ultimate concerns (most intensive and extensive values) and how one is asked to commit oneself to public societal tasks, then a person will be confused and inhibited in responding and may even offer positive resistance. If vast numbers of citizens experience such a predicament, then the morale of a nation and confidence in its leadership can be undermined. By discussing the 'dilemmas of secularism' in Bangladesh, I attempted to examine a problem of this sort insofar as it affected the Muslims of Bangladesh, who then numbered upwards of sixty (now over eighty) million and constituted over eighty-five per cent of the nation's population.

B. Secularism in the 1972 Bangladesh Constitution: The fourth principle of state policy

The official pattern of national identity and purpose of Bangladesh, as given in the Preamble to the Constitution passed by the Constituent Assembly on 4 November 1972, reads:

Pledging that the high ideals of nationalism, socialism, democracy and secularism, which inspired our heroic people to dedicate themselves to, and our brave martyrs to sacrifice their lives in, the national liberation struggle, shall be the fundamental principles of the Constitution;[6]

The promulgation of a constitution less than a year after liberation was a considerable achievement, which I do not mean to belittle when I point to the dilemmas and difficulties that cluster around the fourth of the high ideals, more popularly called pillars of state policy, namely, secularism. To begin with, the word secularism is ambiguous enough in English. In some contexts it suggests ideological commitment (often hostile to traditional religion, but sometimes less so or not hostile at all); in other contexts it merely analyses or describes processes such as urbanization. For some persons, secularism is a highly charged symbol of progress and liberation; for some it carries an equal but opposite symbolic charge reeking of blasphemy and irreligion. Others, myself included, use secularism and secular as evaluatively neutral terms useful for descriptive and analytic terms. Indeed, the related word secularization as spelt out in Donald E. Smith's[7] perceptive analysis, may take at least four different forms (or degrees).

Interesting, the equivalent expression in Bengali for what appears in the Bangladesh Constitution of 1972 as secularism is said to be *dharma-nirapeksata*, which one would expect to see translated as 'neutrality in religion', or 'religious tolerance', not as 'secularism'. Were it certain that the Bengali expression *dharma-nirapeksata* and the semantic and conceptual meaning it carries were to dominate legal, judicial, and rhetorical interpretation of the fourth pillar, then some of the ambiguity and controversy engendered by the word secularism might evaporate.[8] As it is the English secularism rather than the Bengali *dharma-nirapeksata* that has borne the brunt of controversy, it is secularism that is assessed in this essay. A further elaboration of secularism is given in the 1972 Constitution's explanations of the four principles of state policy:

9. The unity and solidarity of the Bangalee nation, which, deriving its identity from its language and culture, attained sovereign and independent Bangladesh

through a united and determined struggle in the war of independence, shall be the basis of Bangalee nationalisrn.

10. A socialist economic system shall be established with a view to ensuring the attainment of a just and egalitarian society, free from the exploitation of man by man.

11. The Republic shall be a democracy in which fundamental human rights and freedoms and respect for the dignity and worth of the human person shall be guaranteed and in which effective participation by the people through their elected representatives in administration at all levels shall be assured.

12. The principle of secularism shall be realized by the elimination of—
   (a) communalism in all its forms;
   (b) the granting of the State of political status in favour of any religion;
   (c) the abuse of religion for political purposes;
   (d) any discrimination against, or persecution of, persons practising a particular religion.

The Constitution does not define secularism/*dharma-nirapeksata* directly. Rather, it lists the abuses, the elimination of which will realize secularism. The first abuse, communalism, goes altogether undefined.[9] It is clearly a pejorative term, however, reflecting the bad experience of communal politics associated with the Pakistani period. Another article of the 1972 Constitution enlarges upon the prohibition of 'the abuse of religion for political purposes'. It states:

38. Every citizen shall have the right to form associations or unions, subject to any reasonable restrictions imposed by law in the interests of morality or public order: Provided that no person shall have the right to form, or be a member of, any communal or other association or union which in the name of or on the basis of any religion has for its object, or pursues, a political purpose.[10]

This provision had major political implications as it would exclude from lawful politics such communalist–fundamentalist parties as the Muslim League and the Jamaat-i-Islami (as well as any explicitly Hindu, Christian, or Buddhist political party). Did it, or could it, prohibit lobbying or public opinion formation on political matters by communal groups as well? This provision attempts a more rigorous curtailment of religio–communal political activity than, for instance, anything in the Indian Constitution. In view of the traditional tendency of Muslims to view political and social affairs as religiously significant, as areas in which the divine injunction to establish a good and just society is operative, the prohibition of all religio–political activity by

Muslims (and others), if that is how the 1972 Constitution was to be interpreted, was a bold move.[11]

C. Secularism in the First Five-Year Plan

The First Five-Year Plan, 1973–78 (Part I, Chap. l, pars. 1.3–1.4) has this to say about secularism:[12]

1.3. Secularism:
True to our secular belief, we stand committed to disband all communal forces from the body politic. The War of Liberation against the colonial oppressors which we waged as one man demonstrated that Bangladesh is able to rise above religious bigotry and differences of caste and creed. Even though decades of obscurantism and religious fanaticism cannot be obliterated in one day, such bigotry will not be able to thrive on the soil of Bangladesh if communalism ceases to be a political weapon. Our struggle for emancipation has highlighted our homogeneity and our struggle against poverty will only strengthen it.

1.4. Socialism:
However the ideal of socialism cannot be translated into reality as easily or as quickly as the other three principles of State policy. In Bangladesh today it remains a vision and a dream .

This statement of the Planning Commission is noteworthy for its own religious (in the functional/descriptive sense defined above) tone and dynamic resolve: 'True to our secular belief, we stand committed . . . to disband all communal forces . . .'. There is more here than mere separation of religion and politics; more than guarantees of human and civil rights. There is a pledge not only to exclude communal forces from politics or to contain them, but to positively do away with them. While paragraph 1.3 concedes that this 'carmot be done in a day', paragraph 1.4 sanguinely opines that it can be done relatively 'easily and quickly'. This however depends upon a big 'if'. 'If communalism ceases to be a political weapon', then 'bigotry will not be able to thrive'. There is no further discussion of how this can be accomplished, but presumably the constitutional prohibition of communal politics was to be the crucial factor.

D. Sheikh Mujib on Secularism

A third, and more cautious, view of the meaning of Bangladeshi secularism was provided by Awami League leader (later prime minister and president) Bangabandhu Sheikh Mujibur Rahman. As he insisted that the Constitution of 1972 was a faithful implementation of the proposals contained in the Manifesto of the Awami League prepared for the election of 1970, we may first consider what the Manifesto says about Islam and the minorities.

Islam. The favoured religion of the vast majority of the population is Islam. On this matter the Awami League has decided that there will be in the Constitution very clear guarantees that no law will be formulated or enforced in Pakistan contrary to the laws of Islam well established in the Holy Qur'an and the Sunnah. There will be guarantees firmly established in the Constitution for preserving the purity of the numerous religious institutions. Adequate arrangements will be made for extending religious instruction at all levels.

Minority. The minorities will enjoy full equal rights in the eyes of the law and will receive equal protection of the law. They will enjoy rights as citizens. The rights of the minorities in the matter of preserving and preaching their own religion, in establishing and operating religious institutions, and in giving religious instructions to the adherents of their respective religions will be protected by the Constitution. No individual of a minority community will be required to pay taxes for the preaching of any religion but his own. No individual will be forced to accept any religious regulations nor be required to participate in any religious worship or programme not connected with his own religion.[13]

The 1972 Constitution of Bangladesh seems to assure the various rights and protections promised minorities, and likewise the majority (Muslims), on a single standard. However, there is no explicit guarantee in the Constitution that would exclude legislation contrary to the law of Islam as established in the Qur'an and the Sunnah, although the pledge to do so was expressly given by the Sheikh in at least one of his pre-election speeches.[14] Explicit references to the Qur'an and Sunnah are, however, rare in the incomplete collection of the Sheikh's pre-election speeches to which I had access. The Sheikh was more apt to observe that in a country with eighty-five per cent of its population Muslim it is unreasonable, or an evidence of poor faith, to suppose that anything repugnant to the teachings of Islam could be enacted. What he would consider repugnant to Islam he does not elaborate beyond very general ethical ideals. For example,

The slanderous rumour is being circulated against us that we are not believers in Islam. In reply to this assertion our statement is very clear. We are not believers in the Islam that is simply a label. We believe in the Islam of justice. Our Islam is the Islam of the holy and merciful prophet, which Islam has taught the inhabitants of the world the unfailing teaching of right and justice.[15]

On the whole, the pre-election speeches of Sheikh Mujibur Rahman contain relatively few references to Islam. There are a number of brief appeals to God and there is the occasional, somewhat exasperated, assertion that he and his followers are at least as good Muslims as those hypocrites who slander them. The guarantees to Muslims and to minorities occur occasionally, though the expression *dharma-nirapek-sata* (religious neutrality, tolerance) does not seem to appear, nor the English word secularism, though some other English words creep in. The speeches available to me concentrated, for the most part, on pragmatic political and economic issues.[16]

It was after independence that, as prime minister, Sheikh Mujibur Rahman began making reference to the four pillars of the state. It would seem from the sampling of his speeches that I have seen that only then did he speak more fully, though still not a great deal, about secularism, religion, and communalism. On 7 June 1972, he said,

Secularism does not mean the absence of religion. You are a Mussalman, you perform your religious rites. The Hindus, the Christians, the Buddhists all will freely perform their religious rites. There is no irreligiousness on the soil of Bangladesh but there is secularism. This sentence has a meaning and that meaning is that none would be allowed to exploit the people in the name of religion, or to create such fascist organizations as the Al-Badr, Razakars, etc. No communal politics will be allowed in the country. Have you understood my four pillars?[17]

Another speech in which the prime minister made extended reference to religion and secularism was delivered to the Awami League in January 1974.[18] In it he remarks that 'the people of my Bangladesh are religious and God-fearing. They can be misled more easily in the name of religion than by any other means'. It is likely that this practical insight, based upon bitter experience, underlay Mujibur Rahman's espousal of secularism/*dharma-nirapeksata*, rather than any ideological commitment or philosophical rationale. The same speech is noteworthy also for its warning that communalism was on the rise again (as early as January 1974) in rural Bangladesh.

One who loves man can never be a communalist. Those of you who are Muslims must remember that Allah is Rabbul Alamin (Lord of all Mankind) and not Rabbul Muslimin (Lord of all the Mussalmans). All men are equal in His eyes, be he a Hindu, a Christian, a Muslim, a Buddhist. That is why those who spread the virus of communalism while talking of socialism and progress are wrong. Socialism and progress cannot coexist with communalism. They are poles apart. Beware of those who want to sow the seeds of communalism in the soil of Bangladesh. You workers of the Awami League, you have never countenanced communalism, you have all your life fought against it. My injunction to you is that as long as you live, see to it that communalism does not take root in the soil of Bangladesh. You should be clear in your minds as to your aims, namely, Nationalism, Democracy, Socialism and Secularism. If you are to build up a socialist economy, you must become a fully trained socialist cadre. Only then will you be successful. Of course, there are many people who want to defeat the aims of a socialist economy, because they cannot accept socialism. They are adopting indirect methods to oppose it. You have to oppose all those who in the name of progress are spreading communalism. You have to organize people from village to village and carry out a campaign among them to explain your aims.[19]

The warning about resurgent communalism was but one of numerous signs that Muslim assertiveness in public life was on the rise again in Bangladesh after the debacle of 1971. Other signs included the spectre of 'Muslim Bangla', an opposition slogan roundly denounced by the Awami League in the election of 1973. There were also Mujibur Rahman's pledges of solidarity with his Arab brethren, his expressions of pride in prohibition of alcohol, in increased numbers of pilgrims to Mecca, and in other tokens of Muslim piety. There was official and popular eagerness to participate in the summit meeting of Muslim states in Pakistan and to resume good relations with Pakistan, epitomized by the warm greeting given Zulfiqar Ali Bhutto when he visited Bangladesh. Conversely, there were reports of outspoken anti-Indian and implicitly anti-Hindu sentiments being voiced at Muslim gatherings; and an editor was arrested (amid public indignation at his effrontery) for printing a piece satirizing belief in God. Meanwhile, Maulana Abdul Hamid Khan Bhashani was launching a movement that could be deemed a direct challenge to the prohibition of political activity in the name of religion. At the time, one could hear any number of private remarks to the effect that the honeymoon with India, advocacy of the offensive policy of secularism, and refusal to tap Muslim sentiments for the task of nation-building had been carried too far.

I refer to those signs as Muslim assertiveness, rather than communalism, because it was not clear that all or most of this upsurge of explictly Muslim sentiment and activity was destined to crystallize in the intolerant obscurantist mould of communalism. Some of this sentiment probably would never degenerate into intolerant communalism and some of it very likely was already bitterly communal and intolerant. One, however, suspects that much of the Muslim assertiveness being voiced by 1974 was still malleable enough to go in either tolerant or intolerant, pluralistic or communal directions, depending upon circumstances and leadership: leadership not only in political affairs but in other sectors of Bangladeshi life: religious, cultural, social, and economic. It seemed crucial, if they were to succeed, that the Awami League goverment and those who sympathized with its aims, channel this resurgent Muslim assertiveness in constructive ways rather than alienate mainline Muslim sentiment and occasion an unintended communal backlash. However, most indications by early 1974 were to the effect that (despite Mujibur Rahman's assurances about Islam) the Awami League / BAKSAL leadership was not effectively addressing Muslim concerns. In particular, the pillar of secularism had become a pretext for the very communalism it was designed to curb.

Bengali Language and Culture: Preferred Sources of National Identity

There is another aspect of the dilemma that the fourth pillar of the 1972 Constitution sought to resolve, namely the problem of motivating popular and élite commitment to the Awami League vision of national identity and national goals (including a socialist economy). Could this be done effectively in a population that is overwhelmingly Muslim without appealing in some way to Muslim solidarity and Islamic ideals?[21] In this context, one thinks of the remark by Wilfred Cantwell Smith, certainly no advocate of communalism, with reference to Pakistan: 'Given the fact that it [Pakistan] is a democracy (formally) and that the great majority of its citizens are Muslims, it must, virtually, pursue Islamic ideals or no ideals at all.'[22] However, could Muslim solidarity and Islamic ideals be tapped without encouraging and legitimating Islamic communalism or fundamentalism? Without, in the last analysis, jeopardizing socialism, democracy, and even the Bengaliness of Bangladeshi nationalism as the Awami League saw it? The resolution of this dilemma favoured by the first Awami League government of Bangladesh was to appeal to Bengali language and culture rather than to a tolerant humane interpretation of Islam and Muslim solidarity as the principal source of national legitimation and motivation.

A. Bengali language and culture in East Pakistan

The first and most basic of the four principles of the Awami League conception of state policy was nationalism. Nationalism was, according to the 1972 Constitution, 'based on the unity and solidarity of the Bangalee nation', which nation was said to derive its identity from 'its lan-

guage and culture'. Selection of language and culture as symbolic sources of national identity was by no means arbitrary.[23] The process,
whereby, most East Pakistanis became conscious of themselves as a
people distinct from West Pakistanis was initially focused on their
popular struggle to secure Bengali as a national language and to thwart
efforts to modify the language substantially to make it more Islamic and
Pakistani.[24] Later, when the martial law regime of Ayub Khan sought to
cut off East Pakistanis culturally from Indian West Bengal, Bengali language and literature (epitomized this time by the writings of
Rabindranath Tagore) again became foci for self-definition of East
Pakistani Bengalis against the West Pakistanis, who were in control of
government and other sources of power. Although the Awami League's
eminently successful campaign for regional autonony was defined largely in terms of political and economic grievances, as summarized in
the Six Points,[25] its widespread acceptance depended upon there already
having been formed among East Pakistanis a sense of their being a distinct Bengali people with common interests transcending (though hardly
eliminating) their particular communal, caste, and class solidarities.
When the regime of Yahya Khan cracked down brutally on the East
Pakistani/Bengali autonomy movement, and not only upon its leaders
but upon East Pakistani Bengalis indiscriminately, the inchoate sense of
Bengali national solidarity rapidly sharpened and intensified. Language,
blood, and country became the emotive symbols of Bengali resistance
and some months later, of Bengali, or Bangladeshi pride in newly
gained independence.

It is interesting that in the first few years after the independence of
Pakistan there were a number of governmental and non-governmental
efforts to critique and modify Bengali language and literature to make
these more appropriate for East Pakistanis. Some of these efforts, especially the official ones, sought major changes to bring the language
closer to Urdu, Persian, and Arabic in linguistic form and more Islamic
(and less Brahmanic Hindu) in literary content. The unofficial efforts
ranged widely, from those most zealous to adopt the Arabic script and
Urdu–Persian–Arabic lexicon and exclude Hindu authors from the
literary canon to those championing Bengali language in its current
form and upholding the unbroken Bengali literary heritage, Hindu as
well as Muslim. However, once conflict over Bengali as a national language erupted into violent conflict, finer points of discrimination gave
way to more simplistic advocacy for or against Bengali language and
culture as such.

B.   *Language, blood and country during the liberation struggle*

When the reign of terror broke out in March 1971, some of the academic and literary advocates of Bengali language and literature (and, by extension, culture) who managed to escape from East Pakistan (or were abroad at the time) served admirably in diplomatic and public relations roles. To Indians, they could present a portrait of an East Bengal that, in stark contrast to Pakistan, was not ideologically Islamic, but was apparently quite secular and tolerant, and in terms of literary and cultural heritage, was not alienated from the Indian Sanskritic tradition (but rather was intimately linked to it by virtue of sharing Bengali literature and culture). To liberal and progressive sympathizers abroad, the same pomait was attractive and conveyed the hope that the plague of communal violence would not convulse the new republic that, with worldwide assistance, was to arise from the ravages of 1971. Bengali intellectuals themselves became symbols of civilized Bengali resistance to the reactionary brutality of the Pakistani army and its fundamentalist Muslim auxiliaries in East Pakistan. The coordinated murder of scores of intellectuals on 14 December 1971, two days before liberation, provided a final group of martyrs in the cause of language, blood, and country.

C.   *Language, culture and literature after liberation*

The broad outline of the desired cultural identity of Bangladesh, as rooted in Bengali language and literature, had been chalked out by the Awami League leadership and its academic and literary associates even before their return to Bangladesh following the surrender of the Pakistani army in December 1971. The task of articulating in greater detail that conception of national cultural identity and propagating it throughout Bangladesh fell in considerable measure upon academic and literary figures, in addition, of course, to the political leaders themselves and their cadres. Bengali departments of the universities were strained to furnish public speakers, produce popular tracts, and compose serious expositions of Bengali national identity as derivable from language and culture. One institution central to the effort to define Bangladesh culturally was the Bengali Academy. Since its inception in the 1950s, the Bengali Academy had been fostering Bengali literature and culture by such means as publishing new editions of older Bengali Muslim authors and translating texts, including (but not exclusively) Muslim texts, into

Bengali. Subsequently, its emphasis shifted to include more secular and contemporary Bengali literature composed in East Pakistan. After Bangladeshi independence, the Bengali Academy was commissioned to prepare the official history of the Bangladesh freedom struggle. It also became responsible for the work of the Bengali Development Board and organized a continuous round of cultural events in which, academics, creative writers, and government officials articulated the meaning of Bengali culture and Bangladesh's national identity.

University departments of Bengali along with individual scholars and creative writers contributed their own variations on the theme of the cultural identity of Bangladesh as a nation based largely on language and literature. The press, radio, television, cinema and, as always, the politicians carried the message that was being distilled to the populace at large. However, was this sufficient to instill a nationwide sense of Bangladesh identity and to motivate commitment to achieve the goals being set by the government?

There were several reasons for doubting that Bengali language and literature, while certainly necessary, would be sufficient as resources to build a cognitively persuasive and emotionally compelling sense of national identity and purpose. One reason was its restricted emotional appeal, another the ambiguity of boundary and content of Bengali literature and the Bengali/Bangladeshi national identity being rooted in that literature. A third reason for doubt is perhaps, implied by the first two: a gross underestimation of (or resistance to) other foci of socio-cultural identity, especially varying types of Muslim commitment and identity.

It is one thing to rally an entire people in defence of their language (which implicates their livelihood and self-esteem) when that language is really in jeopardy (e.g. initially during the language movement of the early 1950s, sporadically under martial law regimes, intensively during the 1971 conflict). It is quite another thing to maintain passionate concern for language and literature long after the threats to the basic language, and the economic and political interests tied to language policy, have passed. Most Bangladeshis may have heard that Rabindranath Tagore was a great Bengali poet and composer of the national anthem, but they can hardly be expected to centre their private and collective lives upon him, or upon the cultivation of Bengali literature, as devoted students of Bengali literature might be inclined to do. Even less, I suspect, can the bulk of the population (the majority being unable to read in any event) adequately appreciate and be moved by sophisticated contemporary poets and prose writers of Bangladesh. Faced with staggering problems in economic, social, political, and religious life, the typical peasants and labourers of Bangladesh cannot live by language and the refinements of literature alone. In material terms, they need food, work, and basic security; in symbolic terms, they need to find meaning in their lives, inspiration for the sacrifices they are called upon to make, and a sense of security and solidarity. They seek leadership offering a message that speaks to them in an idiom they can understand and respect.

The ambiguities of 'language and culture' as defining national identity appear most bluntly when one looks for the demographic boundary of the Bengali nation which is said to derive its identity from these sources. Was *de facto* Bangladesh in 1971, only the core of a nation awaiting completion by incorporation of fifty million Bengali-speakers then in Indian West Bengal? If so, would the greater Bangladesh be an independent state or a member of the Indian union? The repercussions of either prospect would of course be explosive in India and Bangladesh if seriously pressed, and neither was. Yet, removal of the map from the flag of Bangladesh and designation of its citizens officially by the generic name 'Bangalee' (subsequently modified to Bangladeshi) in the Constitution did nothing to relieve the ambiguity (presumably tolerated rather than intended) on this point. On the other hand, however fixed the demographic/geographic boundaries of Bangladesh as erstwile East Pakistan might be,[26] it would hardly make sense to limit the national linguistic and cultural heritage to elements that had been produced within the current boundaries of Bangladesh. That would be to define a purely East Bengali culture and language which would exclude most of the literature and culture of Hindu Bengalis and, for that matter, much of the modern literature by Bengali Muslim authors, e.g. those resident in Calcutta prior to 1947. It would be as stunted a version of Bengali literature and culture as the Urdu enthusiasts and martial law regimes in the Pakistan period had proposed. What then realistically, and specifically in terms of literature, was to constitute the heritage of 'Bengali language and culture' by which the national identity of Bangladesh was to be defined?

Although the Bangladesh Constitution of 1972 gave no definition of what was meant by Bengali language and culture, and in particular what constituted Bengali literature, at least three broad conceptions or models of Bengali literature, come to mind. One is the inclusive pan-Bengali model, which would present Bangladesh with the full gamut and complexity of Bengali language and culture (especially literature): tradition-al and modern, eastern and western Bengali, Hindu and Muslim (and that of other communities), sophisticated and folk. This might seem to be the obvious intention, though much of what I observed in 1972–3, suggested otherwise. What seemed apparent (though not stated in so many words) from talks heard and essays published during that period was that the preferred model was not the full unedited panorama of Bengali language, culture, and literature.

A second plausible model would be one that selectively emphasizes Muslim contributions to Bengali literature and culture, supplemented by folk and regional dialectal elements from East Bengal, and perhaps, ac-knowledges writing being done by the relatively few Hindu writers still active in Bangladesh. Such a model would marginalize (if not indeed stigmatize) both traditional Hindu religious literature and modern Ben-gali literature by Hindus concentrated in Calcutta. This model might be recognizable to most citizens of Bangladesh, but it would accentuate the Muslim contributions to Bengali culture and the Arabic–Persian impact upon the language while denying Bangladeshis any share in the heritage of much of the finest of traditional and modern Bengali literature. It would be tantamount to acceding to one of the fall-back positions of critics of Bengali language and literature in Pakistani days, i.e. to allow East Pakistanis to use Bengali provided they modified its form and redirected it away from the Sanskritic and toward the Urdu–Arabic–Persian tradition, giving exclusive attention to compositions by Muslim Bengali authors. Such a Muslim-cum-East Bengali model might have been congenial to prior Pakistani regimes, and may even have appeared somewhat attractive to post-Mujib regimes in Bangladesh, but certainly it was not in favour during the first Awami League period.

A third conception of Bengali language and culture is an idealized constructed model; an extrapolation from the wider tradition of what is deemed (by its constructors) to be most essential and desirable. It was such a constructed model of Bengali language and culture, as crystal-lized in literature, that seemed to be in the process of definition by official and unofficial spokespersons of Bengali cultural nationalism in the early years of Bangladesh. That extrapolation, reflecting what might be considered guidelines for a canon of suitable literature, was an ex-pression of a rather extreme version of secularism. While it is true that writers from all communities and regions were receiving attention, texts with a narrow communal tone were being passed over or dismissed with disapproval. Texts that were explicitly religious, and such texts dominated Bengali literature until the mid-nineteenth century, tended to be passed over too. Texts written in a subtle humanistic fashion, that could be read either in traditionally religious or in secular terms, tended to be interpreted on the latter level. Ironically, folk songs and tribal (ritual) customs and esoteric songs of Baul adepts were being extolled as integral to Bengali literature and culture, while explicitly Muslim, Hindu, or Christian songs, rites, prayers and devotional texts typically were not. Historical reconstructions of Bengali language and culture tended to minimize both the Sanskritic and the Arabic–Persian influences, presumably because of the pretiominance of traditional religious orthodoxies, the Brahmanic Hindu and the Muslim, respectively, in each of these two 'great traditions'. This kind of radical selectivity could place the scholarly arbitrator of Bangladeshi literature and culture in the awkward position of virtually restricting acceptable Bengali literature and culture to what remain of tribal and folk traditions, plus only those modern Bengali literary compositions and other cultural creations that are secular in character.

This construction of language and culture in Bangladesh being promulgated in the Mujib era might be characterized as aesthetic Bengali secular humanism. The Bengali aspect was evident enough from repeated reminders that it is one's own Bengali language, country, and cultural forms that are of value in themselves, though rarely with any appeal to external or universal standards to justify or confirm such valuation. The aesthetic emphasis was, perhaps, inevitable with so many creative writers and scholars of literature engaged in the task of promoting Bengali language and culture as the key to national identity. However, even foreign observers have noted the unusually high priority which aesthetic, particularly emotionally expressive aesthetic values enjoy in Bengali literature and cultural life generally. This, of course, is at least as much the case in Hindu-majority West Bengal as it is in Muslim-majority East Bengal or Bangladesh, and may or may not disproportionately reflect élite cultural standards. The third characteristic of the ideal pattern that was being promoted is its secular emphasis, about which much has been said already. That secular emphases are to be found in some nineteenth century (especially in Calcutta) and much of twentieth century Bengali (in East and West Bengal, by Muslim as well as Hindu writers) literature and other aspects of cultural life is true enough. However, explicit religious themes dominated most Bengali literature and culture until the mid-nineteenth century, and religious themes continue to be prominent even in contemporary Bengali literature, especially in non-élite circles.

The fourth characteristic of the idealized pattern, humanism, like the aesthetic but unlike the secular, can be traced back through the history of Bengali literature, in works composed by Muslim as well as by Hindu writers. Even medieval texts that are explicitly religious, such as lives of saints and songs reflecting spiritual disciplines, may show a great deal of sensitivity to human (and human-like, in the case of deities) experiences and feelings of protagonists. Also distinctly humanistic, while certainly not anti-religious, are the heroic romances of pre-modern Muslim poets of south-eastern Bengal. The humanism of Bengali culture, and in its literature especially, typically stands in tension (whether implicit or explicit) with both theism and materialism, without necessarily denying either the divine or ignoring the material. It is indeed ironic that in the Mujib-era extrapolation of Bengali language and literature, several of the individuals most often cited for their apparently secular humanism—Chandidas (whose plea for the human, 'than whom there is none higher', reflects Vaishnava Sahajiya spirituality), Lalan Shah and other Bauls (who as Tantriks sing of the 'man in the heart'), and Rabindranath Tagore (whose *Religion of Man* articulates a very spiritual sense of personhood)—all exemplify religiously attuned modes of humanism.

A broadly humanistic ideal is to many persons, myself included, an attractive one. Moreover, with due specifications and adaptations, humanism is compatible with and reinforced by the more humane tendencies within Muslim, Hindu, Christian, and Buddhist traditions, not just with secular views of life. For centuries, if not millennia, a strong humanistic vein has run through Bengali culture, mellowing the religious traditions and political regimes that have played off against one another in the complex pluralistic, history of Bengal.[27] It should not, however, be overlooked that, at least until the last century or so, and perhaps even then, most of those whose humanistic utterances have found favour with the Bengali people have been, as far as can be determined, religious men or women (be they Muslim or Hindu theists, tantric yogis, monists, or exponents of some esoteric type of religious faith and discipline). Even those, whose values and practices were esoteric and unorthodox, often managed to express themselves in an idiom that the more orthodox could in their own way appreciate. The creative interpreters of human experience recorded in the history of Bengali literature traditionally displayed a flexibility and subtlety of symbolic language that enabled them to serve as agents of humaneness and revitalization within their respective religio–communal traditions.

Often enough, and not surprisingly, they were read or listened to beyond their own communities.

Advocates of Bengali aesthetic secular humanism in the Mujib era, on the other hand, seemed for the most part to be hesitant to articulate their humanistic values (and, perhaps, in many cases their private faith in a transcendent divinity) using the traditional idioms and symbolism of Bengali Muslims or Bengali Hindus. It is, of course, as many of us academics must readily acknowledge, a difficulty by no means peculiar to Bangladesh that, exposed to the manifold demands of modern life, one may find it difficult to integrate one's humanistic insights and values with the values and symbolism of one's inherited religio–cultural tradition. However, the very fact of difficulty should give one pause before offering as the paradigm of national identity a truncated version of a humanistic ideal that till now has been only one strand or trait, though a very significant one, of a complex culture rooted in traditional religio–cultural systems.

An Alternative Suggestion: Humanity/Humanism Rather than Secularism

As we have seen, the rationale for accentuating secularism was, in part, to project an ideal of tolerant respect for all citizens regardless of community and to channel commitment toward socialist development priorities of Bangladesh. Also, secularism was intended to prevent political exploitation of Islam by Muslim communalist political parties and fundamentalist organizations. In neither respect did secularism prove to be successful. Jettisoning that unpopular principle did remove a pretext for communal backlash, but it may also have created a vacuum inviting a return to communal intolerance. Substituting an affirmation of confidence in almighty Allah and Islam may well have enhanced the legitimacy of the later regimes in the eyes of many Muslims, but such an affirmation does not explicitly endorse tolerance for non-Muslims nor commitment to national socio-economic development. Therefore, the question that arises is whether there is some other ideal that might complement nationalism, democracy, socialism, and even the affimation (by Muslims) of confidence in Allah and Islam? Such a symbolic ideal, to be effective, should draw upon familiar Bengali cultural themes, orient people toward national developmental goals, and be inclusive of non-Muslim Bangladeshis while not marginalizing or alienating most Muslims. It would be even more desirable if the general ideal could reinforce (and be reinforced by) more particularist versions or analogues of the ideal embedded in each of the religio–communal groups, above all the Muslims, and as many as possible of the ideological viewpoints prominent in Bangladesh.

A. Humanity as a national ideal

I would suggest that the notion of the human, or humanity, could fulfill all the foregoing criteria for a symbolic ideal to enhance the character of Bangladeshi national identity. There are a number of Bengali words capable of conveying to Bengalis positive values intended by the ill-fated term, secularism, and the ineffectual, if inoffensive, *dharma-nirapeksata*.[28] *Lok, manush, manab, manushya* et al. and some of their derivatives are commonplace non-controversial Bengali words. The humane ideals associated with these words have permeated much of Bengali literature and culture, Muslim as well as Hindu, traditionally religious as well as modern and secular. Human/humanity, though not an explicitly religious notion, is certainly not the antithesis of religion, either in common parlance or in intellectual discourse.

The more abstract word, humanism, designating either a general attitude or a systematic body of thought sympathetic to the development of human life, may take a wide range of particular forms, some explicitly religious, some less so, some explicitly secular. There has long existed (especially, since the European Renaissance) a deeply entrenched and much studied tradition of what is called Christian humanism. Muslim or Islamic humanism is not yet an expression commonly used, but there is within Muslim tradition much emphasis upon the value and dignity of the human as such (and not exclusively of the Muslim human).[29] Certain modern Muslim thinkers and writers have been hailed for the humanism they expressed, not least among these being Amir Ali and Muhammad Iqbal.[30] Any number of modern Bengali Muslim writers, from the neo-orthodox, like Muhammad Akram Khan, through liberals, like Muhammad Shahidullah, to rational humanists, like Qazi Abdul Wadud, have displayed pronounced humanist tendencies, and some have been outspokenly humanistic without ceasing to consider themselves Muslims.[31]

While the related themes of the human, humanity, and concern for human welfare permeate Bengali language and culture, choosing a single term to symbolize the ideal of the human or humanity would require some care. Some possibilities are suggested here. This is, however, a matter for those with a far better sense of the connotations and nuances of Bengali language in Bangladesh than I have to determine. The most common words in Bengali for human include *lok, manush, manushya, manab, jan, byekti (vyakti), purush* and, in more Urduized Bengali, *admi*.

The first word, *lok* (human being, humans collectively, world), is the simplest of the lot, which is in itself, a plus. *Lok* also has the peculiarity of designating either human being(s) as such or a realm, or world (e.g. earth, heaven, or hell), which humans or other living beings populate. This bifocal character of *lok* and its derivatives may also be a rhetorical plus, if comments made below regarding human survival in a global natural environment have any force. The adjectival derivative, *lok-hita*, meaning caring for the welfare of humans/humanity/the world, is a common Bengali word, as likewise are *lok-hitoishi* (m.)/*lok-hitoishini* (f.), meaning one who cares for the welfare of humans/humanity/the world.[32] One might utilize or coin related abstract nominal forms, e.g. *lok-hitata* or *lok-hitatva* (concern for the welfare of humanity), or the adjectival *lok-hitabrat* (dedicated to human welfare), or possibly *lok-hitabad* (doctrine/ideal of human welfare), though these may seem cumbersome or artificial. (The simpler *lokbad* might be proposed for doctrine/ideal of humanity, were it not for the entrenched sense of *lokbad* as rumour).[33] For *lokbad* or such abstract terms ending in *-bad* (and meaning doctrine or theory of humanity), there would be the corresponding *-badi* term, meaning one who advocates that doctrine or theory.

Manush (like the somewhat more formal *manushya* and *manab*) is also commonly used for a human being individually or for humans collectively. *Manushya* (like the more abstract *manushyatva* and *manabata*) means humanness/humanity (with secondary connotations of manliness, manhood, liberality, benevolence, goodness). A number of compounds and phrases based on *manush, manushya* or *manab* further extend and specify the sense of human (e.g. *manushya-caritra* and *manab-svabhab* for human character or human behaviour, *manusher dharma, manushya-dharma* or *manab-dharma* for the duties, essence, even religion, of the human).[34] The term *manabata*, with its derivatives (e.g. *manabatabad, manabatabadi*), has been widely used in the sense of humanness/humanism in Bengali writing, including recent statements provoked by the Babri masjid fiasco at Ayodhya and its brutal communal aftermath.[35] Also, *manabata* has been used extensively in writing on Muslim ideals even by such neo-orthodox spokesmen as the late Maulana Akram

Khan.[36] Accordingly, *manabata* and its derivatives may well be the most apt Bengali equivalents of humanity/humanness/humanism.

Jan (living thing, human, humans collectively, the people or populace) is yet another possibility. It has already been used in political terms, e.g. *janata* (the public, the people), *janatantra* (republic), even in proper names of parties claiming to represent the public generally. In this respect, the term is akin to *awami*, also meaning people/people's. Current partisan associations of both terms (but especially the latter) should rule them out as inclusive terms for symbolizing a non-partisan, trans-communal ideal of humanity for Bangladesh, though particular groups may wish to use them in this sense.

Likewise, the Persian/Urdu words *admi, adamzad* (human), and *admiyat* (humanness/humanity), or even the Arabic *insan* and *insaniyat*, though they would not serve as inclusive Bengali terms for the ideal of humanity, might be appropriate in certain orthodox Bengali Muslim circles.[37] *Purush* is sometimes used for human, but tends to emphasize the male, and its compounds and derivatives further stress the vigorous 'manly' qualities rather than essential humanness. *Byekti* designates an individual person, and hence, is often used in the context of individual human rights. However, this stress on the individual has a narrower focus than that being suggested here as an overarching ideal of the well-being of humankind, collectively as well as individually. When all things are considered, *manabata* (or possibly *lok-hitata*) would seem to be a more suitable Bengali term for summing up the ideal of humanity.

If the main communities and ideological groups in Bangladesh were to accentuate the ideal of humanity as embedded in their respective religio–cultural and/or philosophic traditions, one might anticipate some positive results. For one thing, each community or ideological group would be contributing something of its own values and conception of humanity to the sense of national identity and purpose. None, least of all the majority of Muslims, would find itself symbolically marginalized, its religio–cultural heritage apparently being ignored or neglected. Moreover, to the extent that the ideal of humanity can be affirmed and accentuated in the life of any community, so much the more effectively can those within that community who feel strongly about human life, refute and challenge those who would project a less humane, less tolerant interpretation of their own community and its ideals.

It may be too sanguine, indeed naïve, to think that a renovation of Muslim thought in the direction of Bengali Muslim humanism is likely with or without a commitment to humanity by the present or any future government of Bangladesh. Yet, among countries with Muslim majorities, Bangladesh may well be comparatively more humanistic, tolerant, and pluralistic to begin with, and its intellectual and professional élites perhaps, more pragmatic and cosmopolitan. Hence the prospects for constructive renewal of Muslim self-consciousness being arrived at in Bangladesh might well be better than in other, more traditionally orthodox or ideologically narrow, countries where Muslims are in the majority.[38]

A national Bangladeshi commitment to humanity (or humanism) need not, though it might, involve alteration of the Bangladesh Constitution's declaration of principles. Clearly, however, it would entail a change in how Bangladeshi Muslims, especially the more modernized élite, think, talk, and feel about the meaning of being Muslim in relation to national identity and purpose. The leadership of Bangladesh, by advancing humanity (*manabata/lok-hitata*) as a shared non-partisan trans-communal ideal, might reasonably hope to motivate a broad cross-section of citizens, each in his or her particular way, to contribute to such overriding national objectives as economic development and population control, social justice and responsible politics. Obviously, more thought and study would be needed to assess just how constructive and effective humanity/humanism, or yet another more suitable ideal, could be in refining the cultural identity of contemporary Bangladesh. Nevertheless, there may be some point to making the suggestion at this particular time in the ever-changing history of the country.

B. Bangladesh, humanity and the global environment

There is one further consideration, less a domestic than an international one, that also suggests that it may be in the interest of Bangladesh to make the ideal of humanity prominent in its thought and actions at home and in its voice abroad. Bangladesh, among the world's densely populated countries, may be the one most imperilled by deterioration of the global natural environment. If nothing else, continued global warming and melting of polar icecaps could innundate vast portions of Bangladesh.[39] For the sheer survival of the world's most vulnerable countries and populations, it is imperative that global decisions be made and enforced to bring to an end, and soon, the massive industrial and commercial degradation of the natural environment now in process. Bangladesh, out of sheer self-interest, if for no other reason, should be at the forefront of nations pressing for environmental protection.

Two decades ago, Bangladesh took a leading role in forming the South Asian Association for Regional Cooperation (SAARC), a consultative initiative that has had considerable success. Bangladesh might again assume a catalytic role in international collaboration on behalf of the environment. This time, the region is global and the cooperation needed is pan-human. The issues involved in turning global economic and political priorities toward preserving the natural environment, upon which human life collectively depends, transcend religious and secular dimensions of life as well as ethnic and communal solidarities, though all these factors may be involved in one way or another. The effectiveness of Bangladesh in arguing for environmentally constructive policies and changed patterns of behaviour wordwide could hinge upon its credibility as an advocate of human survival and well-being. If Bangladesh can be seen to think, speak, and act well on behalf of humanity in its domestic affairs, it will be far more credible in international environmental debates than if known to be hobbled by communal intolerance and fundamentalist violence within its own borders. Reciprocally, the more Bangladesh can distinguish itself internationally as a champion of global environmental protection in the interests of humanity as a whole, the more readily can the ideal of humanity be appreciated at home as integral to the national well-being and identity of Bangladesh; a Bangladesh, in which the humanity, or humanism, of its Muslim citizens must be a crucial factor.

Notes and References

*This essay contains substantial portions of an earlier essay, 'Dilemmas of Secularism in Bangladesh' revised and redirected to a new question: Could the ideal of humanity, if advocated by Bangladeshi leadership, achieve what secularism could not?'

1. Joseph T. O'Connell, 'Dilemmas of Secularism in Bangladesh', *Journal of Asian and African Studies,* 11:1 & 2 (January–April), 64–82; also appears in Bardwell Smith (ed.), *Religion and Conflict in South Asia* (Leiden: E.J. Brill, 1976).

2. For the political history of Bangladesh, *see* Craig Baxter et al., *Government and Politics in South Asia* (Boulder: Westview Press, 1993); Marcus Franda, *Bangladesh: The First Decade* (New Delhi: South Asian Publishers, 1982); Chandrika J. Gulati, *Bangladesh: Liberation to Fundamentalism: A Study of Volatile Indo-Bangladesh Relations* (New Delhi: Commonwealth, 1988); Zillur R. Khan, *Leadership in the Least Developed Nation: Bangladesh* (Syracuse: Maxwell School of Citizenship

and Public Affairs, 1983); Lawrence Ziring, *Bangladesh: From Mujib to Ershad. An Interpretive Study* (Dhaka: University Press Ltd in association with Oxford University Press, Karachi, 1992); for Islam in Bangladesh, Peter J. Bertocci, 'Bangladesh', in John L. Esposito (ed.), *The Oxford Encyclopedia of the Modern Islamic World* (New York & Oxford: Oxford University Press, 1995); and U.A.B. Razia Akter Banu, *Islam in Bangladesh* (Leiden: E.J.Brill, 1992).

3. For an outspoken fundamentalist indictment of secularism and other aspects of the first Awami League government, *see* Matiur Rahman, *Bangladesh To-day: An Indictment and a Lament* (London: News & Media, 1978); for Jamaat-i-Islami apologetics, *see* Muhammad Nuruzzaman, *Prof. Ghulam Azam: A Profile of Struggle in the Cause of Allah* (Dhaka: Prachi Prakashani, 1992). For a critique from the secular left, *see* Badruddin Umar, *Politics and Society in Bangladesh* (Dhaka: Subarna, 1987, esp. 99–118); for analyses of Jamaat-i-Islami and Muslim fundamentalism in Bangladesh, *see* Rafiuddin Ahmed, 'Redefining Muslim Identity in South Asia: The Transformation of the Jama'at-i-Islami', in *Accounting for Fundamentalisms*, ed. Martin E. Marty and R. Scott Appleby (Chicago: University of Chicago Press, 1994, 670–74); Rafiuddin Ahmed (ed.), *Religion, Nationalism and Politics in Bangladesh* (New Delhi: South Asian Publishers, 1990); and Gulati, *Bangladesh: From Liberation to Fundamentalism*, op. cit.

4. The remarks in this section are based primarily upon observations, discussions, and reading undertaken by me during an eleven month research visit (Sept. 1972–July 1973) in Bangladesh to prepare an anthology of passages (to be translated) constituting a Bengali Muslim self-statement: a project that remains to be completed.

5. Frederick Ferré, 'The Definition of Religion', *Journal of the Academy of Religion*, 38 (1970), 3–16.

6. *See The Constitution of the People's Republic of Bangladesh* (authorized English translation), 1972, passed by the Constituent Assembly of Bangladesh on 4 November 1972, and authenticated by the Speaker on 4 December 1972.

7. Donald Eugene Smith, *Religion and Political Development* (Boston: Little, Brown & Co., 1970), 85–6.

8. The English version of the Constitution is designated as the 'Authorized English Translation', implying that the Bengali text is the Constitution proper. However, the document is said to have been composed first in English by lawyers trained in the British legal tradition as adapted to India and Pakistan. Therefore, secularism may have been the precise term and concept intended by the drafters of the Constitution after all.

9. Presumably, the communalism that was to be eliminated included such elements as: placing religio–communal interests above the national interest, subordinating civil rights to the demands of the dominant community,

obscuring political and economic exploitation by appeals to religion, and creating an atmosphere of communal intolerance and religious bigotry, so that members of minority communities might be subjected to harassment.

10. *See The Constitution* (1973), passim.

11. Perhaps, the bulk of the Muslims of Bangladesh at that time were willing to abide by such a restriction, especially in view of their painful experience with communal politics in East Pakistan. However, what now seems evident is that the 1972 Constitution, accepted less than a year after liberation in a Constituent Assembly with virtually no opposition, went beyond what the majority of Bengali Muslims would eventually find acceptable. Some examples of more radical secularism may be found within the Muslim world, notably in Turkey, but in such cases, changes were imposed by a dominant modernizing élite, not, as in Bangladesh, made subject to democratic elections and intervention by a traditionalist military.

12. *See* Planning Commission, Government of the People's Republic of Bangladesh, *The First Five Year Plan, 1973–1978* (Dacca, 1973).

13. In Sheikh Mujibur Rahman, *Mujiburer Racana Samgraha* (Calcutta: Reflect Publications, 1971) (i.e. AH 1378), 120. English renderings of selections from this volume are mine.

14. Speech of 10 October 1970 in *ibid*, 55.

15. Speech with no date in *ibid*., 65.

16. Rahman, *Mujibarer Racana Samgraha*, 1 (versus charge of conspiring against Islam); 2 (enemies deceive people in name of Islam); 54 (opposes communalism, pledges to protect minorities); 55 (versus charge of undermining Islam); 61 (exploiters appeal to Islam); 64 (Muslims, Hindus, Christians, Buddhists are all Bengalis); 66 (no discrimination for religion or caste); 68 (majority and minority are all Bengalis); 76 (versus the self-proclaimed lords of Islam); 79 (no more molestation of Hindus, Christians, Buddhists); 89 (every resident of Bangladesh is a Bengali and will be protected); 96 (all Bengalis (Muslim, Hindu, Christian, Buddhist) must protect non-Bengalis); 115 (exploiters say Islam is in danger, but we are better Pakistanis than they); 20, 41, 57, 66, 72, 74, 79 (appeals to Allah).

17. Translation of speech delivered on 7 June 1972 (Dacca: External Publicity Division, Ministry of Foreign Affairs, Government of the People's Republic of Bangladesh, 1972), 16–17.

18. Translation of speech delivered on 1 January 1974 (Dacca, Department of Publications, Ministry of Information and Broadcasting, Government of Bangladesh, 1974), 3.

19. Ibid., 13.

20. *See* Umar, *Politics and Society in Bangladesh*, 189–95, for a leftist critique of Muslim Bangla as a communalist phenomenon.

21. For a sensitive reflection on this issue, *see* Wilfred Cantwell Smith, *Islam in Modern History* (Princeton: Princeton University Press, 1957).

22. Wilfred Cantwell Smith, *Pakistan as an Islamic State* (Lahore: Sh. Muhammad Ashraf, 1962), 86.

23. For varying perspectives on the place of Bengali language in the formation of East Pakistani and Bengali/Bangladeshi nationalism, *see* Mo[hammad] Abul Kasem, 'Bangali Musalmaner Rajnaitik Svatantrya-cetana: Bamla Bhasha o Sahitya Carcay tar Pratiphalan (1942–1972)', Ph.D. dissertation, 1988; Fazlur Rahman, *Culture and Conflicts in East Pakistan, 1947–1971: A Study in the Attitude of Bengali Muslim Intelligentsia towards Bengali Literature and Islam* (Dhaka: Sejuty Prakashani, 1990), and articles by M.G. Kabir and A.R. Khan in R. Ahmed (1990). For earlier developments shaping Bengali Muslim identity, *see* Rafiuddin Ahmed, *The Bengal Muslims, 1871–1906: A Quest for Identity* (Delhi: Oxford University Press, 1981),

24. Indeed, the national remembrance day that was observed most passionately in Dhaka before liberation from Pakistan and later, is 21 February, the anniversary of the killing of several young men in the 1952 agitation on behalf of Bengali language.

25. By focusing upon language and culture (including literature) as the primary symbolic factors in constructing a new collective self-consciousness of East Pakistanis as Bengalis, I do not, of course, mean to imply the lack of importance of economic and other *material* factors that divided East Pakistanis from West Pakistanis. Such factors have been amply discussed in appropriate scholarly literature, notably in Rounaq Jahan, *Pakistan: Failure in National Integration* (New York: Columbia University Press, 1972), and Ahmed (ed.), *Religion, Nationalism and Politics in Bangladesh* (1990).

26. The practical difficulties of precisely defining and policing the borders between India and Bangladesh, and the problems of recent and earlier movement of large numbers of persons across borders between India and Bangladesh and between Burma and Bangladesh are a separate matter, though not altogether unrelated.

27. For general accounts of the history of Bengali literature and religion, *see* Md. Enamul Haq, *Muslim Bengali Literature* (Karachi: Pakistan Publications, 1957); Sukumar Sen, *Bangla Sahityer Katha*, 7th ed. (Calcutta: University of Calcutta, 1963), and *History of Bengali Literature* (Delhi: Sahitya Akademi, 1971); Mahmud Shah Qureshi, *Etude sur l'evolution intellectuelle chez les musulmans du Bengale, 1857–1947* (Paris and the Hague: Mouton, 1971); Ahmed Sharif, *Bangali o Bangla Sahitya*, 2 vols. (Dhaka: Bangla Academy, 1983); Asim Roy, *The Islamic Syncretistic Tradition in Bengal* (Princeton: Princeton University Press, 1983); and Richard M. Eaton, *The Rise of Islam and the Bengal Frontier, 1204–1760* (Berkeley: University of California Press, 1993).

28. There are also such related expressions as *manab-dharma* and *manushya-dharma* (humanity, human religion, human nature). Hindus and any others

who are comfortable with such -*dharma* compounds should be free to use them, but they probably are too Sanskritic or Hindu in tone to serve as generic expressions of the ideal of humanity.

29. For discussions of Islamic humanism and related notions of Islamic anthropology (understanding of the human) and cultural tolerance, *see* A.H. Green, *In Quest of an Islamic Humanism: Arabic and Islamic Studies in Memory of Mohammed al-Nowaihi* (Cairo: American University in Cairo Press, 1984); Merryl Wyn Davies, *Knowing One Another: Shaping an Islamic Anthropology* (London, New York: Mansell, 1988); George Makdisi, *The Rise of Humanism in Classical Islam and the Christian West: With Special Reference to Scholasticism* (Edinburgh: University of Edinburgh Press, 1990); Abdullah Ahmed An-Naim, *Toward an Islamic Reformation: Civil Liberties, Human Rights, and International Law* (Syracuse: Syracuse University Press, 1990). For a moving appeal by the national poet of Bangladesh for human life in the midst of communal savagery, *see* Nazrul Islam, 'Mandir o Masjid' ('The Temple and the Mosque'), trans. J.T. O'Connell, *Journal* (Toronto: St Michael's College, 1971), For overviews of human rights and democracy in Muslim life, *see* Anne Elizabeth Mayer, 'Human Right' in John L. Esposito, *The Oxford Encyclopedia*, op. cit., vol. 2, 143–8 and Muhammad Muslih, 'Democracy', in Esposito ibid., vol. 1, 359–60 respectively.

30. 'Despite his [Iqbal's] commitment to the concept of a separate Muslim state, he remained a philosophical humanist, and humanism was truly his message'. Hafeez Malik, 'Iqbal, Muhammad', in Esposito, op.cit., vol. 2, 121–4, 1995, 223.

31. I am indebted to Dr. Shahadat H. Khan for the categorization of neo-orthodox, liberal, and rational humanists among Bengali Muslim intellectuals of the twentieth century (Khan, 1997). His recent thesis is an important study of the rational humanism of the *Buddhir Mukti Andolan* (Freedom of Intellect Movement) in the 1920s and 1930s. It also includes condensed treatment of liberal and neo-orthodox Bengali Muslim modernists. The best account of modern Muslim intellectuals in a Western language remains Qureshi, op.cit. (in French). For Bengali accounts of it, *see* Anisuzzaman, *Muslim Manas o Bangla Sahitya, 1757–1918* (Calcutta: Muktadhara, 1971) and Qazi Abdul Mannan, *Adhunik Bangla Sahitya o Muslim Samaj* (Dhaka: Bangladesh Book Corporation, 1990).

32. One thinks of the nineteenth century Maharashtrian advocate of community service, Gopal Hari Deshmukh, who signed himself as Lokhitawadi.

33. It would also be prudent to dissociate the intended use of *lok* from its use in Lokayata, a classical materialist school of Indian philosophy, lest anti-materialism zealots be given a pretext.

34. Rabindranath Tagore, as the title of the Bengali parallel to his noted Hibbert Lectures, *The Religion of Man*, chose *Manusher Dharma*. He also

employed such expressions as *vishva-manab* in the sense of 'man the universal' or 'humanity as a whole' and *manushyatva* (humanness), as pointed out to me by Dr. Kathleen M. O'Connell.

35. *See* pertinent essays, Mafidul Huq and Arun Sen (eds.), *Dhvamsastupe Alo* (Dhaka: Sahitya Prakash, 1993).

36. Information supplied by Dr Shahadat H. Khan.

37. The Arabic *insan* (man, human), *insaniyat* (humamess), and *insan al kamil* (perfect man), especially the latter, are too theologically determined to serve, even in orthodox Muslim discourse, for humanity/humanness in the public sense intended here. Cf. R. Arnaldez, *'Insan* (A), man *(homo)'*. *'Insan al Kamil*, The Perfect Man', *The Encyclopedia of Islam*, new edn , ed. B. Lewis et. al. (Leiden: E.J. Brill; London: Luzac & Co., 1971, vol. III, 1237–9, 1239–41.

38. For somewhat parallel developments elsewhere in the modern Muslim world, *see* Mourad Wahba, *Cultural Tolerance, Proceedings of the First EASRG Regional Conference* (Cairo: Anglo-Egyptian Workshop, 1982); Muslih, op.cit., Mayer, op.cit. For a valuable, and perhaps unique, recent quantitative-cum-qualitative study of Muslim attitudes and practices in Bangladesh, *see* Banu, op. cit., passim.

39. Other pertinent ecological problems beyond control of Bangladesh acting alone include deforestation leading to silting up and flooding over of rivers, pollution of surface and underground water sources, disruption of monsoons, severity of cyclonic storms, etc.

9

Gender and Islam in Bangladesh: Metaphor and Myth[1]

SHELLEY FELDMAN

Introduction

Islamic political practices often include a symbolic politics that draw legitimacy from either a timeless supra-human authority or a cultural or civilizational heritage that simultaneously regulates social behaviour, and structures sources of power and authority. The increased prominence of Islamic religio–political movements in Bangladesh, and elsewhere in recent times, helps transform our understanding of especially the relationship between religion and state practice, and religion and civil society. Once thought to be a private matter, greater attention is now focussed on how Islamist demands appropriate public discourses to gain institutional control of the state. Contemporary religious parties, for example, incorporate various patriarchal assumptions and in challenging to women's behaviour, they draw renewed attention to how patriarchal relations and gendered ideologies constitute emergent sites of struggle and challenge. The changing role of Jama't-i-Islami in the period between the country's independence under Sheikh Mujibur Rahman through the regimes of Zia, Ershad, Khaleda Zia, and Sheikh Hasina provide an important backdrop for illuminating this process.

In this chapter, I explore the paradoxical determinants and consequences of appropriating a gendered symbolic politics to secure political legitimacy and authority in Bangladesh. I argue that state appropriation of Islamic practices, constituted by gendered references to backwardness and decline, provide the basis both for legitimating development assistance and for arguing against industrial growth and the integration of Bangladesh into spheres of global production. This view depends on an understanding of religious doctrine as a dynamic and changing representational politics constructed in accordance with the interests of specific groups and constituencies. This sociological account views the use of Islam to construct state practices, whether to organize coalitions in order to secure political office, or to establish bureaucratic control of political opposition, as a modern call for authority and legitimacy rather than, as some would suggest, a return to the past.

The representation of, and increased legitimacy given to the Jama't-i-Islami in the period between the country's independence under the leadership of Sheikh Mujibur Rahman through the regimes of Ziaur Rahman, Hossain Muhammad Ershad, and Begum Khaleda Zia set the stage for these political transitions. During this period, images of women, poverty, and economic instability were sustained as well as contested by Islamic demands and the institutionalization of traditionalizing, but not traditional, ideologies.[2] As women move into new areas of work and public participation, they indicate the significance of their contribution to previous forms of production and thus challenge longstanding production relations among particular rural interests. By so doing, women mark the need to contest forms of production that ignored or undervalued their labour and enabled forms of gendered exploitation. Against this backdrop, I argue that women serve as a metaphor for dislocations brought by economic change; they mark a romantic vision of the past and an unknown, dramatically changing future.

Barber identifies these two apparently distinct responses to economic restructuring as that between 'Jihad and McWorld', but, he suggests, it is important also to acknowledge their 'powerful and paradoxical interdependence'.[3] I will explore their paradoxical interdependence by examining how different responses to women's place and position shape the rise of ethno–religious movements as well as how different interest groups construct institutional political authority. However, where Barber argues that Islamic movements are not opposed to democracy, but to modernization as it is manifested in Westernization,[4] I argue that these same 'values, culture and institutions' are a key to understanding support for NGOs as well as secular support for modernization and its attendant attributes of privatization, economic individualism, and the rights of women. These interdependent sources of mobilization suggest several key questions: How might we interpret the interests of those who mobilize for or against participation in the Jama't-i-Islami, and how do they employ valuations of women's rights as a resource for their own vested interests? The basis for this exploration is thus not to explain how Islam functions to constrain women's behaviour. Rather, it is to explore how representations of women that contest relations of domination and control also enable relations of inequality and their justification in a rapidly changing political economy.

Situating the Argument

Zartman[5] argues that political Islam arises 'as a political formula in reaction to the failures of modernization and secular socialism'. In contrast, I posit that the rise of political Islam represents the relative success of the modernization project and the development of an outward-looking entrepreneurial élite tied to global circuits of production and exchange. This new élite emerged amidst a policy of denationalization, privatization, and trade liberalization where the move from import substitution to export led growth slowly eroded the state's commitment to subsidies for non-farm rural and agricultural production. This meant a shift of resources away from inputs that support opportunities to expand production and sustain the economic security of rural petty bourgeois and landed interests.

In the immediate aftermath of these economic reforms, when the emergence of the industrial élite was the most dramatic, the rhetoric of the Jama't provided a ready explanation for the declining status of established rural élites and those, such as first generation urban educated workers facing rising under- and unemployment, who failed to benefit from the economic restructuring during the 1980s. In this policy environment, each political party, including the Jama't, negotiated with each other for political authority over a constituency of young graduates and petty bourgeois interests. Each group was open to mobilization by both the secular parties, the NGOs, as well as the Jama't. Critical to examine here are the ways that each regime built political legitimacy and used gendered differences and a patriarchal rhetoric to secure its interests.

At this stage, it is crucial to acknowledge the sociological distinction between Islamic theology as a set of universalitic impulses and asserted practices, and Islam as ideological tool, a form of symbolic capital that is consciously deployed for particular ends. In this distinction, fundamentalism is not explored as an outcome of the antagonism between the traditionalist clergy and a modernizing secular élite, as some Orientalist and neo-Orientalist views suggest. Rather, fundamentalist discourses unfold in relation to challenges faced by segments of the established élite who employ religious ideologies to mobilize constituencies around the loss of identity, and self-worth in order to create opportunities for social action.[6]

Fundamentalist ideologies deployed by the current 'revival' of the Jama't, for instance, seek to reclaim social practices based on women's unpaid work in agricultural and craft production located within the domestic economy. They emphasize kin relations, social networks, and forms of patronage and obligation established on the basis of communal and reciprocal exchanges between family and community. These relations are associated with feminine qualities that include limiting women's mobility to the private space of the home, and familial networks built upon non-commoditized relations of production and exchange. From this point of view, self-reliant, wage-earning, and entrepreneurial women alter communal and reciprocal relations, benefit from the capitalization of agrarian and non-farm forms of production, and exemplify all that is bad and evil with the modernist transformation of the cultural and political economy. In so doing, women provide a ready target for those seeking to restore, or at least to maintain, control of an economic and political landscape that is rapidly altering their way of life and their sources of capital accumulation.

It is also crucial to differentiate between gender relations understood as the accepted behaviours of women and men, and the ways in which material and symbolic transactions actually construct gender and other social relations. These transactions create both new patterns of accepted behaviour as well as a changing series of responses to the conditions and relations that challenge established traditions and practices. In this context, women's changing forms of work, physical mobility, expressions of religious identification and practice, and engagement in political and social activities must be examined against the backdrop of changing demands on their resources, their familial and community needs, and their individual interests and desires. This context also situates how gendered norms shape people's choices and how such norms are employed as a metaphor for both progress and achievement, as well as loss and decline.

These conditions shape the significance of women's employment in the post-independence period, where women's increased public visibility marks an arena of contestation between petty bourgeois interests and those of the new urban élite, as well as between religious parties and the increasing numbers of non-governmental organizations (NGOs) who target women as programme participants. On the one hand, women's new role in the labour force, their access to credit and training, and greater visibility in education and in other social and political activities make them an easy target for those arguing against the dramatic reorganization of the Bangladesh economy. This is because for rural producers, who depend on the unpaid labour of women to sustain production, the restructuring of agriculture represents a decline in their control of labour power and a direct challenge to their status and economic security. The shift of women from the secluded context of household production to wage labourers in the formal and informal economy, thus embodies all that challenges established norms associated with women's seclusion, unpaid household work, and sources of male and family status.

On the other hand, images of empowerment, equity, and justice are used to legitimate women's increased participation in the labour market and in public life and politics generally. NGOs, for example, support and justify women's needs and desires for increased access to resources by critiquing the conditions that led to women's exclusion from public arenas. Not surprisingly, this argument supports the use of gender differences to legitimate different credit schemes for women and men, and to justify low wages and limited mobility among the new cadres of women workers. Whether argued by donor agents, government bureaucrats, members of the NGO community, or women themselves, the rhetoric of 'upliftment and social progress' is used to secure and legitimate increasing women's access to credit and training, as well as to provide access to entrepreneurs, particularly garment manufacturers, to recruit women as a source of cheap labour.[7]

The contestation between these groups over labour power and different forms of production both invoke the idiom of gender difference and women's changing physical and public presence to legitimate their views about women and about appropriate gender roles. Women's more varied participation in social life thus brings old as well as new forms of production, power, and patronage into question. Taken together, these diverse forms of public participation focus attention on women's bodies, and showcase women as independent subjects who make decisions, secure wage income, and make demands that challenge previous forms of labour control and subservience.

Changing Regimes and Crises of Legitimacy

Efforts to mobilize support for the movement that won independence for Bangladesh replaced Muslim identity[8] with an ethnic, linguistic, and cultural nationalism centred on Bengaliness. This symbolic shift from religious identity to shared ethnicity and language is suggested by the strength and success of the 1952 Language Movement and the declaration of Bangladesh Independence under the banner of Tagore's *Amar Sonar Bangla* as the National Anthem. However, these, and other acts were defined as treasonous by the military government of Yahya Khan of Pakistan and eventually culminated in the attack and murder of students, teachers, and employees of Dacca University, as well as other intellectuals, starting on 25 March 1971. There is considerable support for the finding that the Jama't was responsible for helping to identify those socialist, democratic, and secular intellectuals who were subsequently killed by its front organization with the help of the Pakistan army.[9]

Fuelled by subsequent tensions between Islamic and Bengali identity, Bangladesh society was thus poised to enter the debate over the meaning and form of its policy of state secularism. In the initial resolution to this debate, identity was neither forged nor was mobilization organized in anti-Muslim terms, a point that is significant when interpreting the discourse against secularism and tensions over political choices that followed.[10] However, in the pre-Independence period, contestations between secularists and Islamists were viewed as disagreements over religious definitions of institutionalized politics and the threat of economic autonomy from Pakistan. For example, in a pamphlet entitled 'Don't Blame Centre' the Jama't attacked the Awami League and other secular organizations and groups, and brought out a procession against what they called the 'Secessionist Movement'.[11]

Pakistan's military president Yayha Khan also used members of the Jama't as a counter to the Independence struggle forming a ten-member East Pakistan government which consisted of members of the rightist political parties, including the Jama't, who were defeated in the elections of 1970. Members of the Jama't included elements of the middle class and the upper stratum of the semi-feudal *jotedar*, or affluent landowning classes, who General Ayub Khan (the former military leader and president of Pakistan) had earlier presumed could be contained by giving them a direct stake in the development of East Pakistan. As Sobhan argues:

If enough Bengalis could be set up in industry and trade and introduced into the upper echelons of the bureaucracy and professions . . . . (t)hey would come to depend on the coercive power of the Pakistani ruling classes to secure their gains and would, in turn, serve as their surrogates in East Pakistan.[12]

Important here are the interests identified by membership of the Jama't at the time. Today, these are the same interests that oppose policies that integrate Bangladesh into global production and exchange relations.[13] In contrast, support for Independence came from secular-oriented students, the salaried classes, managers, bureaucrats and professionals, many of whom were deprived of opportunities for advancement under the Pakistani regime, as well as industrial workers, peasants, petty-bourgeois households, and small landholding classes.[14]

How do contestations over the institutionalization of a religious party support a particular class politics, and how might we interpret political choices since Independence between the Jama't and the secular parties? First, both the West and the Middle East refused to recognize the sovereignty of Bangladesh or to provide aid and technical assistance to the new regime in the immediate post-Independence period. This forced political choices in what had been an easy alliance between those who believed in textual readings of Islam and those who supported a syncretic interpretation of Bangladeshi Islam. It also became clear that if Bangladesh was to survive as an independent nation and meet its short term need for external assistance and oil, Mujib could not afford to alienate potential sources of financial aid. Mujib thus moved to gain wider political recognition in the global community, including among the Islamic countries. For example, he participated in the Islamic summit held in Lahore in 1975, took steps to rehabilitate those who collaborated with the Pakistani army during the Independence struggle, recognized the founding of the Islamic Foundation of Bangladesh, and made efforts to have Bangladesh recognized as an independent nation in the United Nations.[15] These initiatives drew attention to the ruling party's interest in mediating differences among possible sources of financial assistance while maintaining a commitment to secularism.[16]

The Mahila Parishad, or Women's Council, which grew out of the Awami League Women's Wing and had over 30,000 members by the 1980s, also valued secularism. Given the Wing's relationship to the Awami League, it is not surprising that the politics of its members were class rather than gender identified, offering very little to rural women. For instance, despite the government's inadequate response to the approximately 30,000 women raped by the Pakistan army and their local supporters during the Independence struggle, there was little effort to mobilize support for these women even among Mahila Parishad urban 'reformers'. Indeed, their failure to respond to various forms of violence against primarily poor women has been partially explained by urban women's naïveté about the conditions of rural women, their sense of middle class vulnerability, and their unwillingness to challenge patriarchal traditions that could result in a backlash against rape victims.[17] Under these conditions, attention was focused on post-war reconstruction and rehabilitation rather than on the politics of a development agenda tied to aid and national policy reform. Challenging the patriarchal state was, moreover, beyond the thinking of both the bureaucracy and those reformers concerned with securing Bangladesh's Independence.

However, even struggles for secularism and democracy were increasingly difficult to manage as the regime became mired in personal greed and corruption, and as relations between the Awami League and the bureaucracy grew more factionalized.[18] This factionalism, coupled with clashes between the regime, the military, and the opposition parties eventually undermined the government's authority. Contributing to its decline was its inability to restore production levels to those prior to Independence, the poor productivity of the nationalized sector, the rapid rise in inflation rates, and the deteriorating standard of rural living that culminated in the 1974 famine.[19] The exploitation of these conditions by the opposition as well as the US further undermined the regime's control and political legitimacy and offered a ripe environment for a military coup.

The Period of Military Rule

Military rule under both Ziaur Rahman (1975–81) and H.M. Ershad (1982–90) significantly altered the political stage[20] and the government agenda which increased Islamic representation in political discourse and featured women in its rhetoric and practice. For example, while Zia doubled the defence budget,[21] he failed to resolve the factional interests and generational differences within the military.[22] This sustained hostilities especially between repatriates representing an anti-Indian constituency with a pro-Islamic world orientation, and young officers and soldiers constituting the more politicized elements of the service.[23]

Zia also dismantled the early socialist principles of Mujib and furthered diplomatic and trade relations with the oil-rich countries of the Middle East as well as generated support from the European Community and North America. He welcomed greater involvement of the World Bank and the International Monetary Fund in reorganizing the Bangladeshi economy and initiated increased trade with countries of the Pacific Rim. The regime also furthered the capitalization of agriculture and rural petty commodity production, turned its commitments to the enhancement of private investment, and promoted the rapid denationalization of the industrial sector to create a new class of entrepreneurs and traders whose interests became central to the politics of the newly created Bangladesh Nationalist Party (BNP), formed under the direct patronage of the military regime. However, notwithstanding these changes, Zia retained subsidies for tubewells and other inputs to peasant producers, a government procurement programme, and infrastrnctural support for roads, irrigation, and grain storage commitments which distinguish this period from those of subsequent regimes. This strategy sustained channels of patronage to rural power brokers and the status of Union Council members whose support was important in building the BNP.[24]

In an attempt to introduce Islam as a political ideology and replace secularism as the organizing principle institutionalized under the Awami League, Zia formally altered the Constitution and inserted, by Presidential proclamation, the words 'absolute trust and faith in Almighty Allah'. As if to emphasize the political shift, Zia visited Saudi Arabia and publicly greeted those who completed the Haj. He encouraged Islamic banks to operate in Dhaka and Chittagong, and mosques and *madrassas* to secure support from the Saudi government. He also provided Islam-oriented parties with a larger space in political fora as a show of Islamic solidarity. Under Zia's Martial Law Administration, the place of Islam on the political stage was also reframed by the actions of many others, who, sensing a 'revival' of the Islamic symbol, began making changes in their political agenda. Thus, although Maulana Bhashani, leader of the pro-Beijing National Awami Party, had advocated the creation of an 'Islamic socialist polity' in Bangladesh during the Mujib period, after August 1975 even the pro-Moscow National Awami Party headed by Muzaffar Ahmad linked religion and socialism in its slogan, 'religion, hard work, and socialism'.[25] Likewise, the Democratic League, another political party, began invoking Islam as the basis for establishing a just society; the Islam-oriented political parties, including the Islamic Democratic League and the Muslim League, framed their political agenda according to the teachings of the Qur'an and on religious practice.[26]

Notwithstanding the increased recognition of Islam in party politics and its recognition in the Constitution, Zia continued to portray himself as a modernist who espoused a progressive version of Islam that included enhancing women's position through increased access to resources and opportunities. He supported women's employment in government and semi-autonomous programmes in health, family planning, and rural cooperatives,[27] which helped transform the configuration of the rural labour force. Moreover, coinciding with the United Nations International Women's Year (1975) and the United Nations Decade for Women (1975–85), Zia ably exploited the 'women in development' banner by establishing, with modest support, a Women's Affairs Ministry, created the Bangladesh Jatiya Mahila Sangshtha (BJMS), the National Women's Organization, which served predominantly middle class women, and reserved parliamentary seats and public sector jobs for women. These efforts were class and gender specific and were implemented in ways that did not directly undermine existing production and gender relations.

Pressured by the World Bank, Zia also promoted the Integrated Rural Development Programme (IRDP) in Population Planning and the Rural Women's Cooperatives, programmes that focused on predominantly poor rural households.[28] The IRDP sought to increase agricultural productivity, while its women's programme centred on reducing the national fertility rate, the latter guided by the assumption that women's increased economic security was a critical factor in reducing family size. Thus, the IRDP provided women with credit and training opportunities,[29] encouraging those activities and investments that did not challenge women's central place within the household. For instance, while credit enabled women to capitalize cattle rearing, vegetable gardening, and home-based sewing, the amount of capital extended limited possibilities for accumulation and economic independence. Additionally, programme staff generally advised against activities that would increase women's participation in market and trade activities. In other words, the purpose of such programmes was to extend and reorganize domestic work rather than to challenge the central place of women in the domestic economy.

However, like other programmes drawing on efforts first introduced at the Academy for Rural Development located at Comilla, the IRDP generated far more opportunities for women than those envisioned by its supporters. For instance, it offered women a place to meet, to make claims on institutional authorities and to secure resources that they sought to control. These new infrastructural resources parallel those provided by many NGOs in the late 1970s. Begun as relief and rehabilitation efforts after the famine, by the late 1970s NGO programmes supported women's interests through consciousness raising and credit extension. Building on Zia's modernist stance toward women, NGOs provided literacy training and population planning to poor rural women, and, with government support and financial assistance from the donor community, they enhanced women's skills and income generating opportunities and participation in the labour market. By offering women new opportunities for participation in wage employment they helped to shape institutional changes that have since sustained the dramatic turn from import substitution to export-led growth.

By supporting government programmes and NGO initiatives to enhance women's resource access and increasing opportunities for middle class rural women in government service, Zia creatively managed a public discourse on Islam that enhanced women's control of resources while sustaining forms of rural production.[30] This approach sustained a 'liberal' interpretation of Bangladeshi Islam while enabling Zia to use other opportunities, including agricultural subsidies, to channel resources and patronage to the countryside. Zia cultivated a 'man of the soil' image, visiting rural communities, and highlighting his role in the liberation war to cultivate political support, partly designed to sustain and consolidate his own political authority. However, Zia's failure to allay the apprehensions of the established rural interests about these programmes gadually eroded his support among this constituency. His failure to mediate these interests, coupled with his move to civilian rule that threatened relations within the military, eventually contributed to his downfall.

Ershad's seizure of power furthered Zia's export-led development strategy and also advanced the centrality of Islam as a political symbol. Ershad put Islam at the centre of his political discourse, extended Zia's move toward denationalization and disinvestment, increased the country's dependence on foreign capital, and further solidified the conditions enabling the creation of an industrial bourgeoisie. He gradually removed agricultural and input subsidies, directed credit toward urban and industrial development, and garnered the interests of the burgeoning urban industrial élite. Moreover, Ershad supported an expanded role for multilateral and bilateral donors by facilitating the shift from commodity and food aid to project assistance furthering national policy reform in concert with structural adjustment lending requirements.

Despite the shift away from agricultural subsidies, Ershad promoted a decentralization policy ostensibly transferring some authority for resource allocation and local level decision-making to the *upazilla*, or sub-district level, although tight bureaucratic control rendered it largely meaningless. However, this change did reorganize the development bureaucracy and created a new vehicle for political control in Ershad's effort to build a base for his new political party. His policy of decentralization altered the patronage connections established by previous regimes and removed support from small scale agricultural and non-farm producers, subverting their efforts to sustain the household economy. These economic reforms increased the likelihood of all family members seeking to secure their own subsistence thus increasing the demand as well as opportunities for women's private sector employment. In so doing, Ershad removed the benefits that had previously accrued to selected rural interests.

In this context, it is not surprising that a space was created especially for the Jama't to combine proselytizing with social welfare initiatives, with financial support provided by the Islamic community, to extend resources to the rural poor. As Kabeer notes, 'The outcome of Saudi munifi- cence has been the creation of alternative networks of patronage which materially bolster the appeal of the Islamic constituency'.[31] Included among these resources, notes Kabeer, are student scholarships, vocational training, and funds for accommodation, employment, and medical aid. Against this backdrop, it is hardly surprising that the Jama't gained the support of large numbers of college and university students, particularly those outside Dhaka. Recruitment of students from Rajshahi and Chittagong resulted in mass unrest and violent exchanges between different political constituencies on their respective campuses. Men who join these cadres were among those who were either frustrated in securing employment in a limited labour market or disenchanted with the existing political system for various reasons; women who joined were both recruits and recruiters of a separate women's front; women generally followed the lead of their male family members in supporting the Jama't. Ershad did, or could do, little to intervene in controlling such politics on these campuses. Unlike Zia, the failure to create a support base among college and university students was indeed one of the principal weaknesses of the Ershad regime.

In the countryside decline in rural resources created the political space for a rapidly expanding non-governmental sector that initially provided limited inputs and services to the rural poor. During the Ershad regime, NGOs broadened their focus, the resources they offered, and the constituencies they served.[32] By the mid-1980s, women accounted for the largest proportion of NGO members, were involved in consciousness raising, literacy, credit, and irrigation programmes, and accounted for a significant proportion of NGO workers. It was also a period when discussion focused on their diverse 'development' strategies, disagree- ments over donor support, and commitment to service delivery versus consciousness raising. The different choices made by the NGOs culminated in a myriad of political alliances and forms of opposition. Despite this diversity, what emerges under Ershad and both the multi- and bilateral lending institutions is a closer working relationship with the NGOs than they previously supported.[33] This, in turn, further reduced government investment in development activities focusing instead on increased support for the private sector, including subsidies for business and trade as well as integration of NGO activities into national planning. This rapprochement highlights the cooptation of the NGOs in what had previously been an adversarial relationship between government and the institutions of civil society.

Thus, through the NGOs as well as the support of government and semi-autonomous government agencies, the gendered politics of developmentalism led to women providing the market and the clientele, characterizing the modernizing economy. Although government resources to rural women did not significantly rise, except in population control, NGO programmes to generate employment and improve women's literacy and health care grew significantly. These new resources provided skills and a degree of self-confidence that eventually enabled rural women to respond to Ershad's industrialization initiatives and the demand for workers in the emerging export sector.

Support for Ershad's 1982 Industrial Policy furthered the government's commitment to structural adjustment that included the development of an export processing enclave in and around Dhaka, credit and tax holidays for an emerging entrepreneurial class, and bureaucratic support to develop and enhance the interests of this ascending class. Built upon the export-led strategy demanded by the World Bank, this policy advertised the competitive wages and docile labour of Bangladeshi women during a time when quotas had begun to restrict imports from Korea and the Newly Industrialized Countries. The result was an expansion of the female labour force leading to an increasing number of women on the streets of Dhaka city, a presence which signified modernity and a new urban landscape. In the course of little over a year, between 1982 and 1983, women were living in hostels that had previously been limited to university students, going to the cinema, shopping in the markets that surrounded the emerging manufacturing sites, waiting for buses, and walking arm in arm along the road. These changes profoundly altered street life and mores in Dhaka, challenging the regime to renegotiate the public presence of women in the context of an increasing use of religious symbols and practices.

Significantly, various examples indicate that independent behaviour among women is no longer limited to a few among the middle class; with the rise in women's employment and income, working class women also seek a greater degree of freedom of expression and mobility than they previously enjoyed. However, rather than travelling alone in a rickshaw or car, working class women often walk collectively along the main streets, representing independence in ways quite different from their middle class counterparts. Important in this example is the challenge embodied in the growing numbers of women in public places, including the labour force and shopping malls, whose behaviour is used to epitomize all that is distinctive about liberalization and modernity. Important too is that reactions to women factory workers, as well as those shopping or attending the cinema, provide a vehicle for criticizing, if indirectly, all women who have benefited from the resources and policies of the Ershad regime.

Despite the failure to generate support for censure of these working women, Ershad took other steps to further the link between the state and Islam. He exempted mosques from paying their electric and water supply bills, instituted a *zakat* fund under his control, required television broadcasts to be preceded by a call to prayer, and required women in the media to be 'appropriately' dressed. He refused to ratify a number of clauses promoted by the World Plan of Action of the UN Decade for Women and part of the Convention on the Elimination of All Forms of Discrimination Against Women which related to inheritance, marriage, child custody, and divorce on the grounds that they contradicted the Shari'a. He also vowed 'to give Islam its rightful place in the future constitution of the country'.[34] Efforts to represent Islam among state policies were viewed by some as a way to promote a nationalist politics, build solidarity and legitimacy for the regime, mask the class cleavages of civil society, and, according to Alam, disempower an opposition from challenging Ershad's political authority.[35]

Ershad's legitimacy was however already in decline, a fact best represented by the March 1988 elections which he 'won', but which were boycotted by the opposition parties and included the votes of only three per cent of the electorate. His increasingly fragile political status led Ershad to negotiate with the rightist opposition and to formally amend the Constitution. On 7 June 1988, backed by the Jama't, the Parliament introduced and passed Section 2A to the Constitution which declares: 'The state religion of the Republic is Islam, but other religions may be practiced in peace and harmony in the Republic'.[36] Despite the passage of this amendment and various other negotiated compromises, Jama't-i-Islami leader Moulana Delwar Hosain Sayeedi accused the government and the secular opposition parties of 'letting women in the street', which, he argued, was eroding Islamic values.[37] This was undoubtedly in response to the mass mobilization against the Constitutional Amendment which included support from women's groups who, in many cases, had never before participated in a public rally.

The compromises, and sustained tension between Ershad and Jama't, on the one hand, and between Ershad and donor demands for economic reforms, on the other, highlight the shift from support for an agricultural élite to negotiation with an increasingly powerful urban élite. For Ershad, compromise meant diversifying his politics of patronage so as to sustain his urban base while not breaking his alliance with the countryside.[38] This was accomplished by rhetorical suppart for a 'traditionalizing' interpretation of gender relations and religious authority, while simultaneously promoting the participation of women in the labour market. Such changes, coupled with an unwillingness to create a civilian power base independent of the military (as had Zia), expanded the political space for the rise of a secular opposition in the form of a strong and coordinated NGO movement. In 1990, a movement for democracy removed Ershad from power and opened the possibility for free elections.

The Democratic Space of Begum Zia

In February 1991, Begum Zia, the wife of former President and Martial Law Administrator Ziaur Rahman, led the BNP in what is touted as the first democratic election in the country. She won 31 per cent of the popular vote. The Awami League, under the leadership of Sheikh Hasina Wajed, won 28 per cent, and Ershad won 12 per cent of the vote. The Jama't-i-Islami, with 18 parliamentary seats, emerged as the fourth largest political party. To secure her office against the Awami League and Ershad's Jatiya party, Khaleda Zia promoted a strategy of negotiation with the Jama't. This strategy was a pragmatic initiative to secure political power and limit the potential effects of an alliance between the Awami League and the Jatiya party. Whether intended or not, this strategy added legitimacy to fundamentalist readings of social behaviour and further undermined a syncretic interpretation of Islamic belief and practice.

Khaleda Zia's relationship with the Jama't is distinct from Mujib's secularist policies and Zia's more cautious, if in the long term equally problematic, rapprochement. Indeed, her political compromises could be said to have pushed further Ershad's constitutional reforms. Through these compromises with the Jama't, Khaleda Zia split the generally non-aligned NGO community, who had an important role in the downfall of Ershad, as well as support for the 1991 democratic elections. Ironically, the challenge posed by BNP's embrace of the Jama't is in stark contrast to NGO support for women's rights and equitable resource access.

For some, Khaleda Zia's collaboration with the Jama't transformed her democratic victory. It extended Jama't's voice and authority in the political arena despite their limited electoral presence. For example, negotiations between the BNP and the Jama't included shared decision-making on, among other things, the distribution of the 30 seats reserved for women, and chosen by parliament.[39] In addition, the secretary-general of Jama't introduced a private member's bill in parliament in July 1992 which sought to make acts that 'defile' the Qur'an or the name of the Prophet criminal. Under this bill the Penal Code would be amended such that

whoever willfully damages, or desecrates the Holy Qur'an or . . . uses the Holy Qur'an . . . in a derogatory manner shall be punished with imprisonment for life, . . . whoever by words either spoken or written, or by signs or visible representations, or by an imputation, immuendoso [sic] or insinuation, defiles, directly or indirectly, the sacred name of the Holy Prophet Muhammad (peace be upon him) shall be punished with death, or imprisonment for life and shall also be liable to a fine.[40]

While this bill did not pass, these sentiments, and the lack of any restraint on the Jama't by the BNP, offered a discursive space and hence legitimacy for the BNP to support more textual interpretations of Islam. The BNP position on this, however, was not so much to employ such readings but to ignore or fail to challenge the increased place of Islam as a source of control rather than religious belief in everyday exchange.

Not surprisingly, a forum of intellectuals and professionals urged the government to resist enacting such a law in anticipation that it could be used as a tool of repression. These progressive forces, often led by women and members of the NGO community, have since become the most direct targets of Jama't attack. Yet, despite these demands, the government did not denounce, investigate, prosecute, or punish crimes committed in the name of fatwas, or take action against those who issued them. Such inaction appears as a direct incitement to violence, since such attacks, according to Human Rights Watch violate the Bangladesh Constitution.[41] Moreover, the lack of democratic leadership under Begum Zia led, throughout 1994, to women being stoned for supposedly committing adultery, presses being destroyed, writers banned or executed for their 'blasphemous' writings, and NGOs firebombed for the programmes they offer to women. The summer of 1994 is also distinguished by protests, demonstrations, hartals, and pitched battles demanding the execution of Taslima Nasreen, the controversial feminist author, and the intellectuals, journalists, and government officials who support her rights. The 29 July *gherao* ('cordon') for example, was a call for a restriction to be placed on NGOs from operating in the country.[42]

These instances of repression are neither rare nor localized. In one well known case, Nurjahan, a woman living with her parents when her first husband abandoned her, was remarried after her parents fulfilled the obligations of an appropriate annulment. Claiming that her behaviour was inappropriate and offensive to local interests, Nurjahan was ordered in a waist-deep hole and pelted with 101 stones. She survived this attack, as did her parents who were also publicly brutalized, only to commit suicide because of the public shame and humiliation suffered by her and her family.[43] This example, and others which substantiate verbal abuse and physical attacks against women, indicates how the BNP–Jama't-i-Islami alliance led to the legitimation of direct repression against women, even when they acted in ways that were appropriate under the law. It also shows how traditional local institutions, often representing well-established élite constituencies, were used to represent the interests of the Jama't, or similar groups or individuals, against particular expressions of change.

Striking too about the strategy of the religious-oriented parties and their allies is the effort to control the information shared in the public press. Thus, several secular-oriented presses in Bogra and Dhaka were set aflame because of allegations that they printed anti-Islamic articles. On 20 May 1994, for instance, in addition to setting fire to the offices of two Bengali newspapers, the marchers demanded the execution of Taslima Nasreen and a ban on four additional newspapers, namely, *Bhorer Kagoj, Sangbad, Janakantha*, and *Banglar Bani*. This was followed by attacks on newspaper offices, threats to their editors, and charges against or warrants for the arrest of editors whose papers were alleged to publish articles with 'malicious and deliberate intent of hurting the religious sentiments of the people'.

Another incident following a nationwide call for a hartal by the fundamentalist parties led to setting aflame the Bangladesh Women's Health Coalition clinic in Zakiganj, Sylhet, by a mob assumed to be led by the sons of a local *pir*. While the mob eventually let the clinic medical officer escape, the clinic was gutted and an adjoining NGO, 'Friends of Village Development in Bangladesh', was badly damaged. This clinic, begun more than a decade ago, offers women health and family planning information and services. Its head is an important voice in the struggle for women's reproductive rights. Despite charges, and the identification of a number of those involved in the attack, the ten people arrested were released the following morning, reportedly following a call from the prime minister's office.

These incidents are part of a pattern of attacks directed against women and the NGOs, who symbolize the transformed Bangladesh political economy. Other incidents include attacks against two internationally recognized organizations, the Bangladesh Rural Advancement Committee and the Grameen Bank, whose programmes support women through literacy, skills training, and credit. Their rural programmes have been censured, their programme workers harassed, and schools and buildings burned.[44] Programmes such as those of BRAC and the Grameen Bank Project are internationally recognized for the alternatives they provide to *madrassa* education and informal credit or moneylending. These alternatives challenge established sources of legitimacy and areas of investment for those élites most directly affected by the economic reforms of the past two decades and those likely to identify with the fundamentalist parties.

Less well documented and explored are the everyday politics of individuals who live in the context of an increasingly Islamic presence, and sensibility about accepted women's behaviour. As the Zia government provided no limits or recourse for those threatened or attacked by this version of political Islam, people were forced to negotiate in ways that do not raise the ire of the 'political extremist'.[45] Like the everyday forms of resistance that frame Scott's (1986) understanding of peasant opposition, people in Bangladesh seek ways to limit their public discussion of and to curtail particular forms of behaviour, especially those of their young daughters. Fearful about the lack of government response, especially when assumed to be a democratically elected party, people living in towns and cities outside Dhaka were the most articulate about these concerns. Academics too, found that university politics left little room for exchange and debate as the various camps took to threats of violence and actual struggles that often led to the temporary closing of campuses. Such everyday forms of censure are most likely to occur when government rules of redress fail to operate, and where benign neglect, if not direct support, provide little protection for a significant proportion of the citizenry.

These events and the new conditions that shape public expression follow upon a complex history of negotiation between a 'syncretic' and more fundamentalist readings of Islam. What differentiates contemporary interpretations about the behaviour and rights of individuals under Islam is that women now take the lead in struggles on behalf of women's specific interests as well as in struggles for democracy and human rights, including the right to public redress and improved welfare. These struggles, moreover, are no longer limited to participation among middle class women but increasingly involve women from all social classes. As players in the political struggles of The Gono Adalat ('The People's Tribunal'), for example, led by the late Jahanara Imam,[46] women demanded that the government bring to trial the leaders of the Jama't-i-Islami for collaborating with the Pakistani army and committing war crimes in 1971.

The government's response to these struggles was to demand 'law and order'. However, this exchange is significant as a way to identify important connections between contemporary attacks on the cultural proscriptions of daily life and the vested interests of those who sought to gain by collaborating with the Pakistani élite in their attempt to maintain a colonial status for Bangladesh. Today, these same groups seek to secure their economic interests by sustaining an active place in national politics. Moreover, such efforts highlight the challenge posed by women as they enter the political arena. In this and other ways, changes in women's behaviour, whether as workers, NGO members, or as participants in collective struggles that call into question government practices, mark women as targets of change and threats to an older, once well established rural élite.

Concluding Comments

Through this regime history I have illuminated important tensions that situate the growth of the Jama't-I-Islami within the changing economic and political forces in the country since Independence in 1971. These competitive forces are constituted by the changing position of Bangladesh within the global economy, her integration within the Islamic community, negotiations between Bangladesh and multilateral agency demands for structural reform, and the political and electoral compromises made by particular regimes to secure their authority. They also are shaped by declining economic and social stability among a growing proportion of the population, and the simultaneous increase in the new urban industrial élite who are beneficiaries of the shift in development strategy from import substitution to export-led growth. Besides, struggles for survival have come to increasingly depend upon individual forms of subsistence. For women, this means that they are no longer able to depend upon the support of family and kin to sustain everyday life. Instead, they must negotiate new ways to secure income given dramatic declines in agricultural and small scale, home-based craft production and in response to the reorganization of the household and village economy. Concurrent with these dramatic changes are new alliances between social classes and among these classes, state bureaucrats, party politics and the military, and the generation of new forms of production and gender relations.

These broad realignments have their counterpoint in a dynamic and gradually coordinated NGO[47] sector which provides an increasingly diversified rural community with educational and credit resources and a growing number of employment opportunities for women. Women's employment too has increased in response to state sponsored initiatives in the small and cottage industries sector and in public services. Besides, women feature prominently in the rapidly expanding private sector. As women increase their demand for work they are targeted as a source of cheap labour providing a ready resource for the country's largest export manufacturers: providers of garments and apparel for the world market. Women's recent participation in both the public and private sector also make them a target for fundamentalist parties as women mark their own achievements as well as the dramatic transformation of the political economy where economic reforms have eroded the security of a once entrenched rural élite. Through discursive and pragmatic attacks on women's public participation, the religious right has confronted women as well as the interests of an emergent urban bourgeoisie who challenged their political legitimacy and control of a once vibrant rural economy. Their demands include a return to a way of life that depended upon the direct control of women's labour and sought 'protection' for women who 'step outside the bounds of social norms'.[48] These bounds are reconstructed in terms of a romanticized past and an idyllic future, playing on the promise of a better life where women could be secure within the patriarchal household.

Ironically, these efforts to limit women's work opportunities have been generated just as their need to work has increased under conditions of high levels of under- and unemployment, low wages, and household income insecurity. However, it is perhaps not ironic that such a discursive frame both targets and masks the concrete benefits women have come to enjoy in the past decade—small but independent incomes, and a freedom of movement and participation in social activities beyond the community—and to ignore women's demands for improved employment conditions, greater public representation, and greater social equity.

Against the backdrop of these changes and achievements, the Jama't-i-Islami builds upon, while simultaneously seeking to reorder gender relations, to secure their own class demands. Their demands alter expectations regarding women's behaviour by exposing the tension between women as objects or victims of new economic and social opportunities and as subjects empowered by interests and capacities that threaten extant forms of political authority and social practice. In this latter view, female wage workers are not victims of the modernization project, as some critics of transnational production suggest, but are invokers of change who challenge urban and rural petty bourgeois interests that seek the direct control of their labour. In these and other ways, women's position is among those most dramatically altered by the economic changes that have occurred with economic restructuring.

While some of these changes reconstitute home-based forms of production, others challenge the ready availability of unpaid labour and rural resource control. For example, changes in women's employment and access to credit and training challenge patron–client networks that had once sustained the power of rural élites over landless and poor rural household members. With support from NGOs and government programmes, wage contracts and institutionalized credit and training have replaced many of the informal networks controlled by this once entrenched élite. In concert with national policy reforms that redirect resources from the agricultural sector to small-scale semi-urban manufacturing and industrial growth, the powers of this semi-feudal *jotedar* class has significantly declined only to be displaced by a new urban élite who enjoy the increased attention of each successive regime as well as the international industrial and aid community. In this reading, securing political legitimacy cannot be viewed solely through the lens of parties or state ideologies but must account for both critiques of particular economic reforms and new forms of global integration which recast gender contradictions within a series of national political and institutional realignments. Contestation over these processes and for economic control places Bangladesh at the centre of changes in global production and accumulation.[49]

As I also have tried to show, although fundamentalist forces have been supported through two military regimes, it is under the movement for democracy, supported by the democratically elected government of Khaleda Zia, that the Jama't emerged stronger, or at least more publically vocal than before. However, despite the rapprochement between the Jama't and the Khaleda Zia regime, opposition by a vocal and organized women's movement, including support from rural women, led to calls for new elections in 1997. This latter election, won by Sheikh Hasina of the Awami League, resulted in the Jama't losing all but three parliamentary seats.

Finally, I have suggested that the traditional interpretation of Islamic practices often marks the country's 'backwardness', and fundamentalist ideology and practice are assumed to shape conditions of underdevelopment and patriarchal domination.[50] Yet, contemporary Islamic movements often employ specific textual readings of Islam to draw attention to the very success of modernization by identifying changes in women's behaviour. By so doing, they highlight their loss of control of women's labour and their decline in a once robust rural economy. Further, their efforts to secure political authority are not calls for a return to the past, but are actually modern political forms that build upon traditionalizing but not traditional social practices. The shift from the mobilization of people on behalf of religious belief to contemporary constructions of Islam as a political frame for affirming and mobilizing on behalf of particular economic interests highlights the embeddedness of the political and cultural economy. These demands for political authority represent a global development crisis reconstituting efforts at nation-building as well as contemporary constructions of nationalism and community identity.

Notes and References

1. This essay is a reconceptualization of 'Representing Islam: Manipulating Gender, Shifting State Practices and Class Frustrations in Bangladesh', in Patricia Jeffrey and Amrita Basu (eds), *Appropriating Gender: Women's Activism and the Politicization of Religion in South Asia* (London: Routledge, 1997).

2. *See* Michael Fisher, 'Islam and the Revolt of the Petit Bourgeoisie', in *Daedalus* (1982), 101–25.

3. Benjamin R. Barber, *Jihad vs McWorld: How Globalism and Tribalism are Reshaping the World* (New York: Ballantine Books, 1996), 6.

4. By Westernization, I refer to particular relations of economic restructuring which undermine a previously entrenched élite constituency. *See* Barber, op. cit., 206–9.

5. I follow Zartman in distinguishing between Islam as religious and cultural practice and political Islam as the site of struggles for state power. (William Zartman, 'Democracy and Islam: The Cultural Dialectic', in *The Annals of the American Academy of Political and Social Science*, 524 (November , 1992, 182). This distinction situates and historicizes Islam as a socially constructed and constituted set of practices that embody changing and often contradictory interests. Given this specification, I limit my discussion to questions of Bengali or Bangladeshi nationalism and nation-state formation, even though broader questions about these issues have figured prominently in recent debates on Islam (e.g. Talukder Maniruzzaman, 'Bangladesh Politics: Secular and Islamic Trends', in Rafiuddin Ahmed (ed.), *Islam in Bangladesh: Society, Culture and Politics* (Dhaka: Bangladesh Itihas Samiti, 1983), 184–219; S.M. Shamsul Alam, 'Islam, Ideology, and the State in Bangladesh', in *Journal of Asian and African Studies*, XXVIII, 1–2, 1993, 88–106). I also omit a history of Islam and a discussion of the question of political legitimacy and institution-building in the post-Mujib period (*see* Talukdar Maniruzzaman, 'The Future of Bangladesh', in A. Jeyaratnam Wilson and Dennis Dalton (eds), *The States of South Asia: Problems of National Integration* (Honolulu: The University Press of Hawaii, 1982), 265–94; Shireen Hasan Osmany, *Bangladesh Nationalism: History of Dialectics and Dimensions* (Dhaka: University Press Ltd, 1992) as well as questions of identity politics and their salience for understanding contemporary social movements).

6. *See* Minoo Moallem, 'The Ethnicity of an Islamic Fundamentalism: The Case of Iran', in *South Asia Bulletin*, XII:2 (Fall), 1992, 25–34.

7. The contrast between NGOs, women, and entrepreneurs is important to make, since the discourse they employ is shared, but they generally support quite different programmes and opportunities for women.

8. The 1947 Partition and the formation of Pakistan was constructed on the basis of a 'natural affinity' between Bengalis and Pakistanis as members of a Muslim community.

9. Others argue that those targeted were named in a list prepared by a USAID official who worked in close collaboration with the Pakistan Intelligence department and the army. *See*, for example, Rangalal Sen, *Political Élites in Bangladesh* (Dhaka: University Press Ltd., 1986), 9.

10. Undoubtedly, the abandonment of Bangladesh by the West and her support by India and the Soviet Union conditioned this discursive choice in the immediate post-Independence period.

11. *See* Rangalal Sen, op. cit., 279.

12. Rehman Sobhan, 'Growth and Contradictions within the Bangladesh Bourgeoisie', in *Journal of Social Studies*, 9 (July), 1980, 8–9.

13. Important in solidifying this position at the time of Independence, and since the return to the discourse of heritage and scripture, is the urban-based foreign born Islamic élite who resist assimilation into indigenous Bengali culture and maintain their adherence to orthodox Islamic practices (*see* Naila Kabeer, 'The Quest for National Identity: Women, Islam and the State in Bangladesh', in Deniz Kandiyoti (ed.), *Women, Islam and the State* (Philadelphia: Temple University Press, 1991), 118 . Outlining these different interests are not meant to align with either of the positions posed, but to emphasize both the continuity and difference in the contemporary arguments and those made during the Independence struggle.

14. *See* Naila Kabeer, in Deniz Kandiyoti (ed.), op. cit., passim.

15. S.M. Shamsul Alam, in *Journal of Asian and African Studies*, XXVIII, 1–2, 1993, 97–8.

16. For an alternative interpretation of secularism as a pragmatic idea imported by Western educated nationalist leaders rather than a commitment to the separation of politics and religion, *see* Talukdar Maniruzzaman, in Rafiuddin Ahmed, op. cit., 184–219, and S.M. Shamsul Alam, op. cit. Posed in this way, secularism is deployed merely as another 'religious' ideology rather than as a different axis upon which to base political practice.

17. A programme for women's rehabilitation in the mid-1980s, addressed particularly to rape victims and prostitutes, does little to indicate that government initiatives to secure resources for these women has challenged the underlying liberal assumptions that characterize women's appropriate behaviour and need for social control.

18. Rounaq Jahan, *Pakistan: Failure in National Integration* (Dhaka: Univer-

sity Press Ltd., 1977); and Talukder Maniruzzaman, in A. Jeyaratnam Wilson and Dennis Dalton (eds.), op. cit., 265–94.

19. These conditions also included the ban on the sale of jute to Cuba demanded of the regime by the US in exchange for food aid which furthered deteriorating rural living standards. *See also* Rehman Sobhan and Muzaffer Ahmed, *Public Enterprise in an Intermediate Regime: A Study in the Political Economy of Bangladesh* (Dacca: Bangladesh Institute of Development Studies, 1981)₆ for a discussion of Bangladesh as an intermediate regime.

20. The political prominence of the military beginning in 1975, suggests the failure of the Awami League to offer a hegemonic project that could mediate the varied interests that had supported the struggle for Independence, particularly those of the military.

21. An increase from 15 to 16 per cent to between 20 and 30 per cent of the annual revenue budget or from $ 34 million or 0.7 per cent of the GNP in the last year of Mujib's rule to $ 130 million or 1.8 per cent of the total GNP by 1978 (*see* B.K. Jahangir, *Problematics of Nationalism in Bangladesh* (Dhaka: Centre for Social Studies, 1986), 80.

22. In fact, in 1975, two factions of the almost 55,000 persons in the army were about equally divided between those who had participated in the liberation struggle and those who were repatriated from West Pakistan. The senior repatriated officers had lost seniority and status to the younger recruits who, because of their participation and experience in the liberation struggle, were able to rise in the military hierarchy.

23. *See* Talukdar Maniruzzaman, in A. Jeyaratnam Wilson and Dennis Dalton (eds.), op. cit., 285.

24. Shelley Feldman, 'NGOs and Civil Society: (Un)stated Contradictions', in *The Annals of the American Academy of Political and Social Science, 554* (Nov.), 1997, 46–65.

25. Talukdar Maniruzzaman, in Rafiuddin Ahmed (ed.), op. cit., 208–9.

26. *See* Ahmed Shafiqul Huque and Muhammad Yeahia Akhter, 'The Ubiquity of Islam: Religion and Society in Bangladesh', in *Pacific Affairs*, 60(2), 1987, 200–25.

27. While employment for such women was limited to selected ministries and programmes, their participation as rural workers began to challenge both the image and the membership of the government cadres.

28. Such households were usually those with small holdings, where agriculture provided the primary source of livelihood. The poorest households, the landless and labouring classes, were generally excluded from access to those modest resources provided by the IRDP (Shelley Feldman, Farida Akhter, and Fazila Banu, 'The IRDP Women's Programme in Population Planning and Rural Women's Cooperatives', Project Manuscript, 1980).

29. A report supported by the Canadian Agency for International Development (CIDA) highlighted the complex and contradictory goals and implementa-

tion strategies of this programme. It identified the class biases and the limited understanding about rural women's needs held by those in the centralized setting of urban based decision-makers. The document, although supported by the Ministry of Local Government and Rural Development, was never widely circulated by the donors and a different version was eventually published by CIDA.

30. One must not overstate this point as reliable statistics on the extent of women's access to resources made available under these programmes are not available. Decades after these initiatives were first taken, grinding poverty is still the hallmark of rural Bangladeshi society with little or no change in the conditions of poorer women in towns and villages. (*Editor*)

31. Naila Kabeer, in Deniz Kandiyotyed (ed.), op. cit., 134.

32. It is important to stress that the relationship between political parties and the NGOs is a contradictory one which has changed significantly over time. Under both Zia and Ershad, negotiation over government registration requirements and control, political support during election time, and the independent status of NGOs led to divisions among them and to changes in their relationship to political parties.

33. *See* Shelley Feldman, in Patricia Jeffery and Amrita Basu (eds.), op. cit.

34. Speech by President Ershad, reported in the *Daily Ittefaq*, 18 February, 1985, cited in Ahmed Shafiqul Huque and Muhammad Yeahia Akhter, in *Pacific Affairs*, 60 (2), 1987.

35. S.M. Shamsul Alam, op. cit., 102.

36. S. Kamaluddin, 'The Islamic Way', *Far Eastern Economic Review*, 23 June 1988, 14–17; also Human Rights Watch/Asia, *Bangladesh: Violence and Discrimination in the Name of Religion* (New York: Human Rights Watch/Asia, 1994).

37. S. Kamaluddin, 'Pulpit Politics', *Far Eastern Economic Review*, 16 Feb. 1989.

38. This includes, but is not limited to, his decentralization scheme which provided rural resources and limited authority for resource distribution to *upazilla* bureaucrats.

39. S. Kamaluddin, 'People's Verdict', *Far Eastern Economic Review*, 15 April 1992.

40. Human Rights Watch/Asia, op. cit., 5.

41. Ibid., 2.

42. Ibid.; also M. Rashiduzzaman, 'The Liberals and the Religious Right in Bangladesh', in *Asian Survey*, XXXIV:11 (Nov.) 1994, 974–90.

43. Reported in *The Daily Sangbad*, cited in Meghna Guhathakurta, 'The Aid Discourse and the Politics of Gender', in *The Journal of Social Studies*, 65 (July), 1994, 101–114.

44. These incidents are abstracted from Tax 1993; Human Rights Watch/Asia 1994; Guhathakurta 1994; various issues of the *Far Eastern Economic*

Review, and personal conversations held during a trip to Bangladesh in 1993.

45. Here I draw on informal discussions held in 1994 and 1996 with NGO workers, academics, and middle class families about the role of the Jama't in their everyday lives.

46. Imam's efforts in the 1990s were built on her own experience during the war. *See*, for example, Jahanara Imam, 'From, Of Blood and Fire' (Bengali diary, 1989), 179–91, in Miriam Cooke and Roshini Rustomji-Kerns (eds.), *Blood Into Ink: South Asian and Middle Eastern Women Write War* (Boulder CO: Westview Press, 1994); also her memoirs in Bengali, *Ekattorer Dingulee* (Memoirs of the Days of Bangladesh Liberation War, 1971), 11th edn, (Dhaka: Sandhani Prakashani, 1992).

47. NGO efforts are envisioned to constrain, if not undermine, previously dominant informal networks of credit and education provisioning which previously excluded women from access.

48. Shelley Feldman, 'Individualism Recast: Changing Relations Between the State and Labor in Rural Bangladesh', Paper presented at the 14th Annual Middlebury College Conference on Economic Issues: Contributions to an On-going Agenda, Middlebury, Vermont, April 1992; also Meghna Guhathakurta, 'The Aid Discourse and the Politics of Gender', *The Journal of Social Studies*, 65 (July) 1994, 101–14.

49. Two characterizations mark the way that Bangladesh is generally compared among Islamic countries. First, edited volumes that focus on Islam, whether as faith, state sanctioned religion, or as ethnicity or community identification, often ignore Bangladesh as an exemplary case. Second, when the Middle East provides the implied framework and backdrop for a discussion of Bangladesh, the region is constructed either as a nation and a people who resist modernization and industrialization, as the recent turmoil surrounding Taslima Nasreen suggests, or as a nation engulfed by poverty, instability, floods, famines, and cyclones.

50. The primary exception to this is in specific discussions of population control and explanations of gender inequality. However, when Islam is invoked as the explanation in such discussion it is usually as a given doctrine rather than as a process of patriarchal control or as forms of class or social domination. In other words, it is a given condition of everyday life rather than an actively reproduced social ideology that requires explanation.

10

Bengali Muslims and Islamic Fundamentalism: The Jama't-i-Islami in Bangladesh

ENAYETUR RAHIM*

Introduction

Events in the Muslim world over the past two decades have dramatically drawn attention to the political and social potential of Islam. During this time, religion, and religious slogans have emerged as powerful political symbols in many Muslim societies, aggravating social and political tension, and often causing violence. Scholars have generally attempted to articulate the dynamics of this phenomenon by projecting a threatening scenario of a 'new cold war' and/or the 'clash of civilizations'.[1] On the other side of the spectrum, the perceived antipathy of the West to what is widely believed by Muslims as their vital interests has been widely interpreted as part of the ongoing hostility in the West against Islam. Although it is necessary to draw a clear distinction between Islam as a religion and fundamentalism as a religio–political ideology, the line is often blurred in both scholarly and popular writings.

This chapter does not propose an investigation of the global phenomenon of what has come to be known as Islamic fundamentalism; its goal is to assess the roles and activities of one such movement, namely, the Jama't-i-Islami, in the context of recent developments in Bangladesh.[2] However, although the primary focus of this study is the Jama't, which has been in the forefront of a 'resurgent Islam' in Bangladesh, its oblique parameters will expand into a wider dimension of political Islam, including the role of the army that has often wrested political power unconstitutionally and used Islamic symbols and slogans to legitimize political authority. Thus, successive military regimes have often solicited the support of religiously oriented political parties, particularly the Jama't, and have equally promoted public expressions of views on political matters by the traditionalist Muslim leaders, such as the *pirs* and mullahs.

Overwhelmingly Muslim, Bangladesh in its earlier incarnation as East Bengal or East Pakistan was an integral part of the Islamic state of Pakistan. However, even during that time, when the apparatus of a theocracy was at least in partial operation, politics in East Pakistan generally revolved around secular issues, and any ascription to religion in politics was at best peripheral or partial. During the period of intense political turmoil, especially between 1969 and 1971, which crystallized the Bangladesh nationalist movement, when Bengali political aspirations transformed themselves from an expression of religious-oriented nationalism to secular nationalism, very few religious-oriented political parties functioned with any degree of success. Islamic parties, like the Nizam-i-Islami Party and the Khilafat-i-Rabbani, consisted of a handful of socially ambitious, well-to-do, and conservative Muslims in urban centres devoid of any popular support. The fundamentalist Jama't-i-Islami, which had begun its activities in former East Pakistan early in the 1950s, had an equally unknown role in the political life of the community until the last days of Pakistani rule.

The Rise of the Jama't

Despite the Jama't's claims to be a national movement in former Pakistan, its presence in former East Pakistan (now Bangladesh) during the initial years after independence from Great Britain was marginal. Thus, in 1947 it had only one *rokn*, or primary member, from East Pakistan;[3] organizationally the Province was also allocated only one administrative division out of a total of 13 for all of Pakistan.[4] Its small office in Dhaka was manned by a lone paid official.[5] Led by Rafi Ahmed Indori, a member despatched from West Pakistan, an organizing committee of the party consisting of four members was formed in 1948. The Jama't then embarked on an active campaign to expand its support-base in the region.[6] To accelerate its activities in East Pakistan, Maulvi Abdur Rahim of Barisal, the only notable presence of a Bengali in the Jama't hierarchy, was appointed *amir* of East Pakistan in 1951. Despite these attempts, its membership of 12 in 1951 rose to only 38 in 1954.[7]

Disturbed by its slow growth, a six member delegation of the central Mujlis-i-Shura visited Dhaka in October 1952 and addressed a number of public meetings seeking to explain Jama't's programmes and goals. These efforts, however, did not lead to any sizable increase in its membership, or significantly strengthen its organizational machinery.

By comparison, in West Pakistan, the Jama't had a larger support-base which came mostly from people of diverse social and economic backgrounds, including those who were driven by the nostalgic goal of turning Pakistan into an Islamic theocracy. Others included younger college students, petty government officials, and *madrassa* students. The Jama't in West Pakistan was also able to draw support from a segment of the refugee population who had migrated from India during and after Partition in 1947. Having been uprooted from their homes in India, they were generally attracted by Jama't's programmes of support for them, especially since the government and the leadership of the ruling Muslim League party paid scant attention to their immediate problems. However, in East Pakistan, the Urdu speaking immigrants from Bihar and other parts of northern India, overwhelmed by the Bengali speaking majority in the province, and the general Bengali askance toward the newly arriving refugees, felt a stronger affinity towards the ruling Muslim League which was organizationally much stronger than the Jama't at that time.[8] The lukewarm support of the refugees for the Jama't, however, increasingly grew in strength as the Muslim League gradually retreated from the East Pakistani political scene not long after the establishment of Pakistan.

The lack of support for Jama't in East Pakistan could also be attributed to the continued influence of the traditionalist religious leaders, namely, the *pirs* and the mullahs, on the religiously conservative sections of the Bengali Muslims. These leaders remained steadfastly opposed to the Jama't for a variety of reasons despite their support for an Islamic polity which the Jama't espoused. The East Pakistani based religious-oriented political parties, the Nizam-i-Islami, the Khilafat-i-Rabbani, and the like, similarly failed to win any significant support from the conservative sections of the population and politically remained largely marginal. As long as the Muslim League was in political power, they generally sided with it, but with its fortunes in decline by the mid-1950s, many of them switched their allegiance to the centrist United Front.[9] Even among college and university students, Jama't support was almost nonexistent at this stage; in sharp contrast to the support the Jama't enjoyed amongst students in West Pakistan, where its student-wing, namely, the Jamia't-i-Tulaba, played a significant role in campus politics, and was equally active in national politics.

A moving force to revitalize the Jama't in East Pakistan was Ghulam Azam (1922–), who would soon establish himself as the principal theoretician and tactician of the party after he joined it as a *muttafiq*, or associate member, in 1954. He rapidly rose through the ranks and was confirmed to full membership (*rokn*) in 1955. In recognition of his leadership role, he was then chosen to a five member Jama't team to present the party's point of view on the constitution to the Constituent Assembly of Pakistan. He became the general secretary of the provincial Jama't in 1956 and its *amir* in 1969.[10] In the latter capacity he is known to have masterminded the Jama't's policy, strategy, and action plan during the Bangladesh war of liberation, 1971, collaborating with the Pakistani army in seeking to suppress the Bengali nationalist movement.

Ghulam Azam had joined the Jama't when he was teaching political science at Carmichael College, Rangpur (1950–5). Unlike Maulana Mawdudi, the founder and principal ideologue of the Jama't, Ghulam Azam had both a religious and secular education. After a *madrassa* education, he received his undergraduate and graduate degrees from Dhaka University, the premier institution of higher education in East Pakistan. Prior to joining the Jama't, Azam was an active member of the Muslim League and was also involved with the *dawa'* movement, known as the Tabligh *jama't*, which campaigned for the 'purification' of the Faith.[11] As a college student, Azam was similarly active in campus politics and was elected general secretary of the student government of his hall of residence in 1946; also serving as the general secretary of the prestigious Dhaka University Central Student's Union for two consecutive terms in 1947–8 and 1948–9.[12]

Ghulam Azam's commitment to Jama't's ideology was tempered by a unique sense of loyalty to his Bengali identity. His deep personal involvement in the Language movement, which ignited the first spark of Bengali nationalism in East Pakistan in the early 1950s, is anathema to many today for the apparently contradictory role he subsequently played by collaborating with the Pakistan army in 1971. He was imprisoned in 1952 for his role in the Language movement, and on his release was accorded a tumultuous welcome by the students. He again suffered imprisonment in 1955 for speaking out against political repression by the Pakistan government.[13] Thus, his political credentials when he joined the Jama't had the ambiguity of pseudo-Bengali nationalism.

As the newly-elected general secretary of the Jama't in 1955, Ghulam Azam's principal job was to popularize its programmes and create a support-base.[14] He was supported in his endeavor by the *amir* of the national organization, Maulana Mawdudi, who arrived in Dhaka in February 1956 to attend an all party Islamic constitutional conference and took the opportunity of placating educated Bengali Muslim public opinion as a means of legitimizing his organization in the province. Thus, at a Jama't conference held in Dhaka in March, Mawdudi pledged his support for the recognition of Bengali as an official language and admitted that East Pakistan had suffered discrimination under the Pakistan government, especially in the government services and the army.[15] Earlier, the Jama't had opposed the acceptance of Bengali as an official language, believing that this would keep the Bengalis ignorant of Islam.[16]

Soon, however, Mawdudi's rhetoric changed, betraying the Jama't strategy not to antagonize Bengali Muslim public opinion. Thus, during his 40 day trip to the province, Mawdudi castigated the demand for provincial autonomy and joint electorates underlying which he saw sinister Hindu machination to become the power broker in the province.[17] Mawdudi even went to the extent of accusing Hindus of playing upon the grievances of the Bengalis in order to gain economic dominance by expelling Muslim refugees who had earlier migrated to East Pakistan from India.[18] Insinuations were also reportedly made about Bengali Muslims' identity as Muslims which caused widespread resentment in the province.

As originally conceived, the Jama't was perhaps not designed to be a party of the masses; it concentrated more on 'revitalizing' the Muslims by inducing them to adopt the 'correct' ideals of Islam.[19] It could not however ignore the reality that political power was critical to achieving its desired goal: the creation of an 'ideal' Islamic society. The Jama't thus took part in electoral politics for the first time in 1951 by participating in the Punjab provincial assembly polls held in March that year.[20] Until that time, its policy was to keep away from elections as it did not want to associate itself with what it described as an un-Islamic system. While participating in the provincial elections, Mawdudi made it clear that reconstruction of Pakistan as an Islamic state could only be undertaken after a change in the leadership of the central government in favour of Islam.[21]

The Jama't had begun taking an active interest in the political process of the country after the passage of the Objective Resolution by the Pakistan Constituent Assembly in 1949 which proclaimed the primacy of Islam in state affairs. The Majlis-i-Shura met in April 1949 and declared that Pakistan had become 'an Islamic state in principle', and as such association with the state was permissible, thus setting the stage for its participation in the elective bodies.[22] An Election Board was established in September 1950 and an election manifesto was issued stating that the 'true' Islamic ideals as enunciated by the shari'a should be the guiding principles of the state.[23] The same manifesto, with minor modifications, was to be used in all future elections, including the 1970 national elections which resulted in the final break-up of Pakistan.

In the first provincial elections held in East Pakistan in 1954, the Jama't was still an unknown entity, and was unable to nominate a single candidate. However, the participation of another Islam-oriented political party, namely, the Nizam-i-Islami Party,[24] with its principal platform the establishment of an Islamic state, in a coalition of secular parties under the banner of the United Front, must have encouraged the Jama't. Indeed, a revived Nizam-i-Islami Party and the Jama't would combine forces with the secular Awami League on several occasions in the sixties, helping to politically legitimize the Jama't in the province. In the process, the Jama't established itself as a viable political entity which could promote the case of an Islamic polity in Pakistan with the tacit support of the secular-oriented political parties, including the Awami League.

After the enactment of the Constitution of 1956, which was hailed by the Jama't for bearing an Islamic stamp, Mawdudi announced plans to participate in the elections scheduled for 1958. However, the army takeover in October that year led to the suspension of all political activities; the Jama't, like other political parties, soon found itself under intense pressure from the military administration headed by General Ayub Khan. In his modernizing zeal, the Sandhurst-trained general, assisted by a Westernized civil–military bureaucracy, refused to permit the Islam-oriented groups any political space and thus obstructed the advocacy of an Islamic state: 'The Jama't's offices were closed down, its leaders were excoriated in government sponsored publications, and its activities, networks, and operations were stopped'.[25] When the Political Parties Act of 14 July 1962 came into force, the Jama't resurfaced within 24 hours. Unlike the other political parties, the Jama't re-emerged 'intact' and had become 'the most organized and robust of all political parties' by the end of 1962.[26]

It is difficult to ascertain the nature of Jama't's participation in the non-party indirect elections, held in 1959, to the odious apparatus of local self-government and rural development crafted by General Ayub known as the 'Basic Democracy', or controlled democracy. Similarly, the Jama't's presence in the national and provincial assemblies created in May 1962 with the 'basic democrats' as members of the electoral college is not quantifiable. It should however be pointed out that the Jama't had bitterly opposed the creation of the institution of Basic Democracy; similarly, it opposed the unchallenged presidential referendum held in 1960 confirming Ayub's incumbency to that high office. Unlike the other major political parties, the Jama't also refused to support Ayub's 'promulgated' constitution of 1 March 1962. Consequently, it incurred the wrath of the regime and paid a heavy price, especially for opposing Ayub's Family Law ordinance of 1961 which sought to regulate Muslim marriages.[27] Led by Mawdudi, the Jama't quickly exploited the occasion by leading an active campaign against the government. Concerned with Jama't's rising popularity, especially among the religious conservatives in West Pakistan, Ayub arrested three leading members of the organization.[28] In December 1963 he took another drastic measure by banning the Jama't and arresting several leading members of the party, including Ghulam Azam. However, the Dhaka high court held the ban on the Jama't to be unlawful; subsequently the Supreme Court also upheld the verdict of the high court and declared the ban null and void.[29] In those circumstances, the Jama't could claim political martyrdom for being singled out for persecution by the regime for its opposition to any anti-sharia law.

Faced with the regime's interminable enmity since 1958, the Jama't sought to redeem itself by aggressively focusing on social work and undertaking a programme of promoting Islamic education in the country. The Jama't became the only political party to develop welfare programmes for the poor, and supported charitable institutions and medical facilities through its subsidiary the Rabitat-i-Alam Islami.[30]

During the Ayub era (1958–69), the Jama't also pursued an ideological and cultural war against any manifestation of Bengali nationalism, regionalism, and secularism. Its agenda was also punctuated by an all out effort to rejuvenate the 'Islamic ideal'[31] through a programme of active religious propaganda, and the fabrication of alarmist anti-Hindu and anti-Indian propaganda to popularize itself. Indeed, this dual extraneous fear helped the Jama't more than any other issues in its programme at this time, especially in winning over support from the conservative, and generally anti-Indian sections of the population, in East Pakistan. A reinvigorated Islam buttressed by the fear of Hinduism and India, the Jama't felt, could challenge Bengali nationalism and the secular leadership.

Autonomy for East Pakistan and the Jama't

When, in February 1966, Shiekh Mujib (d. 1975) launched his celebrated Six Point Programme outlining the scheme for achieving provincial autonomy for East Pakistan, the Jama't, together with all other Islam-oriented parties, including the Nizam-i-Islami and the Council Muslim League, rejected it as a separatist design.[32] However, though it remained steadfastly opposed to the principle of greater provincial autonomy for East Pakistan, in a pragmatic step the Jama't modified its stance on the Six Points and in May 1967 became a signatory to the Eight Point Programme of an electoral alliance, called the Pakistan Democratic Movement, which recognized the Six Point autonomy demand for East Pakistan in a modified form. However, the anti-regime stance of the Jama't in East Pakistan gradually changed to a pro-regime policy in view of the outpouring of Bengali support for Mujib who, as charged in December 1967 with high treason in the Agartala Conspiracy Case for collusion with India in dismembering the state of Pakistan, was considered by the Jama't a greater threat than Ayub. The Jama't reacted forcefully, denouncing the 'conspirators' of the Agartala conspiracy case and offering justification for making Islam the ideological foundation of national politics.[33]

In subsequent months, mammoth protest rallies were organized in East Pakistan by the secular-oriented Awami League and its allies, condemning those who opposed the Six Points. The Jama't countered this by forming post-haste an Islamic Sangram Parisad, an impromptu council of the Islamic right, and took to the streets raising slogans against the autonomy demands.[34] The Jama't also renewed its oft-repeated propaganda campaign, arguing that Bengali ethnic, linguistic, and cultural identities should be subsumed by Islamic identity alone, and urged its student wing to cleanse the college campuses of leftist influences.[35]

A triumphant Jama't promptly claimed victory when, on 25 March 1969, Ayub relinquished authority to another man in uniform, General Yahya Khan.[36] The Jama't considered it advantageous in offering its unequivocal support to the new martial law regime in the expectation of garnering some quick gains. When Yahya announced his goal of holding national elections as a prelude to the transfer of power, the Jama't welcomed the move and decided 'to bring the party close to Yahya Khan's regime'.[37]

In East Pakistan the party's principal attention in its election campaign was directed against the Six Point Programme of the Awami League. Ghulam Azam, the *amir* of East Pakistan, branded the Six Points a programme for secession,[38] calling Mujib a greater threat than the socialists of East Pakistan.[39] Without any tangible popular support in East Pakistan, the Jama't lost no time in declaring the Awami League an enemy of Islam and proclaimed jihad against kafirs.[40] The Jama't workers conducted their electioneering campaign in mosques and other religious fora ignoring the restrictions imposed by the election commission, although such propaganda had little real impact on the average Muslim voter in the province. For the latter, the primary problems were economic, not religious, and the Jama't's effort to manipulate Islamic religious symbols and slogans to popularize its programmes proved futile. Thus, in the national elections of 1970, the Jama't was unable to win a single seat in the National Assembly, and captured just one seat in the East Pakistan Assembly.[41] Contesting from a Dhaka constituency, Ghulam Azam himself was defeated by a huge margin of over 80,000 votes.[42]

This debilitating defeat in the election virtually eliminated the political influence of the Jama't at that time. In a surprise volte face, the Jama't urged Yahya Khan to allow Sheikh Mujib to form a government,[43] but this advice did not deter Yahya from launching his terror campaign in East Pakistan in March 1971. The Jama't lost no time in pledging its unqualified support to the regime against the 'communist–Hindu plot to dismember Pakistan' and formed an 'alliance with the Pakistan army'.[44]

The Jama't devised a two-pronged strategy to support the Pakistani military repression in East Pakistan. It took prompt measures to secure the support of some Muslim countries and world opinion in favour of the military action. Mawdudi himself made several impassioned appeals to the Muslim governments, which included a telegram sent in April 1971 to Muslim heads of states charging India with interfering in Pakistan's internal affairs.[45] A group of Jama't members led by Khurram Jah Murad, the head of the Dhaka city unit, visited a number of countries in Europe to explain Pakistan's position. Simultaneously, the Jama't's headquarters in Lahore despatched several delegations to East Pakistan in support of the military operations there. One such delegation, headed by Mian

Tufail Muhammad, the general secretary of the Jama't, in June 1971 urged the military commanders in Dhaka to expeditiously exterminate the Bengali insurgents and rebels.[46] In extending its support to the Pakistan army, with which it had been at odds till the time of the 1970 elections, the Jama't, after its electoral debacle in 1970, thought it practical to ride high with those who had the guns; perhaps it also honestly believed that it was the army alone who could defend the territorial integrity of Pakistan at that particular juncture in history. From the military's point of view, the Jama't's support for its actions in East Pakistan not only bolstered its case in the Islamic world but also found a willing ally in its attempt to form political committees, known as the peace committees, to bring about an end to the conflict on its own terms.

Days after the Pakistan army launched its bloody reprisal against the Bengali nationalists in the early hours of 26 March, Ghulam Azam met General Tikka Khan, who was in charge of the overall military operations in the province, on 4 and 6 April and pledged his party's full support in safeguarding the unity and integrity of Pakistan.[47] As indicated above, Ghulam Azam and his party also offered primary support to the military-sponsored peace committees, which provided a façade of civilian support to shore up the collapsing civil administration in the province. The formation and activities of the peace committees in support of the regime were widely publicized in the media which was heavily censored by the regime. To directly bolster the regime's military operations, the Jama't also created several impromptu 'counter-insurgency' armed groups, notably, the al Badr, the al-Shams and the Razakars, who were trained and equipped with weapons by the Pakistan army to fight against the Bengali nationalists. Most units of these Jama't supported armed groups included Urdu-speaking Muslims, many of whom had been dispatched from West Pakistan, although the leading roles were played by the Bengali cadres of the party.

In several statements issued from Dhaka, Karachi, and Lahore, Ghulam Azam had no compunction in acknowledging the Jama't's ties to these groups.[48] He urged the authorities to arm 'the patriotic people' of East Pakistan 'so that they could fight the miscreants at large in the rural areas'. He also endorsed the decision of the military to ban the Awami League and outlaw all other groups, or parties who were suspected of supporting East Pakistan's separation from Pakistan.[49]

During the period of the war of liberation (March–December 1971), Jama't-supported armed groups provided logistical and intelligence support to the military; it is widely known that its armed cadres brutally murdered a number of distinguished Bengali professionals, including artists, literati, and teachers, right on the eve of the surrender of the Pakistan army in December 1971. The alliance between the Jama't and the army was further formalized when on 17 September 1971 four members of the party joined the military government in East Pakistan.[50] Immediately after assuming office, the Jama't education minister Abbas Ali Khan announced plans to transform the 'Bengalis into Pakistani Muslims'.[51] Likewise, the Jama't's Lahore secretariat demanded the immediate 'killing of all those responsible for the armed revolt', and the dissolution of the East Pakistan assembly.[52] The Party then urged the regime to declare its candidates who had been placed second in the 1970 elections to be automatically elected as the Awami League representatives had lost their seats by staging an armed revolt against the government.[53] However, this short-lived political stint of the Jama't came to an abrupt end with the humiliating defeat of the Pakistan army by the combined forces of the Indian army and the Bangladesh liberation army (the Mukti Bahini) in December 1971.

When Bangladesh emerged as an independent state, the Jama't lacked any credibility and was forced to go underground. Some of its leaders and cadres were incarcerated on charges of war crimes, and the party along with other religious-oriented political parties were banned in 1972.[54] Sheikh Mujib, now called the Bangabandhu, so detested the Jama't that he made it known soon after Independence that the Jama'ti 'traders in religious politics' would find no place in Bangladesh. In 1973, Ghulam Azam's citizenship was revoked for crimes against humanity.[55] However, by the end of 1973 most of the incarcerated Jama.'t members were released from prison under a general amnesty declared on 30 November, excluding however those against whom there were prima facie criminal charges.

Reeling under the ban imposed by the new government in Bangladesh, the Jama't remained virtually dormant in Bangladesh for the next few years. Ghulam Azam, who had escaped from the province during the last days of the war, took up residence in West Pakistan, and later moved to London; he became increasingly active in portraying a negative image of the new state to the oil rich Arab countries, especially Saudi Arabia, whose help was sought by Bangladesh in shoring up its battered economy. Azam travelled to various countries of the Middle East and lectured at anti-Bangladesh fora in Great Britain, seeking to mobilize Muslim public opinion against the secular regime in Bangladesh. In 1973, when Pakistan was ready to recognize Bangladesh, Azam made strenuous efforts to prevent this, and subsequently urged other Muslim countries not to follow Pakistan's lead. Using the occasion of the Hajj at Mecca, Azam also sought to contact the remnants of the anti-nationalist groups from Bangladesh with the goal of staging a counter-revolution which never materialized.[56]

Legitimization of the Jama't in Bangladesh

The political ban imposed on the Jama't in Bangladesh did not deter the party from conducting clandestine activities, especially in re-establishing its organizational structure.[57] At this stage, the activities of the party were conducted under an organizational umbrella known as the Islamic United Front led by Maulana Abdur Rahim who had in 1977 disassociated himself from the Jama't for its activities in 1971.[58] Following Ghulam Azam's return to Bangladesh on 11 July 1978, made possible by a military coup which eliminated the Awami League leadership in 1975, the Jama't-i-Islami Bangladesh became fully operational in May 1979 with Abbas Ali Khan as the acting *amir*. Just like his mentor Mawdudi who had bitterly opposed the creation of Pakistan but later became its staunchest proponent, Azam returned to Bangladesh ostensibly 'to preserve the infant state's Islamic identity and protect it from Indian agression'. The Jama't headquarters in Lahore had already approved the creation of a separate Jama't-i-Islami organization for Bangladesh soon after the new state had been formed and recognized Ghulam Azam as the *amir* of the new Party.[59] However, the question of Azam's citizenship proved an obstacle in his assuming that responsibility immediately after his return: he still held a Pakistani passport. This, however, did not materially affect the process of the Jama't's political recovery.

The Jama't's rehabilitation in Bangladesh politics was facilitated by a variety of factors. Because of mounting financial difficulties, Bangladesh had to seek aid from the oil-rich Arab countries, including Saudi Arabia. As a precondition, the Saudis put enormous pressure on successive Bangladesh governments to formally recognize the role of Islam in public affairs. In February 1974, Sheikh Mujib himself took the initiative of participating in the summit of the Organization of the Islamic Conference in Lahore at the instance of several Middle Eastern leaders, including Yasser Arafat of the Palestine Liberation Organization (PLO). This was followed by accelerated efforts by the government to strengthen ties with the Islamic countries. As if to placate the Islam-oriented groups,

Sheikh Mujib also re-established the Islamic Foundation, an organization that promotes Islamic ideals and programmes through publications and seminars, in 1975 as a visible symbol of his commitment to rehabilitate Islam.[60]

Another measure of the Mujib government, perceived by many to be a calculated move to satisfy the religious sensibilities of Muslims both within the country and abroad was the publication of the report of the education commission which was released in 1974.[61] The report suggested various measures to restructure the existing system of education, including the retention of the *madrassa* system of Islamic religious education. Although the report emphasized the need for the separation of religion from education, its recommendation in favour of a parallel system of religious institutions was symbolic of the new government's policy of compromising with the Islam-oriented public. A parallel system of religious education would continue to provide an infrastructure for extending the domain of Islam-oriented parties; the *madrassas* would re-emerge as the recruiting centres for Jama't cadres, as well as its sustenance. An indication of Mujib's policy of appeasement of Islam-oriented groups is also evident from the fact that the annual government allocation to Islamic education rose to Taka 7,200,000 in 1973 from 2,500,000 in 1971.

The Jama't's rehabilitation was equally facilitated by events following the assassination of Sheikh Mujib in 1975, and the installation in power of successive military regimes led by Ziaur Rahman (r. 1975–82) and Hussain Muhammad Ershad (r. 1982–90). To create an aura of political legitimacy for their rule, and to win the approval of Middle Eastern Islamic countries, these regimes often collaborated with the Jama't and other smaller parties. In effect, their machinations gradually placed the Jama't at the centre-stage of Bangladesh politics and helped legitimize its status as the champion of the Islamic ideal. General Ziaur Rahman, who assumed power in 1975, soon allowed the revival of religion-based political parties, rescinding the ban imposed by the Awami League government. Zia's overtures to the Islamists was contrived primarily as a means of containing, and if possible crushing the secular-oriented Awami League, which continued to wield powerful mass appeal. Zia took numerous symbolic steps to project himself as an Islamic leader and sought to rally support from Islam-oriented groups both at home and in Islamic countries abroad.

Zia's overtures to the Jama't yielded some dividends. To begin with, the Jama't supported him both in the 'referendum' of 1977 and the presidential election of 1978,[62] However, the Jama't–Zia liaison suffered a setback when the party pressed for the restoration of Ghulam Azam's citizenship. To exert pressure on the government, the Jama't organized a Committee for the Restoration of Citizenship of Ghulam Azam which carried out numerous activities to mobilize support for Azam's citizenship.[63] However, Zia refrained from obliging the Jama't on an issue so sensitive to many in the country. Zia was also concerned about getting too close to Jama't, fearing that his own image as a freedom fighter would be tarnished.[64] The Jama't had however already achieved its principal goal under Zia by gaining political legitimacy; it could wait a few years longer for Ghulam Azam's citizenship!

It was also during Zia's regime that the Jama't reportedly began receiving significant financial assistance from Saudi Arabia and Iran.[65] It also derived significant financial benefit by controlling a number of Saudi-sponsored organizations in Bangladesh, such as the Ibn Sina Trust, Rabitat-i-Alam Islami, and similar other philanthropic and financial institutions. During this period the Jama't also began working towards establishing contacts with other Islamic groups like the Masjid Samaj and the Sirat Majlis committees.

With General Ershad in power since March 1982, the Jama't continued to rebuild itself politically and organizationally. Following Ziaur Rahman, Ershad also began to lean heavily on his personal appeal to the religious minded, projecting himself as a dedicated Muslim committed to serving the cause of Islam. Not unlike Zia, Ershad had little respect for the Jama't's ideology or its political agenda, but his obvious solicitation of the party was motivated by his need to create a support-base for his regime. Although the Jama't appeared fully conscious of Ershad's motives, it agreed to cooperate as it served its goals. Ershad was not a freedom fighter and it was expected that he would assist in the restoration of Azam's citizenship and readily facilitate the party's resumption of political activities.

This short-lived collusion between the Jama't and Ershad was to end abruptly. In early 1983, when the major political parties allied in a movement for the restoration of democracy, the former followed suit although it was not officially inducted into the alliance. Surprisingly, it also bitterly opposed Ershad's half hearted effort to introduce Arabic as a compulsory language at the primary and secondary levels. Like other political parties, the Jama't also boycotted Ershad's 'referendum of confidence' and participated in strikes and demonstrations on the day of the referendum. Similarly, on 15 October 1986, the Jama't boycotted the presidential election organized by Ershad. When, again, Ershad called for parliamentary elections in 1986, it spiritedly opposed it; later, it agreed to participate in these elections when the Awami League decided to do so, and won 10 seats in parliament.

The process of legitimization of the Jama't in post-liberation Bangladesh was now almost complete. It had now re-emerged as a major political player and could no longer be ignored. Tightly knit and well disciplined, the party proved to be dynamic in adjusting itself to the ever changing political environment in Bangladesh and, in the process, gaining acceptance from society at large. From within the short-lived parliament, it soon joined most opposition motions and walkouts and demands for fresh elections, and openly came out in support of the demand for restoration of democracy.

All opposition to Ershad finally crystatlized into a general demand for his resignation which developed into a powerful movement. In a unique move, the Jama't members of parliament resigned en bloc from parliament to force Ershad to step down. Its unilateral, proactive measure was certainly aimed at drawing national attention but it provided momentum to the anti-Ershad agitations.[67] To pre-empt similar actions by the Awami League, Ershad soon dissolved parliament and scheduled new elections on 3 March 1988 which were boycotted by the Jama't and other political parties.

The Islami Chatra Shibir

One of the consequences of the legitimization of the Jama't under Zia, and its greater involvement in political activities during Ershad's long rule was to fully activate its programmes of recruitment, especially at the level of younger members. Although its student wing, known as the Islami Chatra Shibir, is not officially linked to the parent body, and theoretically acts as an independent Islamic movement, their close relationship is hardly a secret.[68] The Shibir gained enormously in membership, especially during Ershad's time; financial incentives made possible by the Jama't's links to the Middle Eastern oil-rich countries as well as political instability at home, and the uncertainty in the job market contributed in large measure to the dizzying growth in Shibir activists who were, as a rule, very carefully selected, recruited, and initiated. Although the exact number of its membership is not known, the Shibir increasingly began playing a leading role in campus affairs in various college and university campuses during Zia's and Ershad's time.

Their training and activities were centred around gaining control of student politics in the major campuses. Notwithstanding their numerical weakness in comparison to the secular student parties, their political preponderance was felt for many years in all major universities, especially at Chittagong, Rajshahi, and Jahangirnagar.

Support for the Shibir on university and college campuses throughout the country seems to be less than ten per cent of the total student population. By all accounts, it is thus a minority group, but a very well organized, militant, and a dedicated minority that neither deviates from its ideology or programme nor yields to intimidation. Indeed, the Shibir is very single-minded in pursuit of its mission and in order to accomplish it no sacrifice is considered too great or too costly. In a political conflict, its cadres do not hesitate to court death. Members of the Shibir move in groups and provide protection to one another. Its most élite corps of activists are well-trained in methods of torture, brutality, and techniques to vivisect the victim's body.[69] In July 1988, at Nawabganj in northern Bangladesh, the Shibir tortured to death, in open daylight, several students of the opposing camp, in some cases even at their homes in the presence of their families. They also terrorized the entire town, ransacked the market place and even assaulted women and children. When asked to explain their extraordinary conduct, the answer was compliance to a command from above. It is thought that Shibir's intentions were known to the district authorities who took no steps to prevent the horrific incidents.[70]

The Nawabganj-style terror was also undertaken by the Shibir in Sylhet, Chittagong, Rajshahi, and in several other towns.[71] In many places the Shibir members ceremoniously desecrated the national flag and other national symbols, which are considered too secular in their origins and orientation by the Jama't and its allies. The response of the secular political parties to the Jama't–Shibir aggressive style of politics was a call to resist such activities and organize strikes and demonstrations directed against the latter. This is exactly what the Ershad regime had wanted: to divert the attention of the mainstream opposition from the real political issues. As the campuses became battlefields for political control between the Shibir and the anti-Shibir forces, the regime got a respite. Violence has since become endemic in student politics: both the Shibir and its opponents have been equally involved in killings and maimings on campuses ever since.

The Revitalization of the Jama't

Following Ershad's resignation on 6 December 1990, elections to parliament were held in February 1991, creating conditions for the Jama't to play a major role in constitutional politics. Its election manifesto, published ahead of other political parties,[72] promised, among other things, the establishment of an Islamic state in Bangladesh, including the implementation of the shari'a as the law of the land, the creation of a governmental system based on the Qura'n and the Sunnah, and an Islamic education system; it also envisaged the provision of a separate workplace for women, and created opportunities for the latter to lead their lives based on the principles of the Qura'n and the Sunnah.

When the results of the February elections were announced, the Jama't had won 18 seats (in a parliament of 300), which later increased to 20 when two reserved seats for women were gained by the party as a reward for its crucial support to the centrist Bangladesh Nationalist Party (BNP) headed by Khaleda Zia. One of the goals of this support to the BNP was to deny power to the left-leaning Awami League and its allies.

Although the Jama't was in fourth position in the elections with a smaller number of seats in parliament than the other three major political parties, namely, the BNP, the Awami League, and the Jatiya Party, it at once assumed the role of a power broker and was able to bargain a deal with the BNP (which, lacking a majority in parliament desperately needed its support to form a government)[73] involving a number of issues critical to its own existence, including two extra seats in the parliament reserved for women. Thus, from the status of a political pariah during the first decade after Bangladesh's independence, the Jama't now became, what may euphemistically be termed as the effective kingmaker. It was further able to elevate its image when in October 1991, the Awami League nominee for the presidency, Badrul Haider Chowdhury, formally sought the support of the Jama't in his failed bid for that high (though ceremonial) office.

Secure in its base in parliament, the Jama't now looked for opportunities to build bridges with other conservative religious groups with whom it had ossasionally been at odds.[74] Such an opportunity presented itself when a much-debated controversy suddenly engulfed the political scene: this centred around the feminist writer, Taslima Nasreen, whose angry criticism of the status of the Bangladeshi women, and her reported remarks on the 'need' for a revision of the Holy Qura'n caused an uporoar in the country and abroad.[75] Although Taslima denied having made such a remark, this did not soothe the ire of the conservatives and fundamentalists: thus, mullahs, *pirs* the other conservative groups were soon drawn into a formal compact (*morcha*) with the Jama't on the issue.[76] The compact adopted a month long programme of protest which eventually proved to be the 'fiercest and most naked attack' on the government since the elections.[77] The Jama't even threatened to turn the protest into a movement to topple the government unless Taslima and other *murtad*s (renegades of the Faith) were punished, and also demanded the enactment of a new blasphemy law.[78]

Although the Jama't's aggressive role in the Taslima Nasreen case provoked counter protests from a number of secular organizations, the controversy once more offered it the opportunity to project itself as the champion of Islam. Similar emotive issues and symbols, especially, anti-Indian and anti-Hindu slogans, were tools which the Jama't often skilfully utilized to create and mobilize support in its favour. Thus, in another calculated move, the Jama't, in concert with other 'like-minded'[79] groups, organized a series of street demonstrations, (a) calling for a ban on 'un-Islamic' books and newspapers, (b) demanding that the government declare the minority Ahmadiya Muslim sect as non-Muslim, (c) proclaiming a jihad against all *murtad*s, and (d) demanding that all NGOs be closed down. The Jama't as well as the other Islamic groups were vehemently opposed to the non-governmental organizations (NGOs), especially for the latter's programmes in support of the empowerment of women. Notably, during the anti-Taslima Nasreen agitations, there was a sudden increase in the incidence of fatwas. These fatwas particularly targeted women charged with sexual misconduct, and were often administered by *gram salish*, or village arbitration councils, which had no formal judicial authority. Although there is no direct evidence of the Jama't's involvement in such cases, its role in openly espousing violence against 'un-Islamic' conduct definitely encouraged such actions by the rural mullahs.[80]

The Jama't's crowning achievement at this time was a high court verdict in April 1993 restoring the citizenship of Ghulam Azam. A triumphant Jama't organized a victory celebration at the famed Dhaka public square, Manik Mian Avenue. While Ghulam Azam felt vindicated by the high court verdict, the trial also resurrected the Jama't's murky record during the liberation war. As if to distance itself from its own past, it soon decided to break off relations with the BNP government which it had earlier helped to form. As a countrywide movement developed demanding the resignation of the government, the Jama't also decided to participate alongside its arch enemies, the Awami League and its leftist allies. This was a singularly unique move on its part to fight alongside those who had earlier refused to accept it as a legitimate political party. The Awami League leadership publicly felicitated the Jama't for its role in the movement,[81] and the latter's leaders were even invited to the home of a top Awami League leader, Abdus Samad Azad, who was latter to be the foreign minister of the Awami League government after the elections in 1996.[82]

Despite its growing power, the Jama't's political role continued to be circumscribed by its inability to gain widesproad popular support in the elections. Although considered the fourth largest political party in the country, its electoral support barely exceeded 12 per cent of votes cast in any election. However, one must not overemphasize this statististical fact to minimize the overall impact of its 'Islamic appeal' on electoral politics in Bangladesh. Thus, during the 1996 election campaigns, the Jatiyo Party headed by General Ershad promised the creation of an Islamic Commission for the promotion of Islamic values in the country.[83] Similarly, the BNP sponsored a Nationalist Ulema Advisory Group to project the party's Islamic image; even the Awami League, contrary to its pronounced secular objectives, promised retention and development of *madrassa* education. The ensuing competition among political parties to publicly display their loyalty to Islam by recourse to various pseudo-religious rituals, such as holding the *milad* in the offices of various political parties including the Awami League, official *iftar* parties during the month of Ramadan, demonstrated the importance of the Islamization of politics spearheaded by the Jama't, and equally pursued by the successive military regimes of Zia and Ershad.

Not surprisingly, the results of 1996 elections did not favour the Jama't. Although, for the first time, it had contested all the 300 seats to parliament, it was able to win only three. Whereas in the 1991 elections, the Jama't, contesting in 167 seats, received 12.13 per cent of the votes cast; in 1996 the percentage dropped to 8.71; the loss of over nine hundred thousand votes and 15 parliamentary seats in 1996 suggests that at least quantitatively, between 1991 and 1996, the Jama't's popular support declined significantly[84]. However, as mentioned earlier, the Jama't never projected itself as a party of the masses; its participation in electoral politics was primarily designed to draw attention to its programmes and goals rather than to gain control of the governmental apparatus. This is because it believes that a real change in society and the governmental system can come only through a revolution, like that in Iran in 1979 under the leadership of Ayatollah Khomeini. Thus, since its birth, the Jama't has concentrated on building a cadre of dedicated followers capable of influencing people and shaping the course of political events rather than scoring big in elections. Its strategy has been to exercise a certain amount of political influence without assuming direct responsibility, which is one reason why it collaborated with successive military regimes both in Pakistan and Bangladesh.

Conclusion

The story of the re-emergence and legitimization of the Jama't in Bangladesh offers interesting perspectives into the dynamics of fundamentalist Islam. Although the Jama't's role in electoral politics has been limited throughout the period discussed, it has certainly succeeded in reintroducing Islam as a powerful political symbol in a country born, partly at least, out of a reaction against excessive emphasis on religion in former Pakistan of which it was a part. Thus, in recent parliamentary elections, even the Awami League, the party supposedly closest to the secular ideal in Bangladesh, has indiscriminately used Islamic religious symbols, emblems, and even rituals to recreate its own image in the Islamic mould. By appealing to the religious sensibilities of the public, using emotive symbols and slogans, the Jama't has succeeded in almost reversing the language-based, secular political ideal that helped to create Bangladesh in 1971.

Among other factors that helped to revitalize Islam as a political symbol in Bangladesh, the activities of successive military regimes who, in their search for political legitimacy, often took recourse to doubtful programmes of Islamization, cannot be underestimated. They adopted measures such as making religious education compulsory at the school level, patronizing *madrassa* education, and proclaiming Bangladesh an 'Islamic State' (by the Ershad regime), which transformed certain aspects of life in the country; they equally encouraged traditional religious leaders, such as *pir*s and mullahs, to play an active role in the political affairs of the country in efforts to isolate the major political parties, and thus helped to create conditions for the re-emergence of Islamic symbols in Bangladesh politics. Likewise, external pressures from oil-rich Islamic countries have had a powerful impact in revitalizing the Islamic symbol in Bangladesh. However, in the final analysis, it was the Jama't's sustained programmes and activities over the years that posed a serious challenge to secular-oriented politics in the country and helped to re-popularize Islamic symbols and slogans.

However, the Jama't's programmes and activities have not been directed toward transforming the political environment of the country alone: it equally promoted ideas and programmes seeking to create 'a truly Islamic' society, and thus placed an overwhelming emphasis on Islamic rituals and practices. In the process of doing that, it often targeted the secular symbols and institutions, and often came into conflict with the secular-oriented movements and parties, stirring up a certain degree of religious fanaticism amongst ordinary citizens, and thus contributed towards a renewed societal intolerance toward non-Muslims and women. This has aggravated social and political tension in the country and put pressure on religious minorities, especially Hindus and women.

One of the principal sources of strength of the Jama't, like other fundamentalist movements and parties, is its well-disciplined organizational structure. Unlike the secular-oriented parties which often lack any specific commitment to an ideology or programme, the Jama't's commitment to its ideological agenda is unquestioned. Organized along the lines of the communist parties, its cadres are loyal and dedicated, and barely question the authority of their superiors.[85] This gives it an organic unity that is rare in traditional politics. At another level, their extreme loyalty to an exclusivist ideology makes the Jama't-Shibir cadres insensitive to alternative symbols and ideologies and promote violence.

The Jama't is also the most literate political organization in the country. Since its membership is recruited after careful scrutiny of their background and commitmment, every effort is made to ensure that its full members (*rokn*) are educated individuals. This is part of the Jama't's programme to train a cadre of dedicated volunteers to bring about long-term changes in the character of society and politics. Its publicity and propaganda apparatus is equally powerful and well organized. Scores of pamphlets and booklets have been published in Bengali and distributed among its members and others. Regular discussion-meetings of its members, including the women's organization affiliated to it, keep them informed of its strategies and current developments.

In recent years, the Jama't has been the principal beneficiary of the rising frustrations amongst the younger generations. A growing sense of hopelessness, especially among college students facing an uncertain future, has led to sizeable increases in its support on college campuses. World events have similarly influenced many to join the ranks of the Islamists. Indeed, the Iranian revolution of 1979 provided a powerful impetus to many in seeking similar changes in their own conditions. Similarly, the success of the Taleban movement in Afghanistan has equally served as a reminder of the revolutionary potential of Islam. The growing power, though not popular support, of the Jama't in recent years may be ascribed to all of these factors.

Notes and References

*The author has immensely benefited from comments by Professors Salahuddin Ahmed, Amanullah Ahmed, Ziya Haider, Hussan Azizul Haque, and Anisuzzaman. Thanks are also due to Ali Zakeria Shirazi and Khalid Afzal Rahim for providing valuable information.

1. *See*, for example, Samuel P. Huntington, 'The Clash of Civilizations', in *Foreign Affairs*, Summer 1993.
2. Although there is a general inadequacy of scholarly discussion on the Jama't in Bangladesh, a number of recent publications contain useful information on the subject. Notable among them are U.A.B. Razia Aktar Banu, *Islam in Bangladesh* (Leiden: E.J. Brill, 1972); Rafiuddin Ahmed, 'Redefining Muslim Identity in South Asia', in *Accounting for Fundamentalisms*, eds Martin E. Marty and R. Scott Appleby (Chicago: Univeristy of Chicago Press, 1944, 669–705); Rafiuddin Ahmed (ed.), *Islam in Bangladesh: Society and Culture* (Dhaka: Bangladesh Itihas Samity, 1983); Partha Ghosh, 'Bangladesh at the Crossroads: Religion and Politics', *Asian Survey*, Aug. 1990, 795–808; Enayetur Rahim, 'Bangladeshe Jamate Islamer Utthan', in *Bish Bachar Pare,* ed. Muhammed Jafar Iqbal (Dhaka: Mohana Pradasani, 1993); Hasan Mohammad, *Jamaat-e Islami Bangladesh; Netritto Sangathan, Adarsha* (Dhaka: Academic Publishers, 1993), and Emajuddin Ahmed and D.R.J.A. Nazeen, 'Islam in Bangladesh: Revivalist or Power Politics?', in *Asian Survey*, Aug. 1990, 395–408.
3. The Jama't consists of members, or *rokn*s and sympathizers, or *muttafiq*s and *hamdard*s who together form a cadre of workers. Members alone, however, may hold office.
4. M.I. Faruqui, *Jama'at-e-Islami* (Lahore: Jama'at-e-Islami Publications, 1957), 73.
5. Leonard Binder, *Religion and Politics in Pakistan* (Berkeley: University of California Press, 1961), 77.
6. *See* Seyyed Vali Reza Nasr, *The Vanguard of Islamic Revolution. The Jama't-i-Islam of Pakistan* (Berkeley: University of California Press, 1994), 124.

7. Kalim Bahadur, *The Jama'at-i Islami of Pakistan* (New Delhi: Chetna Publications, 1977), 129.
8. *See* Rounaq Jahan, *Pakistan: Failure in National Integration* (New York: Columbia Umversity Press, 1972), 134.
9. *See* Keith Callard, *Pakistan: A Political Study* (London: George Alleen 1957), 20. The United Front consisted of the Awami League, Kushak Sramik, and several splinter groups.
10. Maulana Abdur Rahim was the acting *amir* of the Bangladesh Jama't from 1955 to 1969.
11. Muhammad Qamruzzaman *Adhypak Golam Azamer Sangrami Jiban* (Dhaka: Al Falah Printer, 1989), 34–5.
12. In his capacity as a student representative, Azam presented a memorandum to Prime Minister Liaquat Ali Khan when he visited the University campus in 1948, which contained a demand for the recognition of Bengali as a state language.
13. Muhammad Qamruzzaman, op. cit., passim.
14. Shahriyar Kabir, *Ekattarer Ghatak* (Dhaka: Muktijuddha Chetana Bikash Kendra, 1989), 51.
15. *See* Abul 'Ala Mawdudi, *East Pakistan Problem: Causes and Solutions* (Dhaka: Department of Publicity and Information, Jamaat-i-Islami East Pakistan, n.d.), passim.
16. *Tarjuman al-Quran*, vol. 37, no. 6, 1952, 368.
17. Bahadur, *Jamaat-i Islami*, 131.
18. Ibid.
19. Khurshid Kamal Aziz, *Party Politics in Pakistan, 1947–58* (Islamabad: National Commission on Historic and Cultural Research 1976), 154
20. The Jama't was able to get one candidate elected out of the 53 it set up and polled a total of 200,000 votes. It blamed its poor showing on electoral fraud involving the Muslim League ruling party, and negative voting by women voters. Bahadur, *Jamaat-i-Islami*, 64.
21. Bahadur, *Jamaat-i-Islami*, 62.
22. Ibid., 62.
23. Ibid., 63.
24. The party was founded in 1950 and largely comprised orthodox religious leaders.
25. 'Jamaat-i-Islami', in *Oxford Encyclopedia of Islam*, 338.
26. Nasr, *Vanguard*, 153.
27. The Ordinance tampered with the injunctions of the Shari'a by bringing about changes in laws governing marriage, divorce, and inheritance, and thus outraged the sensibilities of the orthodox Muslims. Led by Mawdudi, the Jama't quickly exploited the occasion in leading an active campaign against the measure.
28. Feldman, Herbert, *From Crisis to Crisis: Pakistan 1962–1969* (Karachi: Oxford University Press, 1972), 65–6.

29. Ibid., 66.

30. Ibid.

31. In addition to holding seminars, lectures, and discussion groups, the Jama't's propaganda effort included free distribution of Islamic literature. *See* Shamsul I. Khan, *Political Culture, Political Parties, and the Democratic Transition in Pakistan* (Dhaka: Academic Publishers, 1996), 41; *see also* Ghulam Azam, *A Guide to the Islamic Movement* (Dhaka: Oriental Press, 1968).

32. *The Pakistan Observer*, 17 February 1966. Sheikh Mujib had presented the Six Point formula at an anti-Ayub rally in which the Jama't was represented from East Pakistan by Ghulam Azam together with Khurram J. Murad. The call for the United Front was apparently issued by Mawdudi from Dhaka in early 1966. *See* Bahadur, op. cit., 117.

33. *Dainik Pakistan*, 27 Dec. 1967.

34. *Morning News*, 16 March 1969.

35. Reportedly a number of members of the Taleban from West Pakistan joined the exercise.

36. At the Round Table Conference, the Jama't had offered no constructive proposal but only a vague recommendation for the Islamization of the state, 'the only policy that could keep Pakistan united'. S.M. Zafar, *Through the Crisis* (Lahore: Book Centre, 1970), 204-5.

37. Ibid., 163.

38. *Pakistan Times*, 5 May 1970.

39. He was obviously referring to the National Awami Party, the East Pakistan Communist Party, and several other left splinter groups.

40. Abul Mansur Ahmed, *Sher-e-Bangla* (Dhaka, n.d.), 303–7; *see also* (daily), *Ittefaq*, 28 December 1970.

41. Most of the Jama't candidates lost their deposits for their failure to garner a minimum percentage of votes.

42. For the East Pakistan provincial assembly, the Jama't received 4.5 per cent of the votes cast; in the national assembly its share of the votes was 6 per cent of the votes cast from East Pakistan.

43. Nasr, *Vanguard*, 168.

44. Ibid. In a statement issued on 9 April 1971, Ghulam Azam characterized the Mukti Bahmini as 'armed Indian intruders'. Saiduzzaman Rowshan, *1971: Ghatak Dalalder Baktita of Bibriti* (Dhaka: Afser Brothers, 1993), 11.

45. Bahadur, op. cit., 133. The Saudi sponsored *Rabita Alam Islami*, established in 1962, was also induced to support this effort.

46. Bahadur, op. cit., 133. West Pakistan Amir, Hafizar Ranman Ahsan also held extensive meetings with General Tikka Khan in Dhaka, 7–8 May 1971.

47. *Purba Desh*, 5 April and *Dainik Pakistan*, 7 April 1971; also, Nasr, *Mawdudi*, 45.

48. *Dainik Pakistan*, 2 and 23 Sept. 1971.
49. *Dawn*, 23 June 1971.
50. Nasr, *Vanguard*, 169.
51. Kabir, op.cit., p. 61.
52. Ibid.
53. *Dainik Pakistan*, 24 July 1971.
54. The Constitution of Bangladesh, authenticated on 9 November 1972, declared secularism as a fundamental principle of state policy and prohibited the use and abuse of religion in politics.
55. Azam had left for West Pakistan on 22 November just a few days before Dhaka fell to the allied forces on 16 December 1971. He returned to Dhaka on 19 July 1978 on a Pakistani passport.
56. Kabir, op. cit., 81.
57. The Jama't averted a split when it was forced to operate secretly as some of its activists debated its role in 1971.
58. Kabir, op. cit., 138.
59. Nasr, *Vanguard*, 54.
60. The Foundation was originally established in 1960 as a government-funded institution to indicate Ayub's support for Islam, partly to counter the Jama't propaganda that he was a Western-oriented person who had little respect for Islamic values. The Foundation also administered the largest mosque in Bangladesh, *Baital Mukarram*, in Dhaka. Although its principal goal was the promotion of Islamic ideals, over time it became a centre of conservative as well as fundamentalist activism.
61. The Commission was appointed by Sheikh Mujib in September 1972 with the renowned educator Muhammad Kudrat-i-Khuda as its chairperson. *See* Government of Bangladesh, *Bangladesh Shikkha Komishan Report* (Dhaka: Government Press, 1974), 57–9.
62. The Jama't joined a right-wing coalition in support of Zia.
63. *See* Muhammad Qamruzzamn, op. cit., 98–108.
64. *Weekly Bichitra*, 27 April 1984.
65. *See* Syed Anwar Hussain, 'Islamic Fundamentalism in Bangladesh: Internal Variables and External Inputs', in Rafuddin Ahmed (ed.), *Religion, Nationalism, and Politics in Bangladesh* (New Delhi: South Asia Publishers, 1990), 140–6.
66. During 1986–8, Ershad established 1,845 new *madrassas* and appointed 47,580 *madrassa* teachers. *See The Jagaran*, April 1986. He also promised state salaries for 250,000 *imams* of mosques as well as free electricity and water for the mosques. Ershad also announced plans for the creation of mosque-based Islamic centres in each of the 4451 rural unions. *Bangladesh Observer*, 9 March 1990.
67. Joining the movement, Azam stated that those who usurp political power without coming through the electoral process are enemies of democracy

and their leadership could not be supported. Golam Azam, *Palashi Theka Bangladesh* (Dhaka: Crescent Printing Press, 1988), 26.

68. The Shibir was earlier called the Islami Chatra Sangha in East Pakistan. It was renamed the Islami Chatra Shibir in 1976 partly to avoid criticism of the activities of the Sangha during the liberation war in 1971. *See* Charles Peter O'Donnell, *Bangladesh: The Biography of a Muslim Nation* (Boulder, Colorado: Westview Press, 1984), 31.

69. *Weekly Bichitra*, 7 Oct. 1988.

70. Ibid.

71. Ibid.

72. For details, *see* the Jama't's daily newspaper, *Sangram*, 3 Jan. 1991.

73. Winning 140 seats out of a total of 300, the BNP fell short by 11 seats of the requisite majority in parliament to form a government.

74. Ghulam Azam felt that any group or party that worked for the realization of an Islamic social and political system could be a potential supporter of the Jama't. Ghulam Azam, *Bangladesh o Jamaate Islami* (Dhaka: Jamaate Islami Bangladesh, 1988), 10–11.

75. This remark was printed in the Calcutta daily, *Statesman*, and reproduced in the *Dhaka Times*, 4 June 1994.

76. *Reuter World Service*, 26 June 1994. Faced with death threats, Nasreen was arrested on charges of insulting Islam and was eventually allowed to leave the country.

77. *Reuter World Service*, 6 July 1994.

78. A Jama't member of parliament, Matiur Rahman Nizami, submitted a private Bill to resurrect and modify a British law in the Penal Code of 1860, on 22 January 1994. For a discussion of the Bill see *Sanglap*, 25–8.

79. Among those who supported the Jama't were three religioius-oriented groups, created post-haste, known as Tauhidi Janata, Jagroto Janata, and Sanmilita Sangram Parishad, largely led by and with a membership of traditionalist religious leaders.

80. *See Sanglap*, Aug. 1954, vol. 4, 12–23.

81. *Daily Ittefaq*, 31 March 1996.

82. *Weekly Bichitra*, 6 April 1996.

83. *Independent*, 17 May 1996.

84. Most of the seats held by Jama't in the 1991 parliament were shared between the Awami League and the Jatiya Party.

85. According to an estimate provided by Ghulam Azam to this author, currently the Jama't has 10,000 *rokn*s 100,000 workers, and 400,000 supporters.

Index